Classical Guitar For Dummies®

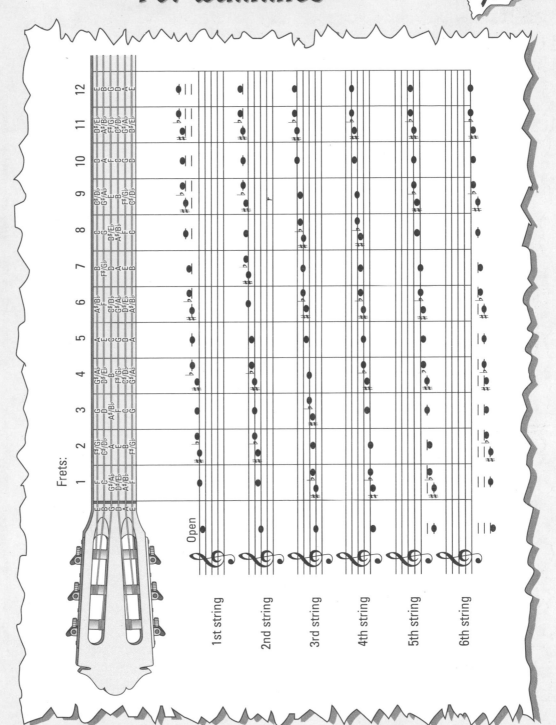

For Dummies: Bestselling Book Series for Beginners

The Circle of 5ths

The circle of 5ths is a way to view the 12 major and minor keys by the order of sharps and flats in their key signatures. Each key is placed on the circle, with the key of C (no sharps or flats) at the top, or 12 o'clock position.

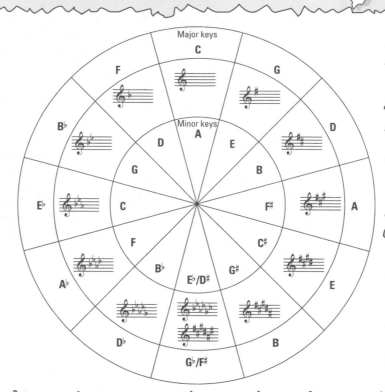

When to Play the Free Stroke versus the Rest Stroke

Use the Free Stroke When You Play	Use the Rest Stroke When You Play
Arpeggios	Slower, more expressive melodies
Chords	Scales, scale sequences, and single-note passages
Light-sounding melodies, or filler notes between melody and bass parts	Loud notes, or notes requiring maximum volume or feeling of intensity
Melodies or passages where the rest stroke can't be applied because of tempo considerations, string conflicts, or awkwardness and impracticalities in the right-hand fingering	Passages that must be drawn out from their surroundings (either other notes from the guitar or in an ensemble setting), assuming no conflict with other strings

Classical Guitar
FOR
DUMMIES®

by Mark Phillips and Jon Chappell

WILEY

Wiley Publishing, Inc.

Classical Guitar For Dummies®

Published by
Wiley Publishing, Inc.
111 River St.
Hoboken, NJ 07030-5774
www.wiley.com

WILEY

About the Authors

Mark Phillips is a guitarist, arranger, author, and editor with more than 35 years in the music publishing field. He earned his bachelor's degree in music theory from Case Western Reserve University, where he received the Carolyn Neff Award for scholastic excellence. He earned his master's degree in music theory from Northwestern University, where he was elected to Pi Kappa Lambda, the most prestigious U.S. honor society for college and university music students. While working toward a doctorate in music theory at Northwestern, Phillips taught classes in theory, ear training, sight singing, counterpoint, and guitar.

During the 1970s and early '80s, Phillips was Director of Music at Warner Bros. Publications, where he arranged the classical guitar folios *Bach for Guitar, Handel for Guitar, Mozart for Guitar,* and *Beethoven for Guitar.* Since the mid-'80s he has served as Director of Music and Director of Publications at Cherry Lane Music, where he has arranged numerous classical guitar book/CD packages, including *50 Baroque Solos for Classical Guitar, 50 Renaissance Solos for Classical Guitar, J. S. Bach: 50 Solos for Classical Guitar,* and *30 Easy Spanish Guitar Solos.*

Phillips is the author or coauthor of several books on musical subjects, including *Guitar For Dummies, Guitar Exercises For Dummies, Sight-Sing Any Melody Instantly,* and *Sight-Read Any Rhythm Instantly.* In his nonmusical life, Phillips is the author/publisher of a series of fun high school textbooks, including *The Wizard of Oz Vocabulary Builder, Tarzan and Jane's Guide to Grammar,* and *Conversations in Early American History: 1492–1837.* For the reference value of his numerous publications, Phillips is profiled in *Who's Who in America.*

Jon Chappell is an award-winning guitarist, author, and writer. He attended Carnegie Mellon University, where he studied classical guitar with Carlos Barbosa-Lima, and then he earned his master's degree in composition from DePaul University, studying classical guitar with Leon Borkowski (a student of Christopher Parkening). While living in Chicago, Chappell served as musicologist for *Guitarra* magazine and played and recorded with such acoustic artists as Tom Paxton, Jethro Burns, and John Prine. He performed with the Chicago Symphony Orchestra twice, including for the premiere of a piece by American composer Gunther Schuller.

When he moved to New York, Chappell served as editor-in-chief of *Guitar* magazine and was founder and the first editor-in-chief of *Home Recording* magazine. He has played and recorded with Pat Benatar, Judy Collins, Graham Nash, and Richie Havens, among others, and has contributed numerous musical pieces to radio, film, and TV, including *Northern Exposure; Walker, Texas Ranger; Guiding Light;* and NPR's *All Things Considered.*

Chappell is the author or coauthor of four other books in the *For Dummies* series — *Guitar For Dummies, Blues Guitar For Dummies, Rock Guitar For Dummies,* and *Guitar Exercises For Dummies* — and has also written several books on guitars and recording, including *The Recording Guitarist: A Guide for Home and Studio* (Hal Leonard); *Build Your Own PC Recording Studio* (McGraw-Hill); and *Digital Home Recording* (Backbeat Books). He has published pieces on music instruction and music technology in *Guitar Player, Rolling Stone, Keyboard, Men's Health, Entertainment Weekly, PC Magazine, Macworld,* and many other publications.

Dedication

Mark Phillips: For my wife, Debbie, and my children, Tara, Jake, and Rachel.

Jon Chappell: For my wife, Mary, and my children, Jen, Kate, Lauren, and Ryan.

Authors' Acknowledgments

The authors gratefully acknowledge the folks at Wiley Publishing, Inc.: Tracy Boggier, Erin Calligan Mooney, Kristin DeMint, and Todd Lothery.

All of the pieces on the CD were performed and recorded by Jon Chappell using a Liikanen A-model classical guitar, AKG C414B-ULS and Neumann KM184 microphones, TL Audio tube preamp, M-Audio interface, and Digidesign Pro Tools recording software. Jon would like to thank Eero Kilpi, Kauko and Keijo Liikanen, Emile Menasché, and John Krogh for their help in the recording of the CD.

Publisher's Acknowledgments

We're proud of this book; please send us your comments through our Dummies online registration form located at http://dummies.custhelp.com. For other comments, please contact our Customer Care Department within the U.S. at 877-762-2974, outside the U.S. at 317-572-3993, or fax 317-572-4002.

Some of the people who helped bring this book to market include the following:

Acquisitions, Editorial, and Media Development

Project Editor: Kristin DeMint

Acquisitions Editor: Tracy Boggier

Copy Editor: Todd Lothery

Assistant Editor: Erin Calligan Mooney

Editorial Program Coordinator: Joe Niesen

Technical Editor: Jonathan Crissman

Media Development Assistant Project Manager: Jenny Swisher

Media Development Producer: Josh Frank

Editorial Manager: Michelle Hacker

Editorial Assistant: Jennette ElNaggar

Art Coordinator: Alicia B. South

Cover Photo: © iStock

Cartoons: Rich Tennant (www.the5thwave.com)

Composition Services

Project Coordinator: Katherine Crocker

Layout and Graphics: Claudia Bell, Reuben W. Davis, Christin Swinford

Special Art: WR Music Service, Jon Chappell

Proofreaders: Jessica Kramer, Shannon Ramsey

Indexer: Steve Rath

Special Help: Alissa Schwipps

Publishing and Editorial for Consumer Dummies

> **Diane Graves Steele,** Vice President and Publisher, Consumer Dummies

> **Kristin Ferguson-Wagstaffe,** Product Development Director, Consumer Dummies

> **Ensley Eikenburg,** Associate Publisher, Travel

> **Kelly Regan,** Editorial Director, Travel

Publishing for Technology Dummies

> **Andy Cummings,** Vice President and Publisher, Dummies Technology/General User

Composition Services

> **Debbie Stailey,** Director of Composition Services

Contents at a Glance

Table of Contents

Introduction

· ·

*1*f you're captivated by the sound of the classical guitar, you're in good company. No less than Ludwig van Beethoven approvingly called the guitar a "miniature orchestra in itself"! We don't think we can improve on that (not that we'd try to compete with Beethoven!), but we do understand his enthusiasm. The classical guitar has the amazing ability to produce expressive melodies, complex chords, flowing arpeggios, and multiple, independent parts simultaneously — all with just six strings. It offers an incredible range of tonal possibilities as well, and it's able to create a broad range of colors and textures, from driving percussive rhythms to sweetly lyrical melodies — and everything in between.

As modern players, we can appreciate that we're playing classical music on the most popular and the coolest musical instrument in the world — the guitar. What could be a better way to have the best of both worlds than to take up the classical guitar? We have access to the music of history's greatest composers — the minuets of Mozart, the bourrées of Bach, and the sonatas of Beethoven. With a classical guitar, we can delight listeners with the subtle intricacies of the Baroque era or inspire their passion with stirring pieces from the Romantic period. And we also get to do this while playing the guitar. How cool is that?

Make no mistake, though, there's a lot more to classical guitar than just being cool. Like any other serious art form, classical guitar requires work. But that doesn't mean you can't have fun while developing the discipline and mastering the skills necessary to play classical guitar. Unlike the world of popular music, the best players in classical music — technically and musically — rise to the top. Our aim is to get you started on the right path so that every minute you devote to practicing and playing takes you closer to your goal of being the best classical guitarist you can be.

About This Book

In *Classical Guitar For Dummies,* we give you everything you need to play melodies, arpeggios, scales, and full-length pieces in the classical style. We present the material in a way that respects the classical tradition yet makes it fun and easy to learn. Here are just some of the methods we use to get our points across:

✓ **Step-by-step instructions:** We guide you through the techniques, exercises, and pieces using plain and helpful language, so that you know exactly what to do to successfully play every exercise and piece that appears in the book.

✓ **Music notation:** We present all the written musical figures in the traditional five-line staff with a treble clef, with notes indicating the pitches and rhythms. In addition, we also supply a tab staff (appearing directly below the music staff) that shows the strings and fret numbers. You can use either system, or even use them in combination, because they convey essentially the same information — just presented in a different way. In some figures we show a neck diagram, which is yet another way to see the guitar represented graphically and which serves to illustrate fingering positions. And have no fear — we show you how to interpret standard music notation in Chapter 3.

✓ **Audio CD:** The CD that comes with this book contains over 140 recorded performances of the exercises and pieces from the book. A written figure that has an accompanying recording on the CD is labeled with the appropriate track number. You can listen to the CD on your computer or CD player, or download the tracks to your portable audio or mp3 player, so that you always have the recorded music to inspire you wherever you go.

Even if you already play the guitar, you'll find this book valuable. You find here a focused approach on learning classical guitar the *right* way — the way it's played in music schools, universities, and on recordings and concert stages the world over. This book covers how to hold the guitar in the proper position, how to strike and fret the strings according to the rules of classical guitar technique, and how to perform the rich body of repertoire that awaits classical guitarists of all levels and experience.

Conventions Used in This Book

We take care to introduce concepts and define terms so that you don't have to wonder what we're talking about if we, for example, use the word *staccato* (which tells you to play notes short and detached, by the way). But we observe certain conventions that we may not explain every time, so following is a list of concepts and terms that we use often throughout the book.

✓ **Up and down, high and low:** When we speak of *up* and *down* on the guitar — whether we're referring to the strings, neck positions, or pitch in general — up means higher in pitch and down means lower in pitch. So the higher strings are the skinny, high-pitched ones — even though they're closer to the floor as you hold the guitar in the playing position.

Going up the neck means heading for the higher-numbered frets (toward the bridge), even though they're slightly closer to the floor than the lower-numbered frets, which are closer to the headstock. Don't be confused by this seeming contradiction of musical direction and physical positioning; knowing which way is up becomes second nature when you begin playing.

✔ **Right hand and left hand:** We say *right hand* to mean the hand that plucks the strings and *left hand* to mean the hand that frets the notes on the neck. Left-handed players sometimes flip the guitar so that the right hand becomes the fretting hand, and some method books avoid any ambiguity by using the terms *picking hand* and *fretting hand*. But we find that a little clunky, so we observe the more traditional use of right hand and left hand. If you're a southpaw who flips, take note!

✔ **Letters and numbers:** In addition to the standard music symbols that appear on the five-line staff, we often use letters and numbers to show you specific ways to use your fingers to play the notes. The letters *p, i, m,* and *a* indicate the right-hand thumb and index, middle, and ring fingers. (The letters stand for the Spanish words for these fingers.) For left-hand fingers, we use small numbers placed just to the left of the note heads: 1 = index, 2 = middle, 3 = ring, and 4 = little. In many cases we provide fingerings because it's the *only* way to play the passage, so try our way first before searching for an alternative.

What You're Not to Read

If you're the type who wants to start playing immediately, this section is for you, because we tell you what you can avoid reading — or at least what you don't have to read right away. For example, feel free to skip over any paragraph flagged with a *Technical Stuff* icon. Although this text offers in-depth information about the topic at hand, it isn't required reading and won't affect your ability to understand the concept fully or to play the music correctly. Similarly, sidebars — those gray boxes filled with text — are entertaining (we think) and offer something extra, but they don't contain vital information you're likely to miss.

If you're *really* itching to play some music and want to just play through the written examples in the book, you can do that, too, and we won't be offended. If you decide to follow that course, we recommend that you at least read the paragraph immediately preceding the example — the one that references the figure number within the text. By reading the paragraph that introduces the figure, you won't miss any instructions that directly pertain to the written exercise or piece.

Foolish Assumptions

We don't assume that you already know how to read music, nor do we assume that you even play the guitar at all. To make the notation a little easier to grasp, we include a tablature staff under every standard music notation staff in the exercises and pieces that appear in this book. Traditional classical music doesn't include tablature, so you're actually getting something extra here in *Classical Guitar For Dummies.* You can use the tab to check the fret and string location of any note or as another way to help figure out the music in case your music reading isn't very strong. We also don't assume that you're a virtuoso, and so we've taken steps to make sure that all the exercises and pieces are easily playable by guitarists that range from beginning to intermediate level.

How This Book Is Organized

We divide this book into logical sections, called *parts,* and within each of these larger sections are chapters that help organize your approach to learning different aspects and techniques of the classical guitar. Learning a musical instrument is a fairly progressive endeavor, so the earlier chapters are easier than the later ones. Also, music, like math (don't worry, no math is involved!), tends to be cumulative, which means that techniques you learn in one chapter are often assumed in later chapters. So we normally recommend that you start at the beginning, read toward the middle, and then finish at the end. We know, we know — it's a radical concept!

Having said that — and this being a *For Dummies* book — you're welcome to flip the book open to *any* page and jump in. That is, just start playing the exercises and pieces and see how you do. But if you do that, or otherwise tackle the book out of sequence (without starting at page 1 and reading straight through, the way you would a novel), we suggest you at least start at the beginning of a chapter. That way you know what to expect, because we always state in the chapter's introduction what we're going to cover.

Part 1: Getting to Know the Classical Guitar

This is the section where you get acquainted with the classical guitar. We take you through the proper way to sit and hold the guitar, how to tune it, and what to do with your right and left hands. We also introduce the notation systems that we use throughout the book, presenting and explaining the symbols of music notation — including the five-line staff and treble clef and how to read pitch and rhythm. But we include something extra that most classical methods don't: *tablature*. Tab (as it's known) is used extensively in popular music for guitar, and we think it's helpful to have here too, as an additional way to help you get your fingers playing the notes on the page.

Part II: Starting to Play: The Basics

This is where you actually get to make some music with the guitar! We start by having you play melodies on individual strings. Then we move to arpeggios, where you roll your right-hand fingers through the strings. Scales are an important tool to get your fingers in shape, and we introduce them here. Finally, you get to use your newly acquired skills to play through some easy pieces.

Part III: Improving Your Technique

This is the part where you get to dig down and absorb the special techniques that make your playing more expressive. First up are left-hand fingering techniques, including barres, slurs, and trills. Then you turn to tone production techniques, including harmonics and an essential technique for playing much Spanish-based music: right-hand tremolo. Part III is also where you venture to the higher frets, playing scales both across the neck and up and down the neck. With your technique tool kit now complete, you can perform pieces that contain barres, slurs, and passages in the higher positions.

Part IV: Mastering Classical Guitar Repertoire

After you master right- and left-hand techniques and get some scales and exercises under your belt (or fingers, as the case may be), it's time to experience the rich history of classical music through the great compositions of the masters. The chapters in Part IV deal with the major guitar composers and the five major periods, or eras, in classical music: Renaissance, Baroque, Classical, Romantic, and Modern. This is where you get to play a complete piece by Bach and to sample the great melodies of composers such as Handel, Mozart, Beethoven, Brahms, and Debussy, all arranged artfully (if we do say so ourselves) for the classical guitar.

Part V: The Part of Tens

The Part of Tens is a veritable Dummies institution — top-ten-style lists that organize information in a fun and memorable way. We put together two lists that we think help round out your classical guitar education. The first is our choice of ten essential great guitarists (though there are so many more than ten) you should know and listen to, with our recommendation of one of their recorded works. Our second Part of Tens lists the ten most important things you can do to make shopping for a classical guitar stress-free, rewarding, and fun!

Part VI: Appendixes

You don't need to read the appendixes to play the guitar or understand the material, but they do provide some useful information. Appendix A gives some tips on caring for and maintaining your guitar and also provides a tutorial on changing strings, complete with step-by-step photos to help you along and to make sure you don't get tied up in knots (though some simple knot-tying is required!). Appendix B contains instructions on how to use the CD and includes the CD track list, which lists all the recorded audio examples on the CD and their corresponding music figures in the text. The track list is essential for browsing the CD, which we encourage you to do!

Icons Used in This Book

We use this icon to signal an opportunity to skip ahead and play a complete piece in the style of the exercise or excerpt we just presented.

This one indicates important information that you want to keep in the front of your mind, as that info has a way of coming up again and again.

This icon tags information that's not absolutely necessary to perform the task at hand but that digs down below the surface to offer greater understanding on a particular subject or point.

A helpful hint, factoid, or other useful nugget that makes some concept easier to grasp or a task easier to perform.

 We use this icon to caution you about issues that could damage your guitar or cause you discomfort. So watch for this one if you — or your guitar — like to avoid pain!

Where to Go from Here

If this is your first brush with music and the guitar — or if it has been longer than you'd care to remember since you practiced — then start right at the beginning, with Chapter 1. However, if you already play the guitar, it's okay to skip Chapter 1 and go right to Chapter 2, which illustrates the special right-hand strokes and left-hand fretting position you use in classical guitar. If you already play the guitar and know proper right- and left-hand techniques, you can skip to Chapter 3, which walks you through some of the notation explanations we use in the book. Finally, if you just want to dive right in and start playing, turn to Chapter 4.

It's a good idea, though, to come back and read what you initially skip over, just to make sure that you're not missing something or perpetuating a bad habit. We'd like to think that you'll read every word here eventually, whether or not you read the text in order from front to back. Even if you think you know the material, a gentle reminder can sometimes be helpful.

Part I

Getting to Know the Classical Guitar

The 5th Wave   By Rich Tennant

You still sound a little flat.

In this part . . .

Whether you're new to classical guitar or the guitar itself, the material in this part covers everything you need to get you playing in the classical guitar style. In Chapter 1 we show you how to hold the guitar correctly, where to place your hands, and how to tune up. Chapter 2 is where we illustrate the correct right- and left-hand techniques used in classical guitar, and Chapter 3 explains the notation systems we use throughout the book.

Chapter 1

An Acoustic Guitar in a League of Its Own

In This Chapter

▶ Defining the term *classical guitar*

▶ Surveying the classical guitar's history in music

▶ Breaking down the classical guitar's parts

▶ Noting the differences between a classical guitar and other guitar types

In the right hands, the classical guitar can produce some of the most beautiful sounds in all of music. With it, a skilled performer can create miniature moments of intimate tenderness or stirring sagas of grandeur and passion. One reason the classical guitar is capable of such wide-ranging textures and emotions is that it's one of the few stringed instruments that can play chords and single notes with equal ease. And many people credit its special emotive powers to the fact that the performer uses both hands to touch the strings directly to make a sound, allowing him to coax out the softest melody or to vigorously ring out triumphant, full-voiced chords. The tonal variations you can achieve on a guitar played in the classical way rival the colors of the entire symphony orchestra. Even the great Beethoven agreed, calling the guitar "a miniature orchestra in itself."

In this chapter, we start off with the very basics, explaining the two different connotations associated with classical guitar to give you a solid understanding of what you're reading about in the first place. (Many people may not realize that simply playing a classical piece on a guitar doesn't necessarily qualify as classical guitar!) We then conduct a side-by-side comparison of the classical guitar and its traditional acoustic counterpart, exploring their differences in physique as well as in technique and musical requirements. Finally, we expound on the allure of this lesser-known stringed instrument to whet your appetite for what's in store.

Classical Guitar: One Term, Two Meanings, and a Bit of History

The first thing you have to sort out is just what's meant by the term *classical guitar*. It can describe both a type of instrument and a style of music played on that instrument. When referring to the instrument itself, you're talking about a guitar that has a particular design and construction, is made of certain materials, and requires playing techniques that are unique to this type of guitar, as compared to other guitars. To mine the depths of all the tonal and textural richness that await you in the world of classical guitar music, you must employ those specific right- and left-hand techniques, which together comprise the *classical guitar style*.

In this book we focus exclusively on the techniques that get you playing the classical guitar style — using a nylon-string classical guitar and stroking the strings with your right-hand fingers. Doing this empowers you to play the music written by the great classical composers throughout history and follow in the footsteps of concert-level virtuosos who for centuries have brought this music to guitar-loving listeners in the same way Vladimir Horowitz did with the piano and Itzhak Perlman did with the violin. The guitar has its own Perlmans and Horowitzes, and you can read about them in Chapter 17.

The guitar as we know it is a relatively young instrument, having evolved to its present form in the 19th century. As such, it doesn't have the rich body of music available for it that, say, the violin does, which has been around for more than 500 years. But the classical guitar has been, how shall we say, *industrious* in the way it has "borrowed" music from other instruments to claim as its own. As a result, studying classical guitar means that in addition to playing music written for the guitar, you play a lot of music that wasn't written for the guitar in the first place, nor written by a composer who would recognize the instrument you hold in your hands. But that's just part of the adventure of being a guitarist; you have to be somewhat of a pioneer with your instrument.

Nevertheless, nowadays composers write for the instrument all the time, ensuring its continued place in the field of serious musical instrument study. Many guitarists, associations, and organizations commission well-known composers to write compositions for the guitar in the same way that wealthy benefactors commissioned Beethoven and Mozart to write symphonies and sonatas.

Some well-known composers from the 20th century who've written for the guitar include Heitor Villa-Lobos, Luciano Berio, Benjamin Britten, Elliott Carter, Peter Maxwell Davies, William Walton, Alberto Ginestera, Ástor Piazzolla, and Leo Brouwer. If you think of the classical guitar as playing just the work of the great masters or having an undeniably "Spanish sound," check out what modern musical thinkers are cooking up for the classical guitar all the time.

After taking a while to come into its own historically, the classical guitar is now a permanent member of the classical music community. Classical guitar is taught in universities and conservatories, it's a frequent program entry for concert and recital halls, and it's found readily in new recordings by major classical music record companies. As far as music for the guitar goes, however, it's definitely in the minority, at least in terms of music that gets heard by the public at large — with rock and pop being the major players in this arena.

What a Classical Guitar Looks Like

Viewed from the front, or facing the instrument in its standing up position, the classical guitar body has an upper section, or *bulge,* where the wood curves outward; a lower section; and an inward curve in the middle separating the upper and lower parts.

The purpose of the guitar's body is to amplify the sound that the vibrating strings make. So the guitar's back and sides are made of stiff, hard wood that reflects, or bounces, the sound off its surface and through the top of the guitar and the sound hole. The traditional wood for the back and sides is rosewood, though lower-priced guitars sometimes use mahogany or maple. For the top, a different wood from the back and sides is used because the top's function is to vibrate freely with the notes that the plucked strings produce. So the wood for the top is softer and more resonant — spruce and cedar are the two most common top woods.

They say a picture's worth a thousand words, so we present a picture of a classical guitar, which allows us to use a lot fewer words than a thousand to describe its various parts and functions. Figure 1-1 shows an illustration of a classical guitar with its main parts labeled. The bulleted list after Figure 1-1 is a corresponding list of those labeled parts with their definitions and brief descriptions of their functions.

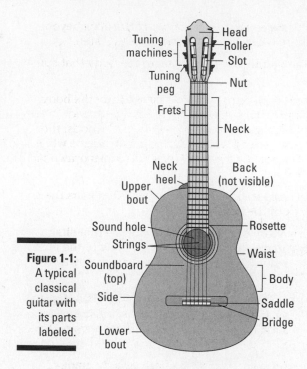

Figure 1-1: A typical classical guitar with its parts labeled.

Here's a list of the classical guitar's parts:

- ✔ **Back:** The flat part of the guitar *body,* parallel to and opposite the *soundboard,* closest to the performer.

- ✔ **Body:** The "box" or sound chamber of the guitar, which acts as a resonator or amplifier for the vibrating *strings.* The body is also what gives the guitar its particular — and beautiful — tone.

- ✔ **Bridge:** A thin, rectangular piece of flat wood that's glued to the top of the guitar and secures the strings at the body. The bridge transfers the sound from the vibrating strings to the guitar's body. Sitting in a slot of the bridge is the *saddle.*

- ✔ **Fingerboard:** Also called the *fretboard,* this is a thin, flat plank of wood glued to the neck and divided into frets. The fingerboard is usually made of ebony, a dense, dark, and hard wood that provides a smooth feel underneath the left-hand fingers as they move up and down and across the neck. Some fingerboards are made of rosewood.

- ✔ **Frets:** Thin metal wires on the fingerboard that run perpendicular to the strings. Pressing down a finger behind one of these shortens the vibrating length of the string, changing its pitch. **Note:** When used in left-hand fingering discussions, *fret* refers to the space below the actual fret wire.

- **Head or headstock:** The slotted section at the top of the neck beyond the *nut* that holds the *tuning machines,* where the strings fasten.

- **Lower bout:** The large, outwardly curved section of the body that surrounds the bridge.

- **Neck:** The long, semicircular piece of wood jutting out from the body, with a *head* on one end and strings stretching the full length and beyond. Usually made of mahogany, maple, or other hard woods, the neck's light weight and grain strength enable it to hold its shape while under the considerable tension produced by the taut strings drawn up to pitch.

- **Neck heel, heel:** The outward-sticking part of the neck that joins the neck to the sides and back of the body.

- **Nut:** A synthetic (formerly ivory or bone) strip of material that sits between the fingerboard and the headstock. Grooves cut into the nut hold the strings in place as they pass through the nut on their way to the tuning machines.

- **Rollers:** The white plastic cylinders inside the slots in the head that go perpendicular to the strings and that create a spool for the strings to wrap around as they're wound up or down to pitch. The rollers rotate by means of the *tuning pegs.*

- **Rosette:** The decorative ring around the *sound hole,* usually made of *marquetry* — inlaid bits of colored wood and other materials (such as mother-of-pearl) arranged in a mosaic-like pattern.

- **Saddle:** A synthetic (formerly ivory or bone) strip of material that sits in a slot in the bridge. The strings rest on top of the saddle, pressing down on it before passing through the bridge holes, where they're tied off (or otherwise anchored).

- **Sides:** The narrow, curved wooden pieces between the top and back of the guitar. The sides are made of the same wood as the back and serve to hold together the top and back and to help reflect sound out of the body and through the top.

- **Slots:** On a classical guitar, the long, oval-shaped holes in the head that expose the rollers and allow the strings to pass through the surface of the head to reach the rollers.

- **Sound hole:** The circular opening in the soundboard, directly underneath the strings in the upper bout. The sound hole helps to project the sound, but it isn't the exclusive source of sound emanating from the guitar.

- **Soundboard or Top:** Also referred to as the *table,* the top is the flat, lighter-colored wood on the body that faces the listener. Its function isn't to remain rigid and reflect sound but to resonate (vibrate) with the strings, amplifying them and projecting the sound in the process.

- ✔ **Strings:** The strings are what the guitarist touches (fretting with the left hand, plucking with the right) to make sound. The six strings travel the length of the neck from the head, where they're wrapped around the tuning machines' rollers to beyond the fingerboard, where they're tied off at the bridge. The top three, or treble, strings are solid nylon. The bottom three, or bass, strings have a nylon core and are surrounded by a metal wrap. (All six strings are referred to as nylon strings, even though the bottom three have an outward metal material.) Strings are available at different prices (usually determined by quality) and are categorized by the degree of tension (such as high and medium).

- ✔ **Tuning machines:** The metal hardware system of gears, shafts, and *tuning pegs* used to wind the strings to different tensions to get them in tune.

- ✔ **Tuning pegs:** The *handles* or *buttons* of the tuning machines that guitarists grip with their fingers to allow them to tune the strings by tightening or loosening them.

- ✔ **Upper bout:** The large, outwardly curved section of the body that surrounds the sound hole and the upper frets of the fingerboard.

- ✔ **Waist:** The narrow, inwardly curved part of the body between the upper bout and the lower bout.

How a Classical Guitar Is Physically Different from Its Peers

A classical guitar is like every other guitar in overall physique. And like other types of acoustic guitars, the classical guitar produces its sound, well, *acoustically* — that is, without the aid of amplification — unlike the Stratocaster of Jimi Hendrix, which must be played through a guitar amplifier (though it is possible to amplify the acoustic sound of a classical guitar with a microphone).

But watch out when you hear the term *acoustic guitar.* A classical guitar produces its sound without amplification, so all classical guitars are in a sense acoustic guitars. But not all acoustics are classical.

Sometimes the best way to know what something is and what makes it special is to know what it isn't. Check out Figure 1-2, which shows a classical guitar alongside a popular traditional acoustic model. Then read through the following list, which sums up some of the major differences between them:

Figure 1-2: A classical guitar (right) with an acoustic steel-string model alongside it.

Acoustic guitar   Classical guitar

✔ **A classical guitar uses nylon strings.** All other acoustics used for unplugged purposes are built for steel strings. And you can't just swap out a set of nylons in your steel string and start playing Bach. The parts that connect the strings to the guitar are built differently, and you'd have a tough time securing a nylon string onto a steel-string guitar. Nylon strings have a gentler sound that suits classical guitar music better than the steel variety.

Some people use the adjective *folk* to mean any unamplified guitar, so it's always a good idea to clarify whether they mean the nylon-string (classical) or steel-string variety — assuming they're aware of the difference. The guitars played by James Taylor, Paul Simon, Bob Dylan, Joni Mitchell, Dave Matthews, and Sheryl Crow are all *steel-string acoustics,* though some folk, pop, and jazz musicians do play their brand of music on a classical guitar, including jazz guitarist Earl Klugh and, somewhat improbably, country music legend Willie Nelson.

Though the instrument is officially known as a *classical guitar,* other nicknames have sprung up that have come to refer to the "instrument played by classical guitarists." Some of these names include *nylon-string guitar, Spanish guitar,* and *gut-string guitar.*

✔ **A classical guitar has only one body size.** Acoustic guitar bodies vary widely with regard to size and shape, with names like *jumbo, dreadnought, orchestra model,* and *grand auditorium* to help you keep track of them all. It's much easier with classical guitars — they're all the same size and they all feel exactly alike when you hold them. So anything you learn on one classical guitar will transfer over to any other without a major adjustment.

✔ **A classical guitar has no cutaway.** Many acoustic guitars have a scoop on the *treble* (toward the skinny, higher-pitched strings) side of the upper bout that allows upper-fret access for the left hand. On a classical guitar, the body is symmetrical.

✔ **A classical guitar neck is wider than the necks on most steel strings and joins the body at the 12th fret.** Steel-string necks are skinnier to facilitate strumming with a pick, and most modern-style steel-string necks join the body at the 14th fret. The wider frets of the classical guitar accommodate playing with the right-hand fingers, and tradition dictates the 12-fret union of neck and body (although some classical guitarists lament the more limited range of a 12-fret neck).

✔ **A classical guitar has no pickguard.** A pickguard helps protect the soundboard from the ravages of a pick. But because you don't play classical guitar with a pick, the pickguard is unnecessary and is left off to expose more of the wooden surface. In flamenco guitars, though, a clear protective plate (called a *golpeador*) is added to protect the top from the percussive taps a performer is sometimes required to play as part of the style.

✔ **A classical guitar has no fret markers.** Acoustic guitars have inlay patterns both on the fingerboard and on the side of the neck. Sometimes these inlays can be quite elaborate, even gaudy. But classical guitars shun such showy displays and present the fingerboard in its natural, unadorned state. Occasionally, a classical guitar may have a single dot fret marker on the side of the neck.

✔ **A classical guitar never has the following images painted or stickered onto its surface:** skulls, lightning bolts, flames, your girlfriend's name, or politically incorrect slogans of any kind.

Antonio Torres: Inventor of the modern classical guitar

Plucked string instruments have been around since ancient times, but the shape that all modern classical guitar makers follow was established by a *luthier* (the term for guitar maker) named Antonio Torres (1817–1892), who lived in Spain and built guitars in the middle of the 19th century. Up until that time, a classical guitar could be found in a range of sizes, which affected the tuning and your entire approach to playing the instrument. For the guitar to be accepted, it had to be standardized, and Torres did that. In fact, an 1863 Torres-made guitar is almost indistinguishable from ones built today. One of the most important things Torres did was establish the string length at 650 millimeters, which hasn't changed. The string length has helped to determine other things, like the body proportions, the neck length, and the guitar's overall dimensions. Many bold makers have tried alternate shapes and materials and added strings, but no one has successfully improved on the basic design of Torres's creation.

Modern improvements have been made, of course, especially in the manufacturing process and in some of the materials (such as synthetic substitutes for the bone or ivory nut and saddle, and better alloy chemistries for the metal tuning parts). But the woods and design have remained largely unchanged since Torres codified them back in the mid-1800s.

Beyond Physique: Other Unique Attributes of Classical Guitar

You may find yourself in a position of trying to explain to someone what's different about the classical guitar when compared to other types of guitar music or guitar playing styles. (You may even want to be clear on what you're getting into yourself!) Sure, the most fundamental difference is that classical guitar is acoustic and played on a nylon-string guitar, but you could say that about other styles and other performers. (Willie Nelson is just one famous example of a nonclassical nylon-string guitar player.) So you have to dig deeper into the essence of classical guitar.

In the next section, you explore some of these key differences — in terms of the physical approach to the instrument — between classical guitar and other acoustic guitar styles.

Player's form and technique

Classical guitar requires that you hold the guitar in a certain way and position your hands in ways that are different from those of other styles of music.

Using these positions makes playing pieces easier, especially when you have to play up the neck or play notes with certain right-hand strokes in order to achieve the fuller tone of classical guitar music. The most important factors are how you hold the guitar, how you place your hands in playing position, and how your right-hand fingers pluck the strings.

The way you hold the instrument

You can hold an acoustic guitar a number of different ways: balanced on your right leg, balanced on your left leg (either between your legs or with your left leg crossed over your right), or dangling from a strap when you're standing up. But the classical guitar is played only in a sitting position, supported by the left leg — either with the left foot elevated or with a special support device (a cushion or frame) between the inner thigh and the guitar's body.

Hand positions

In other styles, you can position the right hand in a number of ways, and no one will correct you (as long as you sound good and aren't doing anything wrong). But in classical guitar, you must hold your right-hand fingers perpendicular to the strings, without touching any other part of the guitar (the top, the bridge). You must also position the left hand so that the hand knuckles (the ones farthest from the fingertips) are parallel to the strings, not sloped away from the strings at the little finger, which some styles allow. And in classical guitar, the left-hand thumb stays braced at the center of the back of the neck or can move toward the high strings, if necessary. But it should never be seen coming up from the bass-string side of the instrument, as you can do in some fingerpicking styles.

Playing style: No picks allowed

To produce sounds on the guitar, you pluck the strings with the fingers of the right hand at a position over the sound hole (actually, the ideal position is not directly over the hole, but a little closer to the bridge than the fingerboard). With the left-hand fingers, you change the pitches of the notes by pressing the strings to the fretboard — a process known as *fretting* — which shortens the strings' vibrating length at a particular fret. (Violinists and other bowed string players don't have frets, so they refer to pressing fingers to the fingerboard as *stopping* the string, a term guitarists sometimes use, too.)

Unlike other forms of guitar playing, in classical guitar, you don't use a pick, or plectrum. (If you play with a pick in another guitar life, leave it at the door when you come into the world of classical guitar!) All the sounds produced by the right hand are created by the unadorned fingers, using the tips with a combination of the fleshy pad and a bit of fingernail (except in the rare cases where you strum downward, "brushing" the strings). The fingernail must extend slightly over the fingertip, and the guitarist must therefore maintain longer nails on the right hand than guitarists who play with a pick, or those who choose to fingerpick with just the flesh of the fingers.

Though classical guitar is played by "picking with the fingers," the term *fingerpicking* isn't used, as it sometimes is with other styles. And don't ever call a serious classical guitarist a "fingerpicker" — unless you want to get a rise out of him!

Musical knowledge and skills

Beyond perfecting the techniques necessary to execute classical music flawlessly (or getting ever nearer to that goal), classical guitarists develop their music-reading skills to cover more repertoire. And having more and more pieces under your belt means you can perform for longer periods of time and with more variety when entertaining listeners. The best classical guitarists are also technically superior to players of lesser abilities (a quality that's not necessarily true in, say, pop music). The following sections outline why classical guitarists focus on improving their reading, mastering repertoire, and honing their technical skills.

The importance of reading music

You can play many types of music without reading a single note of music. Certainly some of the best rock, blues, and folk players don't read music well or even at all, and it doesn't hamper their creative or technical abilities. But classical guitar relies on learning pieces, and the fastest, most efficient way to play through and memorize written music is, obviously, to be able to read music well. That doesn't mean you have to sight read at a level where you can play the music perfectly and up to tempo the first time, but you should be able to read well enough to get a sense of the piece.

The value of mastering repertoire

If you play the classical guitar, you play *pieces* — classical compositions or arrangements written out from start to finish, with the exact notes you're to play and often the way to play them (with indications for articulations, dynamics, and expression). You have to know written, composed music from start to finish, and most of the time you have to play it from memory.

The focus on technical skill, virtuosity, and musicianship

Other styles of music may focus on aspects such as the originality of the material or the inspired results of an improvisation. But in classical guitar, the primary focus is on technical mastery of the instrument. You work and work at improving your skill constantly your whole musical life, and your prowess is measured by how well you play standard pieces of repertoire. Simply put, classical guitarists are measured in the same way athletes are: The best classical guitarists are the most demonstrably technically proficient over their rivals.

One measure of technical proficiency is virtuosity — the ability to play extraordinarily difficult pieces with complete confidence, ease, and mastery. Along with technical prowess comes the not-so-showy quality called musicianship, which is understanding and executing the music with great accuracy, authority, and expression. In this way, the classical guitar has more in common with other classical instruments than it does with other styles of guitar music.

Now, if all this sounds like a lot of rules and that these rules may somehow restrict you in some way, take heart. The opposite is true. You find that the differences between classical technique and other techniques (or no discernible approach to technique at all!) actually enable you to play notes more comfortably, easily, and with greater speed, accuracy, control, and range of expression. It may seem like a lot of do's and don'ts at first, but just as in ballet, architecture, and other art forms, you need to master the basic skills to open up a world of possibilities. To achieve total freedom of expression in playing classical guitar music, you first need to gain total control.

Chapter 2

Getting Ready to Play

In This Chapter

▶ Holding the guitar

▶ Fretting and stroking the strings

▶ Getting your guitar in tune

*I*n this chapter, we get you poised and ready to play classical guitar with the proper posture, hand positions, and approach to the instrument. And lest we forget discerning listeners within earshot — including you! — we also show you how to tune your guitar.

Situating Yourself

Your first step in getting ready to play classical guitar is to make sure you're holding the instrument correctly and with your hands in the proper position. Unlike other styles of guitar playing, where common sense and comfort are often the only guidelines, classical guitar requires you to hold and position the instrument in certain ways, because they allow you to play more smoothly and to master more difficult fingerings you may encounter. But though these requirements are specific, they're not difficult or restrictive in any way.

In proper position, a classical guitar makes contact with four points on your body. This allows you to keep a firm hold on the guitar while your hands enjoy the mobility they need to play freely. The four contact points support the guitar as follows (see Figure 2-1):

1. **Resting on the left leg.** This one's easy, because gravity does all the work! Set the guitar on your raised left leg (or use a support, explained in the section "Supporting the guitar: Leg position") and proceed to the other points from here.

2. **Braced against the right leg.** The lower side of the guitar presses against the inner thigh of the right leg. You can move your leg around a bit if you feel the corner (the spot where the back and sides meet at a 90-degree angle) digging into your thigh in an uncomfortable way.

3. **Touching the chest.** The back of the guitar, just behind the bass side of the upper bout, should lightly touch the center of your chest.

4. **Lightly touching your right arm.** Your right arm rests, but doesn't press tightly, on the side. Avoid pushing the underside of the forearm into the guitar's top, as that may impede its ability to vibrate and project sound.

Figure 2-1:
How to hold the guitar according to the four pressure points.

Taking your seat

Unlike other styles of playing where you can stand or sit, classical guitar is always played from a seated position. You never stand (or kneel, or lie on your back, as some showoff rock guitarists do), and you never use a strap. In fact, a classical guitar doesn't even have the strap pins you often find built into other types of acoustic guitars.

Before you sit down just anywhere to hold the guitar, you should know that classical guitar prohibits certain types of seating arrangements. For one, you can't plop down on the living room couch or a beanbag chair. These two locations, as comfortable as they are for reading or messing around with *other* types of guitar, can't put you in the proper playing position for dealing with classical guitar technique. What you need is a sturdy, armless chair (which rules out easy chairs and desk chairs with arms). Any kind of armless chair will do the job, including a dining room chair, a straight-back chair, or even a folding chair.

The chair you use should be relatively comfortable so that you can spend long periods there without getting uncomfortable or risking strain or stiffness. If you use a normal metal folding chair, you may want to add a pad or cushion for comfort, as you may be spending a good deal of time in that chair — especially if you want to get really good!

Supporting the guitar: Leg position

Another thing you have to attend to, after you find the appropriate chair, is a means to elevate your left foot off the floor about 4 to 6 inches, a trick you can easily accomplish with a footstool that's specially built for the classical guitarist. They're not very expensive (about $25), and you can buy them at any music store. If you don't have a footstool yet, just use a couple of hard-cover books.

So to get started, find yourself a sturdy armless chair and sit toward the edge. Sit up straight with your legs slightly apart so that you can set the waist of the guitar on your left leg. Place your foot on the footstool (or whatever improvised platform you have) and look straight ahead. Your position should look similar to that shown in Figure 2-2.

An alternative to raising your leg is to use a specially made *support* or *cushion* on your left leg, which raises the guitar to the proper playing position while allowing you to keep both feet on the floor. Advocates of the support claim that it's better for your back because it doesn't require you to lift one leg in a sitting position, which causes strain. Figure 2-3 shows this alternate method, using an adjustable support that braces against the inner thigh and cradles the guitar by means of a curved piece that matches the contour of the side of the guitar's body.

Some guitarists alternate the support with the footstool, which mixes it up for the body, preventing them from having to maintain one position for too long. A guitarist may, for example, practice for two hours using the support, and then practice another hour with the footstool. Or he may choose to rehearse with the support and perform with the footstool. This is the approach we like, because we think that the support is more comfortable over long periods of time.

Figure 2-2:
Seated in
the playing
position,
with the
left leg
elevated.

Figure 2-3:
The support
offers an
alterna-
tive means
of raising
the guitar
to playing
position
without
elevating
the left foot.

Embracing the guitar: Arm support

Classical guitarists don't invest in all the doodads and gadgetry available for other types of guitarists, but occasionally, a device or accessory comes along that becomes part of the classical guitarist's bag of tricks. In addition to the support, another common external device you find is the *arm rest.* This fits on the guitar's side, on the bass side of the lower bout, directly under where the right arm sits, as shown in Figure 2-4. The arm rest lifts the forearm off the guitar's top, allowing the top to vibrate freely. Without the arm rest, the right arm inevitably touches the top, even if the guitarist is careful to maintain light contact only. Because the arm rest prevents direct contact between the arm and the guitar, it also serves to prevent wear to the finish from sweat and from friction caused by the arm rubbing against the top and side (especially on instruments with thin tops). Some arm rests lift the right arm off the instrument entirely, which is a benefit to big and tall players, as it helps them maintain good posture and prevents them from having to hunch over the instrument.

Figure 2-4: An arm rest lifts the right arm off the guitar, allowing the top to vibrate more freely.

Placing your hands correctly

When you're in the proper sitting position and feeling comfortable, it's time to turn your attention to your hands. Classical guitar technique requires a specific way to position your right and left hands when playing the guitar, so in this section we take things one hand at a time to get you ready to play your first notes in the correct classical guitar way.

For now, all you're going to do here is *place* your hands in the proper position for playing. Don't worry just yet about actually making sounds or playing notes. This is simply a check to make sure that your hands fall on the guitar in a natural, comfortable, and correct way.

The right hand

Assuming you're seated with the guitar balanced on your left leg (as discussed in the earlier sections, "Taking your seat" and "Supporting the guitar: Leg position"), place your right hand so that it hovers above the strings over the sound hole. Actually, don't center your hand directly over the sound hole, but slightly to the right of it, in the direction of the bridge. Figure 2-5 shows how your right hand should look when placed correctly.

Figure 2-5: Placing the right hand over the strings, over the sound hole but a little toward the bridge.

Let your right forearm touch the edge of the guitar on the bass side of the lower bout. Your hand should be loose and relaxed, with your wrist bent, or angled, in a way to cause the fingers, if you were to outstretch them, to fall perpendicular to the strings, as shown in Figure 2-6. In some playing situations, you may relax this "absolutely perpendicular" approach, allowing your hand to look like the position in Figure 2-1.

You should be able to pivot your right elbow so that your right hand pulls away from the guitar without the guitar moving or going out of balance.

Try wiggling your fingers in the air above the strings. If you feel tension in your forearm muscle, you may be pressing your arm against the guitar's top too tightly. You don't need to hold the guitar in place with your right arm, so try lightening up a bit. The right arm and hand should almost float above the guitar and strings. And no part of your right hand should rest on the top of the guitar. All your fingers should dangle freely above the strings. Make sure your shoulders are relaxed as well.

Figure 2-6:
Angling your right hand so that the fingers fall perpendicular to the strings.

The left hand

When your right hand is in position, turn your focus — and your head — to points leftward. With the guitar balanced on your left leg, open your left hand slightly by separating the thumb from the fingers. Then slip your left hand around the neck and place your thumb on the center of the neck's back, allowing it to rest lightly there. Position your left-hand fingertips to press down the strings on the top of the fingerboard. Figure 2-7 shows how your left hand should look from the back.

Turning your attention to the fingerboard side of the neck, check to see that the hand knuckles (the ones farthest from the fingertips) are more or less parallel to the strings. Don't worry about pressing any strings yet; for now just get your hand in position. Figure 2-8 shows the fingers arched and ready to press down on the strings.

Figure 2-7:
The left hand placed on the neck, with the thumb centered on the neck's back.

Figure 2-8:
The
left-hand
fingers
ready to
press down
on the
strings.

A good check to see if the guitar is well-balanced is to take your left hand completely away from the guitar. The guitar shouldn't move at all, as you don't use the left hand to support the neck.

Approaching the Strings with Your Hands

In classical guitar, left-hand techniques are intuitive and natural — not that much different from left-hand techniques used in other types of guitar playing. In contrast, right-hand techniques are very specific and have to be learned, and they require you to not only position your hand so that the fingers strike the strings at a perpendicular angle but also to execute the notes using specific plucking methods, or strokes, called the free stroke and the rest stroke. This section walks you through these left-hand and right-hand techniques.

Fretting the strings: Left-hand form

Pressing the strings to the fretboard with the left-hand fingers is known as *fretting,* and it's the way guitarists change pitches on the strings. To fret a string, use a left-hand finger to press the string down to the fingerboard with just enough pressure to cause the string to ring clearly (without buzzing or muffling).

To fret the strings as effectively and efficiently as possible, don't place your finger squarely in the middle of the two fret wires; you play a little closer to the higher fret (the one closer to the bridge). This gives you better leverage when pressing down on the string, meaning that it requires less strength to produce a strong, pure sound. Pressing closer to the higher fret helps eliminate buzzing, too.

When fretting a note, approach the string from above, rather than from the side, to get the maximum downward pressure against the fretboard, and keep your fingers rounded (not flat or hyper-extended) by curling your knuckles. This best marshals your finger strength to the tip, where it provides the most effective fretting. Curving your fingers also helps you avoid accidentally touching adjacent strings. And you may be relieved to know that the left-hand fingernails can be kept short! In fact, if you're accustomed to having long left-hand fingernails, you'll have to trim them back to be flush or below the fingertips for the best results.

Figures 2-9 and 2-10 show proper left-hand fretting technique.

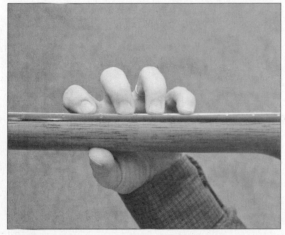

Figure 2-9:
The left hand placed correctly on the fingerboard.

Figure 2-10:
Keeping the fingers curved and approaching the string from above, rather than from the side, to achieve the best sound.

A guitarist's guide to nail filing

After you acquire the proper tools and your right-hand nails are long enough to give you some raw material to work with, follow these steps to shape and finish them so that they can enhance your classical guitar tone:

1. **Use the coarse surface of the file or emery board to get the nails into a basic rounded shape.** If you're using a multi-surface emery board, start with the roughest-feeling grit. File down excess length and then shape the nail's edge to follow the contour of the fingertip in a symmetrical oval. Check your progress frequently by holding your outstretched fingers in front of you, parallel to the wall, with your fingertips at eye level.

2. **In addition to filing the edge of the nail, drag the file between the nail and the fingertip to round out any rough surface on the underside of the nail.**

3. **When the shape is curved and even, switch to a finer grit to smooth out any rough edges left by the coarser surface.** Eliminating snags or rough spots will make your sound smoother as well as prevent snagging on clothing and other fabrics, which can cause the nail to tear.

4. **When you've filed the nails smooth, try using fine grit sandpaper (600 or finer) or the emery board's finishing surface to make the nails even smoother, giving them an almost polished feel that protects them for longer periods between maintenance.**

Preparing to pluck: Right-hand form

Though you don't have to start out with long right-hand fingernails, sooner or later you have to grow and maintain them to be able to effect the tonal variations necessary for classical guitar playing. All classical guitarists agree that combining the nail with the fleshy part of the fingertip to pluck the string is essential in deriving the full spectrum of tonal colors and achieving the wide dynamic range required for classical guitar music.

Preparing your right-hand fingernails for action

To get "good guitar nails," let your right-hand fingernails grow so that they extend about $\frac{1}{16}$ inch beyond the tip. This measurement is only an estimate, so your nails can be longer or shorter, as long as you're able to get some of the nail in contact with the string when you pluck it. You may find it easier to keep your nails shorter as you're first learning to use them, allowing them to grow longer as you develop control. Many players like to have a slightly longer thumbnail for added bass note authority.

It's not enough just to have long fingernails. They also have to be properly shaped — that is, they should follow the shape of your fingertip — and you should keep them smooth and free of nicks and chips. To keep your fingernails at a consistent length and shape, you need to care for them on a regular basis and to invest in some "fingernail paraphernalia." A two-sided diamond nail file and a multi-surface emery board are good options. For more on nail care, see the nearby sidebar, "A guitarist's guide to nail filing."

Making a beautiful sound: The nail-flesh tone

Anyone who studies classical guitar spends long hours perfecting the development of the nail-flesh tone, as it's such an inherent part of classical guitar technique and tone. Being able to combine the nail with the flesh (as shown in Figure 2-11) by angling the finger so that both tip and nail catch the string, in combinations that provide near-infinite degrees of tonal shading, is what makes the guitarist's palette of right-hand sounds so rich.

Figure 2-11: How to pluck to achieve the classical nail-flesh tone.

Stroking the strings: Basic right-hand technique

The *free stroke* is the classical guitar name for the stroke that you probably perform naturally if you already pluck the guitar strings with your fingers. In a free stroke, your fingers and thumb pluck the string in an outward motion, away from the top of the guitar, leaving them "free," or dangling in the air, above the strings and poised to strike again.

The *rest stroke* is what classical guitar players use to produce strong, expressive, and powerful notes — more powerful than those that can be obtained by the free stroke. The "rest" part refers to the finger coming to a stop, or rest, on the next string in the direction of the stroke. Rest strokes are played with the fingers more often than the thumb and enable you to give notes more power and volume than a free stroke yields. But rest strokes are a little less nimble than free strokes, so you use them on notes that aren't moving too quickly.

Many guitarists who first encounter free strokes and rest strokes often wonder when to use one or the other. See Table 2-1 for a handy list that describes which situation falls to the free stroke and which setting is a candidate for the rest stroke.

Table 2-1	Free Stroke versus Rest Stroke
Use the Free Stroke When You Play	*Use the Rest Stroke When You Play*
Arpeggios	Slower, more expressive melodies
Chords	Scales, scale sequences, and single-note passages
Light-sounding melodies, or filler notes between melody and bass parts	Loud notes, or notes requiring maximum volume or feeling of intensity
Melodies or passages where the rest stroke can't be applied because of tempo considerations, string conflicts, or awkwardness and impracticalities in the right-hand fingering	Passages that must be drawn out from their surroundings (either other notes from the guitar or in an ensemble setting), assuming no conflict with other strings

The free stroke

Playing the free stroke doesn't involve any specific trick or technique. It's a very natural way to play the guitar, and the way all styles of fingerpicking (not just limited to the classical style) are performed. In fact, if you think about it too much, you may cause it to sound overly deliberate. Just pluck the string and do it several times to ensure an easy, natural approach.

To play a free stroke, place the index finger of your right hand on the open 1st string. With a brisk motion, bending from the finger knuckle, pluck the string by drawing the finger toward the palm and slightly upward (being careful not to strike the 2nd string as you do) so that your finger ends up above the strings dangling freely, as shown in Figure 2-12.

Repeat the process until you can play several plucks in a row smoothly. (Be sure that you're striking only the intended string and not the adjacent string.) After you're comfortable playing free strokes with your index finger, play free strokes several times in a row using your middle finger. Then repeat the process with your ring finger.

You almost never use the little finger of the right hand in classical guitar, so after you can play free strokes with your index, middle, and ring fingers by themselves, try playing free strokes with the three fingers in combination. For example, try playing index, middle, index, middle; then index, middle, ring, index, middle, ring; then middle, ring, middle, ring; and finally, index, ring, index, ring.

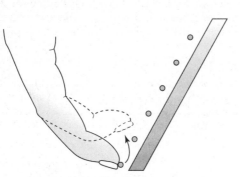

Figure 2-12:
Play a free stroke by plucking the 1st string and leaving your finger above the strings, poised to strike again.

Playing a free stroke with the thumb is just like playing a free stroke with the fingers, except that you move in the opposite direction. To play a free stroke with your thumb, place it on the 6th string. Then push through the string, plucking it, and bring your thumb slightly upward toward your palm so that you don't strike the 5th string. Your thumb should end up above the strings, as shown in Figure 2-13.

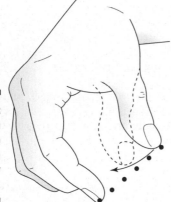

Figure 2-13:
The motion of the free stroke played by the thumb.

The rest stroke

A rest stroke always means coming to rest on the next adjacent string in the direction of the stroke. For the fingers, this means the next lower string in pitch (or next higher-numbered string). For example, if you play a rest stroke on the 2nd string, your finger rests on the 3rd string. Rest strokes must always have a "place to park" after you play the string. Sometimes this creates a problem if you have to play the string underneath with the thumb or another finger, or if that string must be allowed to ring out from being previously plucked. In those cases, you must use a free stroke, even if a rest stoke would be a more musical choice.

To play a rest stroke, plant your right-hand index finger on the open 1st string. Then, in one motion, draw it back, plucking the string and following all the way through until your finger is stopped by the 2nd string. Be sure you don't play through the 2nd string; if you do, you're plucking too hard. To better adopt the rest-stroke motion, it may help to think of drawing or pulling the finger downward into the guitar, rather than away from the guitar, as you do in a free stroke. Figure 2-14 shows the motion of the rest stroke.

Figure 2-14:
The right-hand index finger playing a rest stroke on the 1st string and then stopping, or resting, on the 2nd string.

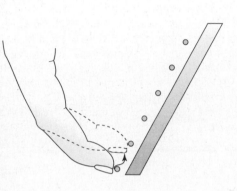

Because the rest stroke has this extra condition of a "landing string," it's a little more limited in its use than a free stroke is. For example, you can't use the rest stroke for arpeggios, which we discuss in Chapter 5. But for bringing out a solo melody, nothing beats the expressive power of a rest stroke!

Playing rest strokes with the thumb is rare, though you sometimes play them this way in order to bring out a solo bass line or low-note melody. In case you do need to play one, you should know that the principles for playing a rest stroke with the thumb are the same as with the fingers, except that your thumb moves in the opposite direction (toward the floor instead of the ceiling). To play a rest stroke with the thumb, plant your thumb on the open 6th string. Then push your thumb so that it plucks the 6th string and follows through to the 5th string, where it stops. See Figure 2-15 for the motion of the thumb rest stroke.

The birth of modern stroking technique

Because they imbue classical guitar music with its unique flavor, you may think the rest stroke and nail sound were always there — preordained, like some version of the "Ten Commandments of Classical Guitar" or something. But the rest stroke is only a recent practice and one largely promoted by Andrés Segovia's mentor, Francisco Tárrega (1852–1909). The rest stroke gave guitarists a much more powerful way to extract notes from the guitar than the free stroke could muster. And while Segovia adopted, embraced, and perfected Tárrega's rest stroke, he differed with him regarding the use of right-hand fingernails. Tárrega and many others of the time were strongly opposed to using the nails. Emilio Pujol, a famous guitarist, composer, and Tárrega champion, thought the sound was "conical, pungent, and nasal," whereas the flesh-only sound "possesses an intrinsic beauty . . . as might be the notes of an ideally expressive and responsive harp." But Segovia persevered and ultimately won out. It's a good thing, too, as, without the use of the nail, the guitarist can't produce a sharp, percussive attack. And when playing the wide range of classical guitar music, we guitarists need to be able to play bright, crispy sounds as well as soft, mellow ones.

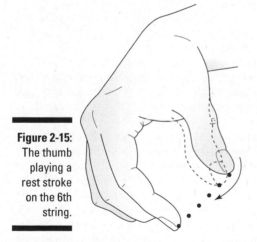

Figure 2-15:
The thumb playing a rest stroke on the 6th string.

Tuning Up

Before you begin playing notes in earnest, your guitar must be in tune. You can tune your guitar either visually, by playing a note and letting an electronic tuner tell you whether the note is sharp or flat, or audibly, where it's up to you to determine whether the note is on pitch and, if not, whether it's sharp or flat.

Although you should be able to tune using either the visual or audible method, we prefer the visual method, as it tends to be more accurate and faster than using your ear. Tuning by listening is important for when a string slips out of tune mid-piece, and you don't have time to access the tuner, but for serious tuning up, it's best to rely on the tuner.

The following sections cover the most common ways guitarists tune up their instruments.

Adjusting the string tension to raise or lower pitch

Regardless of what method you use or what technology you rely on, all guitarists change the pitch of their strings in the same way: by using the tuning peg to tighten or loosen the string. If the string is *flat,* or below pitch, you must wind the peg so that the string becomes tighter. If the string is *sharp,* or above pitch, you must loosen the string.

If your string is sharp, you should loosen the string so that it actually goes flat of the target note. Then you should tighten the string so that you come up to pitch from below. In other words, all strings should be tuned up from below — even if they start out sharp. Tuning up from below ensures that even tension results between the string areas above and below the nut.

As you look at the headstock from behind, rotate the pegs counterclockwise to raise the string in pitch, and clockwise to lower the string in pitch.

Tuning visually with an electronic tuner

Using an electronic tuner means you're taking a cue from a "higher authority"— a source you trust to be in tune, which you use to adjust your guitar. In the case of an electronic tuner, however, the source doesn't produce an audible pitch to compare your guitar strings to. Instead, the electronic tuner gives you a visual readout of your guitar's tuning on a meter, LED (light-emitting diode), or other visually oriented display that lets you know whether you're sharp or flat of the mark.

An electronic tuner can be an advantage in a noisy environment or when your ears aren't completely up to the task of determining perfect tuning (either because you're not yet sure of their ability in that area or you're tired). Tuning by matching each string's pitch to a display is also much faster than using your ear. Electronic tuners used to be the province of electric and acoustic guitarists, but more and more classical guitarists are using them because of these important advantages.

Just because an electronic tuner allows you to tune without the aid of your ears doesn't mean you shouldn't develop your ears to tune. Hearing the subtle differences between out-of-tune strings — and being able to get them in tune — is very important in developing your ear skills. But being able to tune visually is faster, more reliable, and more accurate in certain situations than relying on your ears.

All electronic tuners work in a similar fashion: You play a string on your guitar and the tuner tells you its pitch (A, B♭, C♯, and so on) and whether you're flat or sharp of being perfectly in tune with that pitch. For example, if the electronic tuner reads "G" when you play the open 5th string (A), you know you're a whole step under, or flat of, your target. You tune the string up until you see the display change from G to G♯ to A.

After you have the desired pitch in terms of its letter name, you refer to the other part of the display or meter that tells you whether you're flat or sharp of that pitch (see Figure 2-16). When you see that the meter is dead center (or whatever means it uses to signify perfect tuning), you're in tune. You can then play another string and the tuner automatically senses the new pitch. You don't have to touch the tuner at all to tune all six strings. A chromatic electronic tuner (one that isn't restricted to just the open strings) can sense fretted notes accurately as well. So you can tune up according to the notes of a basic E chord or an up-the-neck barre chord if you want.

Figure 2-16: An electronic tuner uses visual feedback to help you get in tune.

Tuning by ear

Long before guitarists had the modern convenience of electronic tuners, they tuned by listening to match two tones to each other. You too must be able to hear if the guitar goes out of tune, and you sometimes have to make a quick adjustment using just your ear, because accessing the tuner is impractical or impossible. By listening to your guitar when you tune, you're using an audible, rather than visual, approach.

You can tune your guitar audibly by using any of the following methods. We recommend getting familiar with all of them, even if you prefer one over the others; you never know what situation you and your guitar may find yourselves in, but you always have to be in tune when you play. Typically, though, if you have a reliable fixed source available, you take from it the six notes that match each of your six open strings. You can also take just one note from the fixed source (such as the E, 12 white keys below middle C on a piano or keyboard), tune the appropriate string first (the open low E, in this example), and then tune the other five strings to that.

Tuning the guitar to itself

As long as your guitar isn't hopelessly far from the mark as far as where the strings should be pitched, you can get your guitar "in tune with itself" by tuning all the strings according to one string that you designate as the "master," or reference. This method is also called *relative tuning*. For example, if you decide to base your tuning on the open low E string, you leave it unchanged and tune the other five strings in relation to it.

To tune the guitar to itself using the open 6th string as a reference, refer to Figure 2-17 and follow these steps:

1. **Play the 6th string, 5th fret, and let the note ring. With the 6th string still sounding, play the open 5th string (A). Compare the pitches of the two strings.** If the A string is lower, or flat, compared to the 6th string, reach your right hand over your left hand — which remains pressing down on the fret of the ringing 6th string — and tune the A string higher until it matches the 6th string exactly. If the A string is higher, or sharp, compared to the 6th string, tune it lower until it matches exactly. You may have to repeat this procedure several times to get the 5th string perfectly in tune.

2. **Play the 5th string, 5th fret, and let the note ring. While the string still sounds, play the open 4th string (D). As in Step 1, compare the pitches of the two strings.** If the open D string is flat compared to the fretted 5th string, reach over with your right hand and tune it higher until it matches the ringing 5th string exactly. If the D string is sharp, tune it down until you achieve a match.

3. **Play the 4th string, 5th fret, and let the note ring. Play the open 3rd string (G). As in previous steps, compare the open string to the fretted string.** If the open string is flat or sharp compared to the fretted string, tune it in the appropriate direction so that it matches the fretted note exactly.

4. **Play the 3rd string, 4th fret (*not* the 5th fret), and let the note ring. Play the open 2nd string (B). Compare the open string to the fretted string and adjust the open string up or down in pitch accordingly to match the fretted 3rd string.**

5. **Play the 2nd string, 5th fret, and let the note ring. Play the open 1st string (high E). Compare the open string to the fretted string and tune the open string accordingly.**

After you complete Steps 1 through 5, go back and repeat them at least once, as some strings may have slipped or stretched a little as you continued to tune.

Figure 2-17:
A neck diagram showing how to match fretted strings against open ones in the relative tuning method.

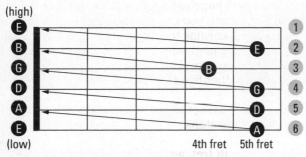

Tuning to a fixed source

Using the relative method to tune will get your guitar in tune with itself, but to ensure that you're in tune with the outside world — such as other instruments and to the standard reference of A-440 (440 cycles per second) — you need to tune to a fixed source that provides an accurate standard pitch. An in-tune piano, an electronic keyboard, a pitch pipe, and a tuning fork are all examples of fixed sources that you can use to tune to. To become the most self-reliant, we recommend becoming familiar with tuning to a pitch pipe or tuning fork, as you can always have these devices close by — tucked into the pocket of your guitar case.

When tuning to a fixed source, first play the note from the source, which you use as a reference. Then play the string on the guitar that corresponds to that pitch. While both the fixed source and the string are ringing, compare their pitches to determine if the string is higher or lower than the fixed source. You may have to play either the source or string a few times to decide (especially if they're already close in pitch, or just a little out of tune). Then raise or lower the string's pitch accordingly to match the fixed source. Following is a list of the most common sources that are reliably fixed (that is, able to maintain perfect "in-tuneness"), and which you can use to tune to.

✔ **Piano or keyboard:** If you play your open strings against their corresponding pitches on the piano or other keyboard, you can compare them and make adjustments to the guitar accordingly. Figure 2-18 shows how the keys of the piano (or electronic keyboard) correspond to the open strings of the guitar.

When tuning to a piano, it helps to hold down the damper, or sustain pedal (the farthest one to the right). This allows the piano note to ring while you use both hands to get the guitar in tune.

✔ **Pitch pipe:** Pitch pipes are small, harmonica-like devices with six individual tubes, or pipes, that, when blown into, produce the pitches of the open strings (although they're usually an octave higher). The advantage of a pitch pipe is that it's small and convenient — fitting easily inside a guitar case or on the lip of a music stand (try *that* with a piano!). Figure 2-19a shows a typical pitch pipe used for tuning the guitar.

Another advantage of the pitch pipe (other than its portability) is that you can hold it, hands free, in your mouth (using your lips or teeth) while using both hands to tune the guitar.

✔ **Tuning fork:** A tuning fork (as shown in Figure 2-19b) is a very stable fixed source (it won't wear out, as a pitch pipe can), but it produces only one note, usually A-440. That equates to the 1st string, 5th fret, but you can use that pitch to match your open 5th string, even though the notes are in different octaves. If you tune your 5th string to the tuning fork, you then adjust your *6th* string (the fretted one) to the 5th. It's no more difficult to tune a fretted string while it's sounding than an open string. The advantage of using a tuning fork over the relative method (described earlier) is that you can get the open 5th string in tune with standard pitch before tuning the rest of the guitar in the relative method.

In addition to using a tuner, tuning fork, or fixed reference, you lucky owners of *Classical Guitar For Dummies* have one more resource with which to tune your guitars: the CD that comes with this book. We set aside Track 99 for tuning. Listen to the notes of the six open strings played one at a time, slowly, and match your own strings to the ones you hear on the CD. Repeat the track as often as is necessary to get all six strings in tune. (See Appendix B for more information on using the CD.)

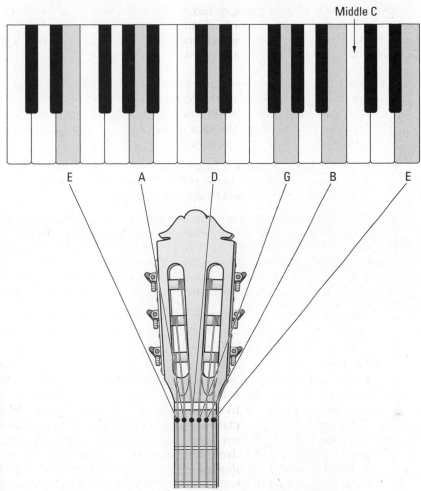

Middle C

E   A   D   G   B   E

Figure 2-18:
The keys of
the piano as
they corre-
spond to the
open strings
of the guitar.

Figure 2-19:
a) A typical
pitch pipe
used for
tuning the
open strings
of the guitar.
b) A tuning
fork.

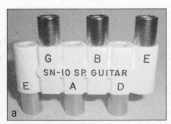

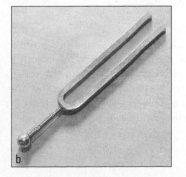

Chapter 3

Deciphering Music Notation and Tablature

Reading music is a part of all classical music, and classical guitar is no exception. You may know and accept this already, but if you still harbor a little anxiety about reading music, fear not: We make it quick and easy, and give you more than one way to approach the written music examples that appear in this book. And you can take comfort that you're not completely at the mercy of the printed page, because you can always use the CD if you're not sure how something is supposed to sound.

But we think you can more quickly absorb how to play music if you read music even a little, rather than not at all. So in this chapter we get you familiar with all the written symbols and notation practices used in this book — including tablature — so that you can better understand the written exercises and pieces that appear here and elsewhere.

Knowing the Ropes of Standard Music Notation

Music written for traditional classical guitar uses *standard music notation* — the stuff of clefs, staves, and notes — just as you find in music for the violin, flute, piano, trumpet, and saxophone. So we start off by getting familiar with the symbols you see when looking at "normal music." In the following sections we show you the blank slate on which composers write music notation, and we cover the three main elements of music: pitch, duration (rhythm), and expression/articulation.

The composer's canvas: The staff, clef, measures, and bar lines

Our current system of writing music has evolved from centuries of different approaches, and it's come a long way since the medieval era. When composers sit down today to write music, they don't write on just any old piece of paper. The blank canvas for a composer isn't really totally blank, as in a solid white sheet of paper. It's a series of horizontal grids that can receive the notes and other music symbols from the composer's pen.

Figure 3-1 shows a blank canvas, according to the way any musician first sees it, just waiting for a masterpiece to be written on it! The following sections explain its components.

Figure 3-1: A blank staff with a treble clef, measures, and bar lines.

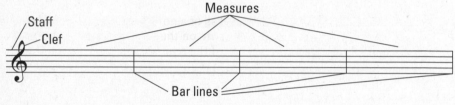

Staff

The grid of five horizontal lines and four spaces onto which all notes are placed is called a *staff*. The bottom line is referred to as the first line, and the top line is the fifth line. The space between the first and second lines is the first space.

Notes can appear either on a line or in the space between two lines. The placement of a note on the staff designates the note's pitch (how high or low it is) and its letter name.

Clef

The staff appears with a *clef* (the squiggly thing at the beginning of the line), which defines what the pitches are on the lines and spaces. Guitar music uses the *treble clef,* also called the *G clef* because the curlicue of the clef symbol (which looks sort of like a fancy *G*) wraps around the second line from the bottom, which is its way of telling you, "This is G." You can determine any note placed on the staff by counting up or down the lines and spaces starting from G.

Measures and bar lines

Just as you need a staff and a clef to tell you the notes' pitches, you must also have some sort of context in which to place notes in time. Most music has a beat, or pulse, that gives the music a basic rhythmic unit that the notes play off.

The beat in turn is usually "felt" in larger groups of two, three, or four; you represent this division in written music with vertical lines that separate the music into sections called *measures,* or *bars.* The section between two vertical lines is a *measure* (or *bar*), and the vertical lines themselves are called *bar lines.* Grouping music into measures is a way to keep it manageable by organizing the notes into smaller units — units that support the beat's natural emphasis. Measures allow you to keep your place in the music and to break it down into smaller chunks for easier digestion.

Pitch: The highs and lows of music

Pitch is the highness or lowness of a note. Music notation uses the staff, the clef, and the placement of a note on the staff to show pitch (see the preceding section for a description of the staff and clef). Take a look at Figure 3-2 and Table 3-1 for a breakdown of the various symbols and definitions used for pitch.

Figure 3-2:
Music
showing the
elements of
pitch.

Pitch names: G A B C   G F♯ E D   A B C A   G♯ B♭ A♭ B

Table 3-1		Symbols Used to Show Pitch
Number in Figure 3-2	**Symbol Name or Term**	**Description**
1	**Note**	A musical symbol whose position on the staff indicates its pitch and whose shape indicates its duration. The notes on the five lines of the staff (from bottom to top) are E, G, B, D, and F. You can remember these using the saying "**e**very **g**ood **b**oy **d**oes **f**ine." The notes placed on the four spaces in between the lines (from bottom to top) spell out the word *face* (F, A, C, and E).

(continued)

Table 3-1	Symbols Used to Show Pitch *(continued)*	
Number in Figure 3-2	**Symbol Name or Term**	*Description*
2	**Ledger lines**	Notes can fall above or below the staff as well as within the staff. To indicate a pitch that falls higher or lower than the staff, use ledger lines, which you can think of as short, temporary staff lines. Note names progress up or down the ledger lines (and the spaces between them) the same way they do on the staff lines. So, for example, the first ledger line below the staff is C, and the first ledger line above the staff is A. Try counting down two notes from the bottom line E and up two notes from the top line F to verify this for yourself.
3	**Sharps, flats, naturals, and accidentals**	The first seven letters of the alphabet — A through G — make up the *natural* notes in music. You can easily see these if you look at just the white keys of a piano (or other keyboard instrument). In between some of these natural notes (white keys) are other notes (the black keys) that don't have names of their own. These in-between notes are known as *sharps* or *flats* and are named according to their adjacent, surrounding natural notes, with either an added sharp symbol (♯) or flat symbol (♭) following the letter name. When you see F♯ in music, you play F one half step (one fret) higher than the natural version of the note. A note with a flat symbol next to it, such as D♭, tells you to play the note one half step lower than the natural version. A *natural sign* (♮) restores a note that's been modified by a sharp or flat to its natural pitch state. In effect, it neutralizes the sharp or flat. *Accidentals* are notes outside the key (defined by the *key signature*) and are indicated in the music by the appearance of a sharp, flat, or natural sign modifying a note. Whenever you see an accidental in a measure of music, that sharp, flat, or natural affects all the notes of that pitch following it for the rest of the measure (see the preceding section for the definition of measure).

Number in Figure 3-2	Symbol Name or Term	Description
4	**Key signature**	The listing of flats or sharps at the beginning of the staff, immediately to the right of the clef, tells you which notes to play flat or sharp for the entirety of the piece (or at least a major section of the piece), unless otherwise indicated with an accidental. For example, the music in Figure 3-2 has a *key signature* of one sharp — F♯. That means any time you encounter any F (whether in the staff or on a ledger line), you play it a half step (one fret) higher. In other words, the key signature sends out the loud and clear message: "All Fs are hereby sharped until further notice!" For an explanation of the major and minor key signatures and their corresponding sharps and flats, head to Chapter 6.

Written high, sounding low

Guitar music is written in treble clef, but the actual sound of the pitches you play is an octave lower. For example, when you see a third-space C on the staff, you play the 2nd string, 1st fret. And you'd be playing the note correctly, according to the way guitar players play written notes on the treble clef. But the note you play actually *sounds* middle C (which is the first ledger line below the staff in music for other sound-as-written instruments, such as the piano). So the guitar is kind of a low-pitched instrument (at least compared with other treble clef instruments, such as the flute, violin, and oboe). But writing the *actual* sounding pitches would be very awkward to read, as it would put so many of the notes many ledger lines below the staff.

Duration: How long to hold a note, what determines rhythm, and so on

While the placement of a note on the staff indicates its pitch, the *shape* of the note indicates its length in time, or *duration,* in relation to the beat. The longer in duration the notes are, the more slowly they move, or the more time there is between their respective starting notes. The shorter the notes' values, the faster they come. Without rhythm, the notes have no motion. We need both pitch and rhythm together to make music.

Rests also pertain to duration; these symbols indicate musical silence and have specific values, just as notes do.

You can increase the length of individual notes or rests by placing a *dot* to the right of the note head or rest. You can also increase the length of a note by adding a *tie,* which connects one note to another of the same pitch immediately following it. We explain all these elements, along with other common symbols used to indicate duration, in Table 3-2; the table corresponds to Figure 3-3, which shows the symbols in the context of a musical excerpt.

Figure 3-3:
Music
showing
duration.

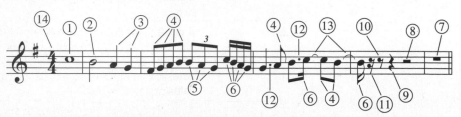

Table 3-2	Symbols Used to Indicate Duration	
Number in Figure 3-3	**Symbol Name or Term**	**Description**
1	Whole note	An open note head with no stem; receives four beats in 4/4 time.
2	Half note	An open note head with a stem; receives two beats in 4/4.
3	Quarter note	A solid note head with a stem; receives one beat in 4/4.
4	Eighth note	A solid note head with a stem and one flag or beam; receives half a beat in 4/4.
5	Eighth-note triplet	A group of three eighth notes appearing with the numeral *3,* to be played in the space of two eighth notes' time.
6	Sixteenth note	A solid note head with a stem and two flags or beams; receives one quarter of a beat in 4/4.
7	Whole rest	A small rectangle that hangs down from a staff line indicating an entire measure's rest in any meter.
8	Half rest	A small rectangle that sits on a staff line indicating two beats' rest in 4/4.
9	Quarter rest	A symbol that indicates one beat of rest in 4/4.
10	Eighth rest	A symbol that indicates a half beat's rest in 4/4.
11	Sixteenth rest	A symbol that indicates a quarter beat's rest in 4/4.

Number in Figure 3-3	Symbol Name or Term	Description
12	Augmentation dot	A *dot* appearing to the right of the note head or rest that tells you to increase the note's or rest's length by half of the original value. For example, a quarter note is one beat, so a dotted quarter note equals one and a half beats.
13	Tie	A curved line that joins two notes of the same pitch. You play the first note for its full value, and instead of restriking the second (tied) note, you let the note sustain for the combined value of both notes.
14	Time signature	A two-digit symbol that appears at the beginning of the piece that helps you count the beats in a measure and tells you which beats to stress, or give emphasis to. The top number indicates how many beats are in each measure, and the bottom number tells you what type of note (half, quarter, eighth, and so on) gets one beat. For example, in 3/4 time, you play three beats to the measure, with the quarter note receiving one beat. In 4/4 time, you play four beats to the measure, with the quarter note receiving the pulse or beat. Knowing how to read (and play according to) the time signature helps you to capture the feel of the music.

When you tap your foot to the music on the radio, at a concert, or on your portable music player, you're tapping (or stomping or clapping) along to the beat. If you count to yourself 1-2-3-4, or 1-2-3 — or however many beats logically make up one measure of that song or piece — you can figure out the time signature. Most popular music is in 4/4, as is most of the music in this book. Some song forms are specifically written in a certain time signature. For example, a waltz is written in 3/4. So the next time someone says, "Do I hear a waltz?" listen and tap along in units of three to determine if he's correct.

The different types of note values relate mathematically to the other types of notes. For example, a whole note is equal to two half notes, and a half note equals two quarter notes. Therefore, a whole note is equal in total duration to four quarter notes. Figure 3-4 shows the relative durations of the most common note types.

When "playing" a rest on the guitar, you often have to stop a string from ringing. Be careful not to get into the bad habit that some beginning guitarists do and look only where to play notes rather than where to "play" or observe rests. When you see a rest, make sure that you're not only *not* striking a note during that time but also that you stop any previously struck string or strings from ringing through the rest.

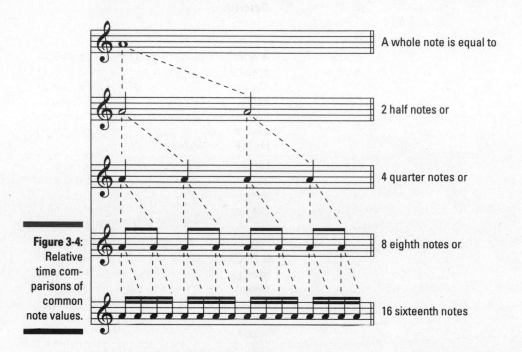

Figure 3-4: Relative time comparisons of common note values.

A whole note is equal to

2 half notes or

4 quarter notes or

8 eighth notes or

16 sixteenth notes

Expression, articulation, and other symbols

Beyond the primary elements of pitch and duration, you often see other symbols and terms in written music. These additional markings give you a range of instructions, from how to play the music more expressively to how to navigate instructions to repeat a certain passage. Figure 3-5 and Table 3-3 show just some of these expression and *articulation* (how notes are struck) symbols and other markings.

Figure 3-5: Expression, articulation, and miscellaneous symbols and terms.

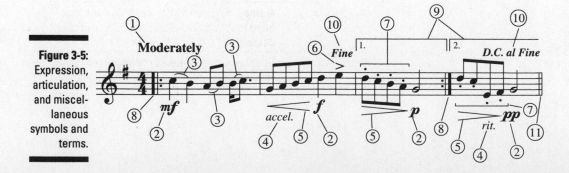

Table 3-3	Expression, Articulation, and Miscellaneous Symbols and Terms	
Number in Figure 3-5	**Symbol Name or Term**	**Description**
1	**Tempo heading**	A word or phrase that offers guidance on the speed and/or general feel of the piece. In much classical music, tempo headings are written in Italian (such as *Andante, Adagio,* or *Moderato*), but it's also common to see the words written in the composer's or publisher's native language (as in Figure 3-5, with *Moderately*).
2	**Dynamic marking**	Letters that tell you how loud or soft to play. The letters are the abbreviations of Italian words and terms, such as *mf* for *mezzo-forte* (medium loud), *mp* (*mezzo-piano,* medium soft), *f* (*forte,* loud), *p* (*piano,* soft), *ff* (*fortissimo,* very loud), and *pp* (*pianissimo,* very soft).
3	**Slur**	A curved line between two notes of different pitch that tells you to connect the second note smoothly to the first. Slurs appear in music requiring a *legato* (*ligado* in Spanish) approach, where the notes blend together in a sustained, uninterrupted fashion.
4	**Accelerando and ritardando**	Instructions that tell you to play gradually faster (*accelerando,* abbreviated *accel.*) or gradually slower (*ritardando,* abbreviated *ritard.* or *rit.*).
5	**Crescendo and decrescendo (diminuendo)**	Symbols that resemble open wedges (called "hairpins" by some musicians) or the abbreviated versions *cresc.* and *decresc.* (or *dim.*) that tell you to play gradually louder (*crescendo*) or softer (*decrescendo, diminuendo*).
6	**Accent**	A small wedge-shaped or caret-like marking above or below a note that tells you to emphasize the note by striking it harder than normal.
7	**Staccato dot**	A small dot placed above or below the note head that tells you to play the note short and detached.
8	**Repeat signs**	Special bar-line-type symbols that tell you to repeat the measures between the signs.

(continued)

Table 3-3 *(continued)*

Number in Figure 3-5	Symbol Name or Term	Description
9	**Ending brackets**	Lines that separate different endings in a repeated section. In Figure 3-5, play the measure under the first ending bracket the first time. On the repeat, play only the second ending, skipping the first ending.
10	**D.C. al Fine**	A score direction that tells you to go back to the beginning (*D.C.* stands for *Da capo*, Italian for "from the top") and play to the part marked *Fine* (Italian for "end"). **D.C. al Coda** tells you to go back to the beginning and play until you see the words *To Coda*. Then skip to the part of the music marked *Coda* (which indicates the final part of the music — *coda* is Italian for "tail") with the coda symbol (which resembles a set of crosshairs or a cross covering an oval). **D.S.** (for *dal segno*, or "from the sign") tells you to go back to the sign (a slanted, stylized *s* with two dots on either side and a slash bisecting the *s*).
11	**Double bar lines**	Two bar lines spaced close together, indicating the end of a section or, if the lines are a combination of a thick and thin pair, the end of a piece.

Relating the Notes on the Staff to the Fretboard

Classical guitarists are no different from other musicians dealing with written music in that after they identify and understand the symbols of standard music notation, they have to relate them to their instrument. And by "relate," we mean *play*. At the most basic level — executing the correct pitch and rhythm — you must be able to play the note you see on the staff correctly on the guitar.

Associating a note on the staff with a string and fret location (even if the fret is zero — meaning an open string) is the first step to reading music on the guitar. A good way to begin associating notes on the staff as they relate to the guitar is to consider just the pitches of the open strings, as shown in Figure 3-6. The diagram above the staff shows the guitar neck if you were to hold it upright, facing the headstock, with the low E string appearing at the far left.

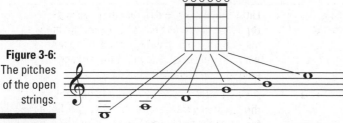

Figure 3-6:
The pitches of the open strings.

You can use these pitches to help tune your guitar to a piano or other fixed-pitch source. See Chapter 2 for more info on tuning your guitar.

To help you correlate the notes of the treble clef with the frets on the guitar, check out Figure 3-7, which shows notes from E to F on the staff as they correspond to the fingerboard. Don't worry about playing anything yet — just get used to the idea that when you see, for example, an E on the 1st (lowest) line of the treble clef, it corresponds to the 4th string, 2nd fret on the guitar.

Figure 3-7:
The notes on the staff corresponding to the frets on the fingerboard.

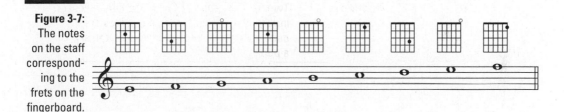

Figure 3-8 shows the entire range of notes (including sharps and flats) on the guitar on the treble clef using ledger lines above and below the staff. All 12 frets of each of the six strings are shown on the staff, which allows you to see how to play some pitches on multiple strings. The lowest possible note is the open low-E string, three ledger lines and a space below the treble staff. The highest note is E, three ledger lines above the staff.

Though the notes extend off the staff in each direction by at least three ledger lines (see "Ledger lines" in Table 3-1 for more info), in reality you encounter far more passages of notes using ledger lines below the staff than above it. So be sure you get familiar with those low pitches, as you'll be playing them quite a bit.

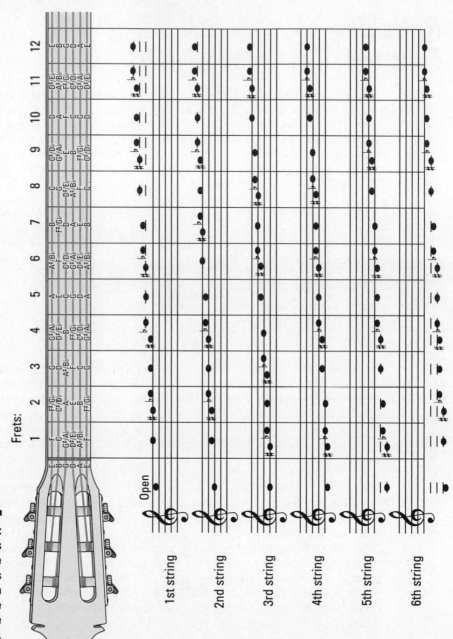

Figure 3-8:
The guitar's entire range of notes shown on the treble clef and the fretboard.

Relishing the Usefulness of Guitar-Specific Notation

Guitarists who read standard music notation observe all symbols and practices regarding clefs, *staves* (plural of *staff*), pitches, and rhythms that other musicians do. But music written for guitar also employs additional symbols that instruct you to perform the music in certain ways that are specific to the instrument. If these symbols appear, observing them helps you perform the music in an easier, more efficient way, or enables you to better realize the intent of the composer or arranger.

These extra symbols don't change anything regarding the pitch or rhythm; their purpose is to instruct you on how to perform the piece in the best way. In the following sections, we explore some symbols you encounter only in music written for guitar.

Fingering indications for the right and left hands

If you see little numbers and letters in the treble staff, it usually means someone (the composer or arranger, a teacher, or the editor of the music) has gone through and thoughtfully provided you with the suggested, the best, or even the *only possible* working fingering indications. *Fingering* is the term guitarists use for the choice, or assignment, of specific fingers to play a given note or passage of notes. And in classical guitar, the issue of fingering comes up a lot!

Numbers without circles appearing next to or near note heads tell you which left-hand fingers to use, as follows: 1 = index finger; 2 = middle finger; 3 = ring finger; and 4 = little finger. (You don't use the left-hand thumb in fingering.) Letters above or below notes indicate right-hand fingers, with the letters signifying the Spanish words for the thumb and the index, middle, and ring fingers: *p* = thumb (*pulgar*); *i* = index (*índice*); *m* = middle (*medio*); and *a* = ring (*anular*). Except for some special percussive techniques and in flamenco style, you don't use the right-hand little finger. Figure 3-9 shows a passage of music with some left- and right-hand fingering indications.

Figure 3-9:
Music with
left- and
right-hand
fingering
indications.

Sometimes you have to use the same left-hand finger to fret two consecutive notes on the same string at different frets. This requires you to actually move your left hand up or down the neck. Keeping your finger in contact with the string as you move to the new fret helps to guide your left hand. The guide finger is indicated in notation with a short, straight line appearing to the left of the second of the two finger numbers, slanting in the direction of the left-hand movement (up or down). Figure 3-10 shows the 1st finger acting as a guide finger moving down one fret from A to A♭.

Figure 3-10:
Notation
indicating a
guide finger.

Unlike the piano, where each note on the staff indicates one and only one piano key, the guitar often provides more than one place to play a given note. For example, you can play the second line G on the open 3rd string or on the 4th string at the 5th fret. If the music requires you to play a note or passage of notes on a certain string, you see a number inside a circle, which indicates the string. For example, if you must play a second-line G on the 4th string (instead of as an open 3rd string), you see a *4* inside a circle. Figure 3-11 shows a passage that's playable only if you take the downstem G on the 4th string, 5th fret.

Figure 3-11:
A number
inside a
circle tells
you on
which string
to play a
note.

Stepping up to the barre

You often have to fret more than one string at a time at the same fret, and you do this by taking a finger and flattening it out to form a "bar" — or, as it's known in classical guitar lingo, _barre_ (Chapter 8 tells you how). You may see various ways to indicate a barre in guitar music, but we use a capital _C_ (because it stands for the Spanish _ceja_ or _cejilla_) for a full barre (all six strings) and a _C_ with a vertical line bisecting it for a half or partial barre (fewer than six strings). A roman numeral tells you at which fret to place the barre, and a dotted line indicates how long you must hold the barre in place to successfully execute the passage underneath it. Figure 3-12 shows how barre notation appears in classical guitar music.

Figure 3-12: What barre indications look like.

Taking on tablature, a nice complement to standard notation

In _Classical Guitar For Dummies,_ we add a tablature staff (called "tab" for short) to the standard notation staff. _Tablature_ is a six-line staff that represents the guitar fretboard (see Figure 3-13). Note that each line represents a string of the guitar, with the top line corresponding to the 1st (high-E) string and the bottom line corresponding to the 6th (low-E) string. A number on a line provides the fret location for that note. (Tablature doesn't tell you which finger to use, but you may be able to get that information from the standard music staff.)

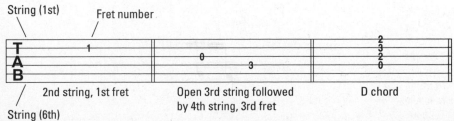

Figure 3-13: The six-line tab staff shows notes as fret numbers on lines.

Remember when we said that all musicians have to be able to understand the symbols of standard music notation and *then* relate them to their instrument? Tablature skips that step! The good news is, you can use tab right away, with no previous experience in reading music. The bad news is, tab is more limited than standard music notation. For one thing, it works only for guitar, so it doesn't teach you the more universal skill of reading music, and it doesn't indicate rhythm.

Tab does, however, work very well in conjunction with the standard music staff. All the notes in the tab staff align vertically with the notes appearing above in the standard music staff. If you're ever unsure as to where to play a note appearing in the music staff, all you need to do is shoot your eyes straight down to the corresponding string-and-fret location in the tab staff. Conversely, if you find yourself in the tab staff and you're uncertain of what's supposed to be happening with regard to rhythms or rests, take a quick trip uptown to see how that passage is displayed in the music staff. Figure 3-14 shows how the notes on the standard music notation staff relate to the tab staff and vice versa.

Figure 3-14: Standard music notation and tab play nicely together in the same system.

Tab staffs aren't traditional for classical guitarists (and may cause some classical guitar purists to raise an eyebrow). That being said, we don't think that having the additional tab staff accompanying the music staff hurts anything; we think that providing as many ways as possible to get you *playing* the guitar is a good thing. So, yes, we encourage you to read music because we think it's the best system going, but we also include tab because it's yet another way to show the same thing (for the most part) and because some people have an easier time with tab.

Part II
Starting to Play: The Basics

The 5th Wave   By Rich Tennant

©RICHTENNANT

"I think if you trimmed your nails, your arpeggios would be a little cleaner."

In this part . . .

Part II is where, as they say, the rubber meets the road — or the fingers meet the strings, in our case. Yes, you actually get to play real music in this part, beginning with Chapter 4, which has you playing melodies on each of the guitar's six strings, and concluding with Chapter 7, where you get a chance to use all your previously learned techniques to play simple pieces in the official classical guitar style. Chapter 5 covers another important technique — arpeggios — which involve playing the notes of a chord individually in a flowing, sustained manner. Chapter 6 introduces you to major and minor scales using both open strings and fretted notes.

Chapter 4

One Note at a Time: Playing Simple Melodies

....

In This Chapter

▶ Playing one string at a time

▶ Producing melodies using two or three strings

▶ Making music with all six strings

▶ Practicing pieces using all six strings

....

All journeys begin with a single step, and all melodies begin with a single note. The difference is, melodies stay that way — as a collection of single notes, played one after the other. Think of any melody as simply the next note following the last, and you can produce all the world's greatest melodies, from a Bach minuet to the epic theme of Beethoven's Ninth Symphony. In this chapter, you practice playing one note at a time.

This chapter focuses on melodies on just the first four frets of the guitar. Playing the natural notes on the lower frets gets you to recognize pitches and rhythms on the staff and convert them to playable notes on the fretboard. By adding in sharps and flats, you can play all the possible notes on the first four frets of the fretboard, from low E to high G♯ (also known as A♭) above the staff.

If you observe the posture and hand position guidelines we present in Chapter 2, you find that playing the music presented in this chapter comes quite naturally.

For the first four frets of the guitar, you use the left-hand 1st finger (the index) for notes at the 1st fret, the 2nd finger for the 2nd fret, the 3rd finger for the 3rd fret, and the 4th finger for the 4th fret (for more on fingering, see this book's introduction and Chapter 3). In other words, the fret numbers correspond directly to the left-hand fingers. This makes it easy to play notes at the lower frets of the guitar because, for example, "1" means both the 1st finger and the lowest fret. This all changes when you start to move the left hand up the neck, but you may find this correspondence helpful when starting out.

Practicing Notes on One String

The natural notes are represented by the unadorned first seven letters of the alphabet: A, B, C, D, E, F, and G. They're the ones that equate to the white keys on the piano (which groups them seven times, or in seven octaves, with a few keys left over). Sharps and flats (which correspond to the piano's black keys) are the half-steps in between the natural notes. In this section, we show you how to play natural notes and sharps and flats.

When playing actual pieces of music, you find that the right-hand thumb generally takes the notes that fall on the 6th and 5th strings and that the fingers handle the 3rd, 2nd, and 1st strings. The 4th string is kind of a gray zone as far as fingers are concerned and can be played with either the thumb or the fingers, depending on the context. No rule exists that says you must play the low strings with the thumb and the high strings with the fingers, though; it's just that these strings fall under the thumb naturally. In fact, when you play scales starting in Chapter 6, you play all six strings with the fingers.

Figure 4-1 shows the notation of the natural notes on the lower frets of the guitar, including the open strings. Some you play with your right-hand fingers and some you play with your thumb, and we cover all the notes you see here using a variety of fingering combinations. The tab staff underneath indicates that in this figure you never go above the 3rd fret (remember, tab shows fret numbers, not fingers).

Figure 4-1:
The natural notes on the lower frets of the guitar.

Figure 4-2 shows the natural notes plus all the in-between notes, here written as sharps. Remember, though, you can also refer to each sharp note by its flat counterpart (for example, F♯ is the same as G♭; for more on flats and sharps, see Chapter 3).

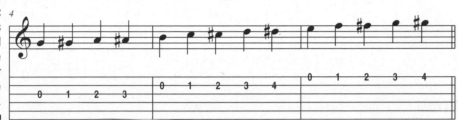

Figure 4-2: All the notes that fall within the first four frets of the guitar.

Exercising your fingers: Strings 1, 2, and 3

When we say "playing with the fingers," we mean the *right-hand* fingers, and we mean fingers as opposed to the thumb — not that we're opposed to thumbs. (In fact, you couldn't play the guitar without opposable thumbs!) For this section we focus on using the fingers to play the notes on the top three strings.

Notes on the 1st string

A good place to start is the 1st string because it's an outside string, which means you'll have an easier time singling it out from the other strings. We begin with the natural notes that fall within the first four frets of the guitar, which are E (open), F (1st fret), and G (3rd fret).

In classical guitar, you alternate fingers to make playability more efficient and feasible (you can't play fast notes with just one finger). In Figure 4-3, start out using the index and middle fingers in an alternating pattern of *i-m-i-m*. Also use the free stroke, which we describe in Chapter 2. Repeat the figure as many times as it takes to produce a steady rhythm so that you feel comfortable playing the notes along with the recording on the CD. Note that we include the fretboard diagram above the staff in measure 1 to remind you where the notes fall.

Track 1

Figure 4-3:
Playing
quarter
notes and
rests on the
1st string.

Note the term *sim.*, appearing in measure 2. This is short for *simile* and tells you to continue in a similar fashion — in this case, to continue alternating your right-hand finger strokes.

Even if you think you play this exercise well, it's a good idea to check the performance on the CD that accompanies this book. Note that the CD version has a count-off (a percussive click that precedes the first note of music; for more on how to use the CD, see Appendix B), which establishes the tempo before the guitar enters. You should give yourself a count-off to set up a steady rhythm for yourself. Also, are your right-hand free strokes as even and confident-sounding as the ones on the CD? Check again to make sure that your rhythm is steady and that all the notes ring loud and true.

Figure 4-4 shows a passage that uses the sharp and flat notes that fall on the 1st string. Play this passage slowly at first, until your confidence in playing the sharps and flats is as secure as it is when playing the natural notes.

Track 1, 0:31

Figure 4-4:
Sharps,
flats, and
natural
notes on
the first four
frets of the
1st string.

Now try the exercise in Figure 4-5, which mixes it up a bit with a combination of quarter notes and eighth notes. Remember, eighth notes come two to a beat, or at twice the rate of quarter notes. (For more on note durations, see Chapter 3.)

Track 1, 0:49

Figure 4-5:
Quarter
notes and
eighth notes
on the 1st
string.

Check that the row of knuckles at the base of your left-hand fingers stays parallel to the fretboard. Keep your left hand turned slightly inward so that your 4th finger is up close to the fretboard, at about the same distance as the 1st finger.

Notes on the 2nd string

After you've had a thorough workout on the 1st string, try the three natural notes on the 2nd string: the open B, the 1st-fret C, and the 3rd-fret D (see Figure 4-6). We continue the quarter- and eighth-note rhythm, but we throw in some dots and ties to keep you on your toes.

Track 1, 1:19

Figure 4-6: Quarters, eighths, and various rhythms on the 2nd string.

Figure 4-7 employs all the available pitches on the 2nd string within the first four frets — the natural notes B, C, and D, plus the in-between notes of C♯/D♭ and D♯/E♭.

Track 1, 1:48

Figure 4-7: Playing notes in the lower frets on the 2nd string.

Notes on the 3rd string

Now that you've played notes on the first two strings, add notes on the 3rd string to your repertoire (see Figure 4-8). The 3rd string has only two natural notes, the open-string G and the 2nd-fret A. Fret the A with your left-hand 2nd finger. And ratchet up the rhythm with some even faster-moving 16th notes along with your eighth notes.

Track 1, 2:08

Figure 4-8: Sixteenth and eighth notes on the 3rd string.

At any given, or fixed, tempo, 16th notes are played twice as fast as eighth notes. So to make sure you're not trying to play something that's beyond your fingers' (or your brain's) ability, be sure to play any examples that involve 16th notes at a relatively slow tempo — at least at first, while you're mastering the rhythms.

The in-between notes on the 3rd string are G#/Ab (1st fret, played with the 1st finger) and A#/Bb (3rd fret, played with the 3rd finger). Note that the 4th-finger note on the 3rd string is B — a natural note, and the same pitch as the open 4th string. This means that when you see a B in the music (the third line on the treble clef), you can play it on either the open 2nd string or the 3rd string, 4th fret. For Figure 4-9, play it as a 4th-fret note on the 3rd string so that you get to use your left-hand 4th finger.

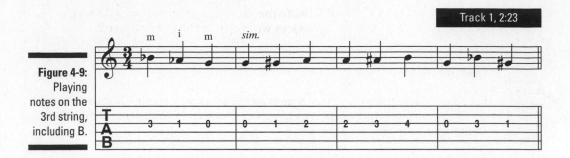

Figure 4-9:
Playing
notes on the
3rd string,
including B.

Remember, tab numerals indicate fret numbers, but when you're playing the first four frets the fret numbers correspond to the left-hand fingers. So while you're learning the notes on the fretboard and trying to balance the tasks of reading the staff and associating a finger with a string/fret location, take comfort that you can use the tab as a fingering reminder (even though the tab numbers really refer to frets). This shortcut should help take a little of the sting out of learning to read music on the guitar. As a bonus, tab can take the ambiguity out of a note on the staff that can be played in two different locations on the guitar.

Workin' (mostly) the thumb: Strings 6, 5, and 4

The right-hand thumb is different from the other fingers in that it strikes the strings at a different angle. The thumb also usually plays a different role in the music, playing bass notes instead of the melody notes that the right-hand index, middle, and ring fingers perform. That's why we deal with it separately here. We give the thumb its own music and its own set of strings to play so that we can focus on thumb-specific issues.

Just as you did when playing notes with the fingers, you start out playing one string at a time using the right-hand thumb on an outside string. You can use both the free stroke and the rest stroke with the thumb, but it's rare in classical guitar to use a rest stroke for the thumb, so in the following sections, play all the thumb notes with the free stroke.

Notes on the 6th string

The thumb often plays *bass* notes, and bass notes typically move slower than *treble* notes — the higher ones that usually take the melody — so in that spirit we start out with whole notes, half notes, and quarter notes on the "bass-est" string of all, the 6th. Note the use of dots and ties as well, and, if necessary, review how these devices work by referring to Chapter 3.

Use your thumb to play the three lowest natural notes on the guitar: E, F, and G, as shown in Figure 4-10.

E, F, and G have the same letter names as the notes you play with your fingers on the 1st string (beginning with Figure 4-2), but the thumb notes on the 6th string are two octaves lower.

The 6th string is the low E string. Its letter names, or pitches, are the same as the 1st, or high E string's (except two octaves lower), so the pattern of in-between notes is also the same. The F#/G♭ and G#/A♭ are found on the 2nd and 4th frets, respectively, and are fingered with the corresponding left-hand fingers (see Figure 4-11).

Track 1, 2:48

Figure 4-10: Playing E, F, and G on the 6th string using the thumb.

Track 2

Figure 4-11: Playing notes on the 6th string.

Notes on the 5th string

Figure 4-12 employs the three natural notes on the 5th string: A, B, and C. Be sure you're able to strike the 5th string cleanly, without bumping into either the adjacent 6th or 4th string.

Track 2, 0:18

Figure 4-12: Playing A, B, and C with the thumb on the 5th string.

Because the natural notes A, B, and C fall on the open string, the 2nd fret, and the 3rd fret, the sharp and flat notes — A♯/B♭ and C♯/D♭ — fall on the 1st and 4th frets, and you play them with the 1st and 4th fingers (see Figure 4-13).

Track 2, 0:40

Figure 4-13: Playing the notes on the 5th string.

Notes on the 4th string

We finish our coverage of the low strings by playing the notes on the 4th string with the thumb. Figure 4-14 shows D, E, and F played in a variety of rhythms: half notes, quarter notes, and eighth notes. For extra credit, try Figure 4-14 using only your fingers, noting that you may have to pull your right hand slightly up (toward the ceiling) to maintain the proper finger-striking angle. In some situations, such as when the thumb plays the 6th or 5th string for a bass note, you may have melody notes that fall on the 4th string, and you must use right-hand fingers to play those notes.

Track 2, 1:02

Figure 4-14: Playing D, E, and F with the thumb on the 4th string.

Play the following 4th-string notes (which include the natural notes, sharps, and flats) using your right-hand fingers as indicated, and then using just your thumb (as the 4th string is sort of the crossover point for thumb and finger playing in the right hand). Figure 4-15 introduces D♯/E♭ and F♯/G♭, fretted by the 1st and 4th fingers, respectively.

Track 2, 1:34

Figure 4-15:
The notes
on the 4th
string.

Playing across Three Strings

In this section, you gather together your experience in playing the top three strings individually in order to play them together. Being able to play on more than one string increases the range of notes you can play in a passage, but it also means you have to switch among the strings while you play notes, traveling across the neck as well as using left-hand fingers to play up and down the neck.

Finger fun on the first three strings

Playing music that involves more than one string means you have to pass from one string to the next with equal ease. In other words, you must be able to play two notes on different strings as easily and effortlessly as playing them on the same string — even though it's a bit trickier to cross strings.

Not only should it be effortless for you, the performer, but the listener should also be unaware that you've crossed strings. The melody should flow with an evenness of tone and attack that masks the fact that you're changing strings.

Two-string playing with the free stroke

Figure 4-16 shows a two-string melody in quarter and eighth notes that goes between the 2nd and 1st strings. Play this with the free stroke according to the right-hand fingering indications in the score. Then switch the fingering to begin with *m* instead of *i*.

After you can switch between two strings comfortably, with no breaks between the notes and with a nice flow in the notes, try Figure 4-17, which starts on the open 3rd string, works its way up to the high G on the 1st string, and then comes back down again. This gets you playing a melody using the top three strings of the guitar.

Track 2, 1:45

Figure 4-16: Playing on two strings.

Track 2, 2:17

Figure 4-17: A melody on the top three strings.

Three-string playing with the rest stroke

You learn the mechanics of the rest stroke in Chapter 2, and now it's time to put them to use in playing a melody on the top three strings. Remember, you use the rest stroke in classical guitar playing to bring a more powerful stroke to the strings — one that helps bring out a melody in terms of volume. This strong, deliberate delivery is most effective on slower melodies.

Take care to maintain the same smooth transitions between strings that you strive for with the free stroke in earlier exercises and that you now apply to Figure 4-18. The rest stroke requires a little more effort and movement because the fingers come to rest on the lower-pitched string rather than being already poised and dangling above the strings, ready to strike. But the increased effort of the rest stroke is worth it for the richness of tone it brings!

Track 3

Figure 4-18: A rest-stroke melody on the top three strings.

To hear the effect the rest stroke has, take a moment to listen to Figure 4-18 on the CD. Try playing the passage yourself using the free stroke and then comparing the difference in tone when using the rest stroke.

All thumbs again on the three lower strings

When your thumb can play notes on the bass strings individually, you're ready to play passages whose notes fall on all three low strings. Because you use just one right-hand digit to play all the notes on the three bass strings, you don't have the extra step of interpreting right-hand fingering indications, as you do with melody playing. The downside is, sometimes your thumb has to scramble to play faster notes, such as eighth notes, because you can't divide up the duties among different members, the way you can with finger notes. But so that things don't get too frantic with your thumb, keep your tempo at a reasonable pace in the following two exercises. As always, check the CD to hear our recommended tempo for playing any particular exercise or piece.

Figure 4-19 shows a passage of bass notes on the lower three strings that proceeds mostly *stepwise* (no skips), or from letter to letter (A, B, C, and so on). Play this exercise slowly at first, ensuring that successive notes you play on different strings sound as smooth and even as successive notes you play on the same string.

Track 3, 0:28

Figure 4-19: Stepwise motion on the lower three strings.

Bass parts — which, in classical guitar, you almost always play with your thumb — often perform non-melodic roles, so that means they often skip around to different notes rather than proceed in a more stepwise fashion. Figure 4-20 has your thumb playing in intervals comprised largely of skips rather than steps, which helps prepare you for bass parts that jump around.

Figure 4-20:
A bass line contain-
ing mostly
skips.

Cruising through All Six Strings

This section is sort of a milestone in your classical guitar playing: This is where you get to play all six strings of the guitar. That means that any passage of written music you see that uses a range from low E (three ledger lines and a space below the staff) to the G♯ above the staff is fodder for your note-reading pleasure. But to make this collection of notes a little more manageable, we break it down by section, so that first you use just your fingers to play the notes, and then you divide the note-playing duties between your fingers and thumb.

No thumbs allowed!

When playing most music you use a combination of the thumb and fingers to play the notes. But guitarists really need to be able to play all six strings with just their fingers, too, so we focus on that in this section. Particularly, playing all six strings with your right-hand fingers helps you when playing scales, which we cover in Chapters 6 and 11.

Figure 4-21 presents a passage that you *could* play using a combination of thumb and fingers (using the thumb to play the low notes) but that we're asking you to play here with just your fingers.

Track 3, 1:30

Figure 4-21: Playing a six-string melody using just the fingers.

Your entire right hand and arm must move toward the 6th string — up toward your right shoulder — to comfortably play the lower strings with your fingers. Even as you move your hand, make sure to maintain the proper angle between your fingers and the strings. (Refer to Figure 2-6 in Chapter 2, if necessary.)

Fingers and thumb, unite!

The goal when learning to play across all six strings is to get the right-hand thumb and fingers — two physically separate tone-producing mechanisms — working as a team.

The thumb and fingers must work together as a cohesive, coordinated, music-making unit, so now you try an exercise where the notes are handed off, the way a baton is in a relay race. Figure 4-22 is simply the notes of the guitar played from low to high in a variety of rhythms. Try playing this ascending and descending passage slowly, and pay particular attention to the transition from the 4th string to the 3rd string, where you switch from the right-hand thumb to the fingers. This change of digits should be imperceptible (or nearly so) to the listener.

Track 3, 1:52

Figure 4-22:
A melody
running the
entire range
of the lower
frets.

![Sheet music with standard notation and tablature for Figure 4-22]

Make sure the flow is steady (you neither drag nor rush the beat) and the *dynamics* (loudness) of the notes is even when going from the thumb to the fingers. Rhythm and dynamics are the two primary elements to be aware of when trying to effect a smooth transition between strings.

Figure 4-23 features a melody that moves back and forth in a meandering way, rather than primarily in one direction, as in the previous exercise. Note the interplay between the 4th and 3rd strings, which we've written in specifically to get you used to switching from the fingers to the thumb.

Track 3, 2:22

Figure 4-23:
A meander-
ing melody
on all six
strings.

![Sheet music with standard notation and tablature for Figure 4-23]

Flowing through Melodic Pieces Using All Six Strings

In this section we give you a chance to unleash all your lower-fret know-how on three full-length pieces, using all six strings to produce the gamut of natural, sharp, and flat notes. But don't worry; we keep things manageable for you by having you play just the melody. In other words, you don't have to worry about playing more than one note at a time. (You have plenty of opportunity for that beginning in Chapter 7.)

You use both your thumb and fingers to play these melody notes, but we've arranged the music such that you don't have to alternate between them that quickly. So it shouldn't be too hard to go from fingers to thumb and back again smoothly. Just be sure to pay attention to the right-hand fingering indications. Also, these tunes are familiar, so use your ears as well as your eyes to help guide you to the right notes.

If you're ever in doubt as to whether you're playing the right pitch according to the standard music notation, you can check your left-hand string/fret choice against the tab number. And of course, you're encouraged to check your results against the performance on the CD, especially for the rhythm, tempo, and flow.

Following is a list of important information about the songs that will help guide you:

- ✔ **A Theme by Haydn:** This melody by the classical composer Franz Joseph Haydn is now used as the German national anthem. It has a majestic feel to it and so should be played in a slow and stately fashion. This arrangement has a lot of open strings, so it's not too hard on your fretting fingers.

- ✔ **"Turkey in the Straw":** For this piece we turn to an American folk song called "Turkey in the Straw" in the key of E. E has four sharps, and these are indicated in the key signature. Be sure you play all F's, C's, G's, and D's one fret higher than where you'd normally play them if they were in their natural state. This is a good stretching exercise for your left hand because it uses the 1st and 4th fingers frequently. It's also good practice for reading and playing 16th notes.

- ✔ **"Scarborough Fair":** Now you switch to F minor, which is a flat key containing four flats (B♭, E♭, A♭, and D♭). This arrangement is the melody to "Scarborough Fair," a haunting song that traces its roots back to medieval times, even though it was made into a popular hit in the 1960s by Simon and Garfunkel. In this arrangement, the melody starts out low, but then shifts to the higher octave in bar 11, giving you an opportunity to play flat notes on all six strings.

Track 4

A Theme by Haydn

Moderately slow

Track 5

Turkey in the Straw

Scarborough Fair

Chapter 5

Rolling the Notes of a Chord: Arpeggio Technique

*W*hen you play a melody, you play one note at a time, one after another. And when you play a chord, you play several notes at the same time. An *arpeggio* is like a cross between a melody and a chord. You take a chord and, instead of playing its notes all at once, you usually play them one at a time (though in some cases you can play two of the notes together in harmony, which we explain in "Adding Harmony to Select Notes," later in the chapter). Because when you play an arpeggio you take the notes of a chord and "break them up," so to speak, arpeggios are sometimes called *broken chords*.

Arpeggiated pieces differ in the number of notes that make up the arpeggios and in the order in which you strike the strings. This unique combination of chord progression and plucking pattern gives each piece its distinctive character or flavor.

An arpeggio can bring a new texture to a piece, and you can find endless variations within the various available patterns. Many pieces of music rely heavily on arpeggios to provide an accompaniment to a melody. Think of Beethoven's *Moonlight Sonata* and you can actually hear the arpeggios in your head. And some pieces are comprised of nothing *but* arpeggios. A famous example is Johann Sebastian Bach's Prelude no. 1 in C from the *Well-Tempered Clavier*.

Guitars are particularly well-suited to playing arpeggios, and much classical music is devoted to the artful employ of arpeggios in various settings. You can see a whole galaxy of these varied, graceful, and beautiful arpeggios in the compositions of Carcassi, Sor, Giuliani, and Tárrega — all of whom you read about and whose pieces you get to play in Chapter 14.

Eventually, we bring out — or emphasize — certain notes from within an arpeggio, but we wait until Chapter 12 to do that because it involves applying more expressive techniques. For now, we help you get used to playing basic arpeggios.

Playing the Notes of an Arpeggio: The Basics

You play arpeggios using free stroke, and the idea is to go for a general lightness in touch and a full, flowing sound. You don't have to worry about stopping the strings from vibrating after you pluck them. Instead, you allow all the notes in an arpeggio (usually three or four) to sustain, or ring out. (This is also true of other instruments played with plucked strings, such as the harp.) Each note lingers a little while and resonates, decaying naturally (or else it stops completely if you strike that string again). When playing the arpeggios in this chapter, focus on getting all the notes to sound even, without any one note sticking out in loudness or prominence from another.

Note that unlike the melodies you play in Chapter 4, the notes in an arpeggio are each played on a separate string. Just as you do when playing melodies, you separate the duties of the thumb from the rest of the fingers when playing arpeggios: The thumb handles the slower-moving bass parts, while the index, middle, and ring fingers handle the fleet-fingered stuff. Arpeggios usually entail playing successive notes on different strings — so, for example, after *i* (the index finger) plays, another finger (*m* or *a* — middle or ring) plays the next note.

It's always a good idea in learning any new technique to start slow and work up to speed, but this is especially true when playing arpeggios. You can keep working to play them faster and faster — much as you can with scales (which we cover in Chapter 6). Arpeggios are made to be played at any tempo, and it's okay to go for speed for speed's sake. The only rule is that your arpeggios must be clean and steady. Otherwise, you can feel free to train for the "fastest arpeggio player in the world" award.

You have our permission to treat all the arpeggio exercises in this chapter as drills and to revisit them constantly: when warming up, when seeking to increase your speed, or when you want to build up strength and endurance in your fingers. And though these exercises are designed to help you develop arpeggio technique in your right hand, we don't want to make it too boring for your left hand. So we give you just enough activity to keep things interesting on the fretting front, but not so much that it causes a distraction for you or slows you down. We want you to focus on getting your right hand fast and nimble. (Your left hand gets a workout soon enough in Chapters 8 and 9.)

Working Your Way across the Strings: The Thumb and Fingers in Order

In this section, you play one string per finger in patterns using various meters, with the thumb always playing the lowest string and the fingers always playing the higher strings. You start in low-to-high order of thumb, index, middle, and ring — or *p, i, m,* and *a,* as they're indicated in the notation.

Assigning each finger to one string

For the following two exercises, as with all arpeggios, you can anchor, or pre-place, your right-hand fingers on the strings you play (some guitarists refer to this as "planting"). For your convenience, the thumb (*p* in the notation) always plays the 4th string, and *i, m,* and *a* always play the 3rd, 2nd, and 1st strings, respectively.

Figure 5-1 shows a four-note arpeggio pattern in quarter notes. The score indication says *let ring,* which is your one-time reminder that you don't do anything to stop the strings from vibrating. So, for example, the first quarter note E doesn't really cut off as the next note (G) sounds.

Play the two four-note arpeggios in Figure 5-1 slowly and steadily, aiming for the thumb notes to be even in loudness with the finger notes.

When writing music for guitar, composers and arrangers often split the thumb and finger notes into two parts (also called *voices*) — downstem notes for the thumb and upstem notes for the fingers. See Figure 5-2 for an example of this two-voice notation at work.

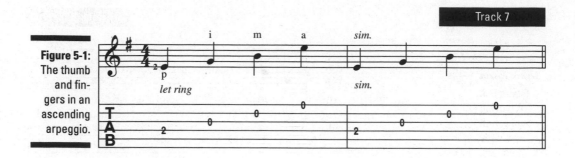

Figure 5-1:
The thumb and fingers in an ascending arpeggio.

Figure 5-2 shows the same *p-i-m-a* pattern as Figure 5-1 but in a different rhythm and using the upstem and downstem notation. The stems and beaming in the notation have no effect on the sound of the notes played.

Try playing Figure 5-2 slowly at first — slowly enough so that the eighth notes are no faster than the quarter notes in Figure 5-1 — and gradually get faster, as arpeggios in general benefit from being played fast and light. And make sure you don't emphasize your thumb, even though you may hear the thumb notes more prominently when playing up to tempo. Work to get the notes between your thumb and fingers to sound smooth and even.

Figure 5-2:
A four-finger arpeggio in a flowing, eighth-note style.

Moving the thumb around

You continue with the same right-hand pattern in the previous figure: *p-i-m-a*. However, in Figure 5-3 you have to move your thumb to different strings during the exercise, alternating between the 4th and 5th strings. Your fingers, though, still play the three upper strings as before — index on the 3rd string, middle on the 2nd, and ring on the 1st.

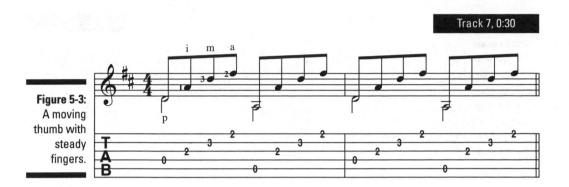

Figure 5-3:
A moving thumb with steady fingers.

Track 7, 0:30

Figure 5-4 combines left-hand movement with the right-hand pattern you practice in Figure 5-3. So in addition to moving your thumb from the 4th to the 5th string (and back again), you also change left-hand fingerings — in this case, from an E minor chord to a D chord.

Figure 5-4:
Left-hand and right-hand movement.

Track 7, 0:43

Figure 5-5 also features left-hand movement and a shifting right-hand thumb, but the meter is 6/8, which is played as two groups of three notes per measure. The pattern here dictates that your thumb strikes every third note instead of every fourth, as in previous exercises, so the activity is heightened a bit. And because you have three notes per group instead of four, as you did in the previous exercise, you need one less finger to fill out the pattern. So don't use your ring finger *(a)* here at all. The pattern for the measure then becomes *p-i-m, p-i-m.*

Figure 5-5:
The thumb gets busy in 6/8 time.

Figure 5-6 shows an arpeggio pattern that moves through a series of four related chords (C, Am, Dm, and G), indirectly forming an interesting group of bass notes, called a *bass line,* that tends to call attention to itself even if you play the thumb notes dead even with the finger notes. That's okay, because it's only natural for the ear to pick up on the movement of the bass against the more static-sounding finger notes and to perceive this as a melody of sorts. In Chapter 10, we ask you to emphasize the thumb notes when they take on a melodic role, but for now, play them with equal emphasis as the finger notes, as you've been doing all along in this chapter.

Figure 5-6:
Moving chords, changing bass notes.

Figure 5-7 is in 3/4 time, which has three beats per measure. In this pattern, the bass notes come only once every six notes, so your fingers get to play a bit more before being "interrupted" by a new thumb note. Instead of just ascending the strings as you do in previous exercises (playing strings 3-2-1 with *i-m-a*), you get to change directions here by coming back down. In other words, you play *i-m-a* going up and *a-m-i* going down.

Track 8, 0:18

Figure 5-7:
Arpeggio
in 3/4.

You can see the difference between 3/4 time and the 6/8 meter in Figure 5-5 in how the beams group the eighth notes together. Three-four is three beats of two eighths each, while 6/8 is two beats of three eighths each. In fractions, 3/4 and 6/8 may be equivalent, and they may have the same number of eighth notes, but the grouping and the stress between these two meters is different.

Varying Your Right-Hand Strokes

The exercise in Figure 5-7 in the previous section gives you an idea of what it's like to play the right-hand fingers in an order other than just *i-m-a*. In this section, we deliberately set out to break up the *p-i-m-a* juggernaut we establish earlier in the chapter by mixing things up a bit! We do that with both our approach to the finger combinations themselves and by breaking up the fingers' unbroken link to one another by inserting the thumb into their midst. Real classical music often doesn't follow a strict pattern (or it doesn't follow one for very long), so playing combinations of fingers that don't fall into predictable patterns ensures that you don't become too reliant on playing patterns.

Changing the finger order

Up till now you've played every figure using consecutive fingers — for example, *p-i-m-a* or *p-i-m-a-m-i*. Now you get to play the fingers "out of order," starting with Figure 5-8. So instead of playing *p-i-m-a*, you play *p-a-m-i*. This exercise is in 16th notes, which come four per beat (versus eighth notes, which come two per beat), so be sure to count off a little slower when you first tackle this exercise.

Track 8, 0:43

Figure 5-8: Playing the fingers in reverse order.

Ideally, you should be able to play the finger notes in any order with equal facility because the music can call for the *filler notes* (our nickname for notes that aren't either the bass note or the melody) of an arpeggio to come in any order. So stay loose and be ready for any combination of fingers that comes your way, making sure you don't show favoritism to the *i-m-a* pattern.

In the exercise in Figure 5-9, your thumb plays only once every eight notes (striking just on the *downbeat,* or first beat, of every measure), so your fingers get a real workout as they fill out the rest of the eighth-note rhythm. This finger pattern is neither the ascending *i-m-a* nor the descending *a-m-i* you've seen thus far. This exercise helps your fingers gain independence and prevents them from developing a preference for strictly ascending or strictly descending patterns.

Figure 5-9: Giving the fingers a workout by letting them fill out the measure.

Alternating the thumb and fingers

Figure 5-10 features a pattern that alternates the thumb with only one finger, the ring finger. So your thumb has a lot to do — playing every other note, and each time on a different string. But at least you don't have to think much about the finger notes. Simply play your ring finger on the outside string after every thumb note. Normally, you'd substitute a stronger finger here, such as your middle or index, but playing this exercise using your ring finger helps you build strength and dexterity in what's often the weakest finger of the right hand. We like to look out for the underdog!

Figure 5-11 is a pattern also featuring an alternating thumb. Take a moment to look at the score and notice the downstem notes (the ones played by the thumb): They occur on every quarter note, so your thumb is pretty active here. Your index, middle, and ring fingers take turns alternating with your thumb. But when *i, m,* and *a* play, they each stay on a single string throughout, while their friend the thumb has to jump around the strings. (Your fingers get their chance to switch strings in Chapter 10, by taking advantage of the "strong finger rule.") So your fingers have it pretty easy here, which means you can focus on your thumb to make sure it negotiates all those string skips with utmost accuracy.

Track 8, 1:17

Figure 5-10:
Alternating
the thumb
with the ring
finger.

Track 9

Figure 5-11:
An alternat-
ing thumb
pattern
using the
thumb and
two fingers.

The pattern presented in Figure 5-11 is sometimes referred to as *alternating thumb,* and it's a very important pattern in many styles of guitar playing, not just classical. You can hear an alternating thumb pattern at work in a lot of acoustic guitar songs, such as "Dust in the Wind," "Classical Gas," "The Boxer," "Landslide," and "Alice's Restaurant." You can also hear an alternating thumb pattern in the playing styles of Paul Simon, James Taylor, John Denver, Gordon Lightfoot, Chet Atkins, and Merle Travis. Classical music doesn't call for preset patterns the way popular music does, but having good alternate thumb technique serves you well in all styles of music, including classical.

Adding Harmony to Select Notes

Up till now you've been playing one note at a time, whether it's a thumb note or a finger note. In this section we introduce the idea of two notes together, played simultaneously. Anytime you play two notes together, you produce what's known as a *double-stop.* The term comes from the string players' lingo of "stopping" a string, which we guitarists call fretting.

Two notes sounded together create harmony, which is different from a chord (which is three or more notes sounded simultaneously). A double-stop is any two notes sounded together, whether a bass note and a treble note (played by the thumb and a finger) or by two fingers (any combination of the index, middle, and ring fingers). You often see a melody with harmony (as you hear commonly in vocal music), so a guitarist has to be able to play two-note harmonies just as easily as Simon and Garfunkel can sing them.

Classical guitarists play a double-stop in one of two ways:

- ✔ **Pinch:** A *pinch* is the non-technical nickname some guitarists have for playing a thumb and finger together. Playing a bass note and a melody note (with the thumb and finger, respectively) is also a double-stop, but guitarists call this particular case a pinch because it mimics the action of actual pinching, which you do with your thumb and another finger.
- ✔ **Two-finger double-stop:** Another way to sound two notes simultaneously is to double up your fingers (as opposed to a pinch, which is the thumb and a finger) so that they play two strings at once instead of one.

In the following sections, we explain the different uses for each of the double-stop techniques and help you get used to playing them.

Feeling the pinch with your thumb and fingers

Even when playing arpeggios where no melody exists, a pinch adds a nice punctuation to a bass note. You can harmonize selected notes of your arpeggios through the judicious use of pinches. In Figure 5-12, the pinches occur once every four notes, or one on each half of the measure.

Track 9, 0:28

Figure 5-12: Pinches the strings with the thumb and fingers.

In Figure 5-13, you combine two arpeggio techniques: a pinch and an alternating thumb. This means that the pinches come every other note! But don't despair — the thumb notes are manageable because they don't move around much. Take a quick glance at the score and note that the thumb plays only the 5th and 4th strings. Also, notice the interesting pattern in the finger notes: *a-i-m-i.* Practicing the exercise in Figure 5-13 just for the sake of scrambling your finger order helps you develop independence of your right-hand fingers.

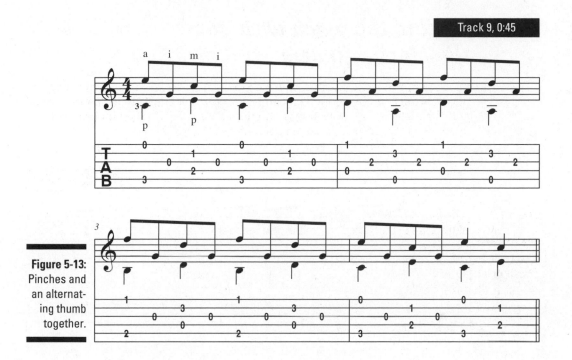

Track 9, 0:45

Figure 5-13:
Pinches and an alternating thumb together.

Doubling up two fingers at once

In this section we explore the most common ways to play a double-stop with two fingers. You can play two notes with the right hand in one of two ways: with a thumb and finger (a pinch, which we describe in the previous section) or with two fingers. To play a two-finger double-stop, you simply bring the fingers down simultaneously on the appropriate strings. When the notes occur on adjacent strings (such as the 2nd and 3rd strings), you usually play them with adjacent fingers — the middle and index fingers, in this case.

Figure 5-14 has you doubling up your middle and ring fingers to play the top two strings simultaneously. To get the feel of two fingers playing together, try plucking the top two strings with those fingers in isolation before attempting the complete exercise. After you do that a few times and the strings are sounding simultaneously, try the exercise in Figure 5-14 at a slow tempo to make sure your doubled-up notes fit right in between the index-finger notes that surround them. Then try bringing the whole pattern up to speed.

Track 9, 1:02

Figure 5-14:
The fingers
play two
notes simul-
taneously.

Playing Pieces with Arpeggios

After you roll, pinch, alternate, and double-stop your fingers till they're ready to cry uncle, it's time to see how they can be put to use playing some nice musical arrangements.

In this section, we present four pieces that include the techniques you encounter throughout this chapter. Keep in mind that most real music doesn't take just one pattern and follow it slavishly throughout an entire piece, so in that spirit we mix things up here a bit as well. These selections include a number of arpeggio techniques — changes in finger order, doubled finger notes, pinches, and alternating thumb patterns.

Here's some information about the songs that will help you master them:

✔ **"Walking Down and Up":** This piece starts with an easy *p-i-m-a* pattern that carries through the first four measures. Actually, it's just a two-measure phrase that repeats, with your thumb playing the 4th string in the first measure and the 5th string in the second measure. This four-measure phrase is a good one to isolate and practice over and over, especially if you're warming up or coming back to the guitar — or arpeggio playing — after a long break.

In measure 5 the piece switches gears, and your fingers play an *a-m-i* pattern while the bass line ascends in half notes, starting from the open low E string. Even though the music changes character between measures 4 and 5, make sure to keep the tempo rock-steady and play the thumb notes with equal emphasis in both halves of the piece.

✔ **"Lowland Lullaby":** For the first four measures, you may hear the bass notes almost as a slow-moving melody rather than as just the low notes of the chords above — despite your best efforts to play them at the same volume as the finger notes. That's okay, because these bass notes seem to take on a life of their own. If fact, if you promise not to tell anybody, you can try adding a little emphasis to the thumb notes to better enjoy their melodic character. The double-stops that appear on beats 2 and 4, however, should in no way overpower their surrounding single-finger notes.

Work to get the *m-a* double-stops to sound with equal intensity as the *i* notes — which is to say, fairly soft. In measure 5, the pattern changes, and the first half of each measure leads off with a pinch followed by an *m-i-m* finger pattern.

Go through the left-hand fingerings before trying the right-hand patterns, as this piece contains some unusual chords.

✔ **"Pinch Parade":** This piece has sort of a theme-and-variations idea at work. The notes on beats 1 and 3 in the first half are the same as in the second half. But what happens in between these beats is quite different when you compare the two halves. Starting out, the pattern is *pinch-finger-pinch-finger,* with a quarter-note feel, so it's a very sparse-sounding arpeggio.

In the second half, however, you see the measures filled out with eighth notes and an alternating thumb pattern in the bass. The rhythm changes from quarter notes to more fluid-sounding eighth notes in measure 6. Be sure not to slow the tempo here just because the rhythm becomes more active (and challenging). In fact, start off the tempo at a fairly slow rate, because though the first half is relatively easy, the second half has an alternating thumb scheme and two pinches per measure.

Note how the alternating thumb scheme helps contribute to the flowing sound. In measure 7 you have to play a "mini-barre" (where your first finger plays two strings at the same fret) in your left hand on beat 3, which sometimes poses a problem for beginning guitarists, because the left-hand index finger has to flatten out to successfully fret the top two strings at the 1st fret. Don't worry, though — the clean sound will come in time as you build up strength and calluses in your left-hand fingers. For now, focus on getting that right-hand part steady as a rock.

✔ **Prelude in D:** This prelude comes from the famous classical guitar method of Italian guitarist and composer Matteo Carcassi (1792–1853). (For more on Carcassi and his music, see Chapter 14.) Here, you play quite a few notes per chord, and those notes change direction frequently, so pay special attention to the right-hand pattern as you prepare to practice this one. For the right-hand strokes, start by playing all free strokes. After that becomes comfortable, try using rest strokes on all notes that you play with your *a* finger (all 1st-string notes) to bring them out as a little "melody" within the arpeggio.

You can also make things easier for your left hand by using the guide finger in measure 2 (the first finger on beat 1) for a smooth-sounding transition from measure 1. (See Chapter 3 for an explanation of how guide fingers work.) In measure 3, your 1st finger plays the 3rd string, 2nd fret, and then plays that note again in measure 4 as part of the new chord. When changing chords, keep your 1st finger stationary and firmly planted on that fret as your other fingers move.

Track 10

Walking Down and Up

Lowland Lullaby

Pinch Parade

Track 13

Prelude in D

Chapter 6

Practicing Scales in First and Second Position

In This Chapter

▶ Understanding major and minor scales

▶ Playing scales using open strings and fretted strings

▶ Trying out scales using fretted strings only

▶ Practicing pieces based on scales

*W*hen you mention scales to anyone who's ever taken music lessons, you may provoke an involuntary shudder as they remember the bad old days of endless drilling and mind-numbing repetition. But scales don't have to be a bore and a chore. After all, scales are the basis of most melodies and most music in the world. And you have good reasons to master them. If you give them a chance, scales can help you get better faster at playing classical guitar pieces.

In this chapter, we help you build the foundation for your guitar practice. We show you how to play the two different types of scales — major and minor — as well as how to play scales in different places on the fretboard. Because this chapter has you just starting out, we stick to the lower half of the fretboard — Chapter 11 takes you farther on up the neck of your guitar.

Introducing Scales, the Necessary Evils

A *scale* is a very regular, ordered sequence of single notes. In this way it can be thought of as a type of melody — although it's a pretty boring and predictable one. But scales have the advantage of preparing you to play all types of "true" melodies (you know, the tunes to songs and pieces), whereas playing one particular melody doesn't necessarily help you prepare to play any other melody or music. Scales have other uses, too, such as being the most efficient way to limber up your fingers and improve your technique. In this section, we explain why scales really are crucial if you ever want to play classical guitar — or *any* instrument, for that matter — well.

In order to communicate about scales, musicians refer to them by the key they're in, which identifies the starting note, how many sharps or flats are in the scale, and whether the scale is major (happy-sounding) or minor (on the depressing side). In addition, scales can land on a number of places up or down the neck. This section helps you figure out which notes to play and introduces you to their different locations on the fretboard.

To keep things interesting while practicing scales, we recommend that you give yourself some extra challenges or tasks to perform, such as playing at different tempos, mixing it up with various rhythmic groupings (eighth notes, eighth-note triplets, and 16th notes), and applying accents (emphasis) on the first note of each group in the beat. Be sure to vary your right-hand strokes, too, so that you play scales using combinations of *i-m, m-i, m-a, a-m, i-a,* and *a-i.* And don't forget to take a few passes using the rest stroke along with those free strokes.

Why scales are important

On the guitar, knowing your scales prepares you for many things. For example, you can use scales to warm up your fingers — working the individual movements of each left- and right-hand finger so that they "wake up" and get primed for the big event, whether that's performing at a recital or simply playing a prelude all the way through for the first time.

Playing a scale also quickly exposes you to the notes of a key by having you play them one after the other, in succession and in a steady rhythm. This process shows your fingers where the notes are, helping you memorize their locations, and it lets you hear the notes of the scale and the key. Hearing the notes is vital to developing your ear — which is arguably just as important a tool in your musical bag of tricks as your fingers!

You memorize and practice scales because they're the *most efficient way to master the notes and fingerings that come up in the pieces you play.* Playing an A major scale, for example, is helpful for music containing melodies in the key of A. Scales help you get acquainted with the notes of a key and they make any new music in that key just a little less foreign. If you can play a scale with great speed and flowing grace, it's a cinch to play a melody based on that scale. And because you only need to know 12 major and 12 minor scales, we're not talking about an insurmountable amount of material to conquer, either — considering most of the world's music is contained in the 24 keys based on those scales.

How you name them: Applying key signatures

As we explain in Chapter 3, key signatures appear at the beginning of each staff and tell you which notes you always play as sharps or flats, in any octave, unless otherwise indicated (with accidentals). Knowing your key signatures is a great way to better understand the music you play. But the key signature doesn't provide the complete information as to a piece's key; it only narrows down the choice to two: the major and the corresponding, or relative, minor.

Most music is based on major keys, which means that most melodies are based on major scales — the scale that the major key produces when you begin on the key's name-tone and play the notes up and down the distance of an octave (eight notes). Minor keys are often thought of as sadder or more mournful than major keys. A minor scale is more foreign to our ears because it doesn't have the familiar *do-re-mi* sound that the major scale does — a sound that seems to have been drummed into our heads since birth!

The main difference between a major scale and its *parallel* minor scale (that is, the minor scale that starts from the same pitch, or letter name) is that the 3rd degree (or step) of a minor scale is a half step lower than that of the corresponding major scale. For example, starting from C, the major scale begins C-D-E, but the minor scale begins C-D-E♭.

To determine whether a piece of music with, say, one sharp in the key signature is in the key of G major or E minor, you need to look at more than just the key signature. Pieces typically end on the *tonic* (the name-tone of the key), so rather than looking at the beginning of a piece (where the note may very well *not* be the tonic), look first at the piece's final note. If you're still not sure, try playing through a bit of the piece from the beginning to see if it sounds more like G major or E minor. You may have to develop your ear a little more to recognize the right and wrong notes for the minor scale (which, among other things, helps you realize when you've made a mistake).

Just because the major scale dominates the music world at large doesn't mean that minor scales don't get to have their say in this book. Technically speaking, playing a minor scale is no more challenging than playing a major scale. Later in this chapter, you get to brood with the minor scale in all its gloomy glory.

Relatively speaking

The major and minor keys that share a key signature are said to be *relative* to each other. The key of A minor is the relative minor of C major, and C major is the relative major of A minor. To take another example, the key signature that has one sharp (F#) signifies *either* G major or E minor, so E minor is the relative minor of G major, and vice versa. In classical music, a piece based in a major key often features passages in the relative minor key, and the score allows for this without a change of key signature.

Associating key with number of sharps or flats: A quick-reference table

Table 6-1 shows the 24 major and minor keys, in order of their number of sharps and flats.

Try to memorize the number of accidentals in a key, as well as which ones they are. For example, if someone asks, "What's the key signature of A major?" an appropriate response would be: "Three sharps: F#, C#, and G#." Note that the table is separated vertically into sharp and flat keys (starting with sharp keys on top). We think it's easier to memorize the keys by whether they're in the sharp family or the flat family. We include C major and A minor in both categories because they have no sharps and no flats, which allows us to start each category with zero sharps and zero flats.

Table 6-1:	The 12 Major and Minor Keys	
Key	*No. of Sharps*	*Key Signature*
C major, A minor	0	
G major, E minor	1	
D major, B minor	2	
A major, F# minor	3	

Key	No. of Sharps	Key Signature
E major, C♯ minor	4	
B major, G♯ minor	5	
F♯ major, D♯ minor	6	

Key	No. of Flats	Key Signature
C major, A minor	0	
F major, D minor	1	
B♭ major, G minor	2	
E♭ major, C minor	3	
A♭ major, F minor	4	
D♭ major, B♭ minor	5	
G♭ major, E♭ minor	6	

Using the circle of 5ths, a helpful tool

The *circle of 5ths* (see Figure 6-1) is a great way to view and memorize the 12 keys by the order of sharps and flats in their key signatures. Each key is placed on the circle, with the key of C (no sharps or flats) at the top, or 12 o'clock position. Move clockwise from C and you progress through all 12 keys, beginning with the sharp keys, by ascending 5ths (a 5th is an interval encompassing five notes, such as C to G or G to D). If you start at C and move counterclockwise, you pass through all 12 keys in descending 5ths. Note that in either direction, when you arrive at the 6 o'clock position, you switch from sharps to flats, or vice versa, because F♯ major and D♯ minor are equivalent to G♭ major and E♭ minor. That's where the keys of the circle meet — each with the same number of sharps or flats.

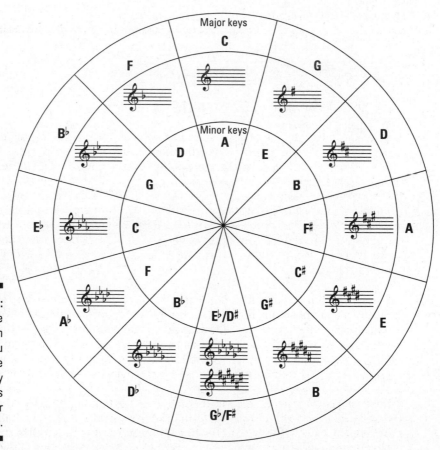

Figure 6-1:
The circle of 5ths can help you memorize the 12 key signatures and their keys.

Variations on a minor theme

The major scale comes in only one version (the familiar *do-re-mi-fa-sol-la-ti-do* sound you hear when you play the white keys of a piano starting from C), but the minor scale comes in three different versions: the natural minor, the melodic minor, and the harmonic minor. The three are identical for the first five notes; that is (sticking with C as the starting note), they all begin C-D-E♭-F-G. Where they differ is in their 6th and 7th degrees. One may use A while another uses A♭, and one may use B while another uses B♭.

In this book, for the purposes of practicing minor scale fingering and of familiarizing you with the fretboard in the higher positions, we concentrate on what's probably the most common type of minor scale — the natural minor. Its one-octave formula, compared to its parallel major scale, is 1-2-♭3-4-5-♭6-♭7-8 (or, starting from C: C-D-E♭-F-G-A♭-B♭-C).

Where they start and end: A primer on positions

In addition to the type of key, we refer to *positions* throughout this book, especially in this chapter. This term refers to a four-fret span of the fretboard where the left-hand index finger plays the lowest-numbered fret, the middle finger plays the next lowest, and so on. "Position" is just a word that means "keeping your hand in one place" while the fingers press the strings. We use positions because it's easier to keep your hand in one place to play notes than to move your hand up and down the neck to grab notes with any old finger. Scales and positions work well together because keeping your hand in one place — in a position — is the best way to ensure a smooth and efficient execution of a scale.

Classical guitar has about 12 positions. We say "about" because you can technically play in positions higher than the 12th fret, but you almost never do. You usually won't find music for classical guitar that contains passages that require you to go above the 12th position, as these would be out of the guitar's range (similar to writing notes that extend beyond the keyboard of a piano) and unplayable. In this book, we don't have you play above 9th position.

Position playing (which means keeping your left hand stationary while your fingers do the work) allows you to play scales that are one and a half to two octaves in size — plenty of notes to capture most of the melodies that are based on those scales. Being able to play in different positions allows you to accomplish several things:

✔ **You can play notes anywhere on the neck.** It may sound obvious, but 5th position enables you to play higher notes than 1st position does, and 1st position enables you to play notes lower than those in 5th position.

✔ **You can play a note on a different string or with a different finger.** For example, in 1st position, you can play the high E only as the open 1st string. But in 2nd position, you can play it as either the open 1st string or as the 2nd string at the 5th fret. You can choose whichever solution facilitates easier playing or smoother execution.

✔ **You can determine the tone quality according to where you play a given pitch.** In the previous example of the E on the open string versus the E on the 2nd string, 5th fret, the fretted version is darker and fuller than its open-string counterpart, which may be more appropriate for, say, a slow-moving, expressive melody.

The following sections begin your scalar explorations in 1st position, which simply means the first four frets of the guitar, with each left-hand finger number (1, 2, 3, and 4 for the index, middle, ring, and little) corresponding to the same-numbered frets. You really start to appreciate the possibilities the entire fretboard has to offer when you leave the confines of the lower frets and venture up the neck. And you get to do that in Chapter 11. We start the process a little later in this chapter by playing notes in 2nd position.

Scales are meant to be played in a flowing manner, so they're almost always presented in eighth notes, eighth-note triplets, or 16th notes. Scales may seem more boring to play than actual pieces, but that's all the more reason not to let yourself go on automatic pilot when practicing them. To prevent things from getting too predictable, we provide a balanced diet of the various rhythmic food groups.

Playing Major Scales in 1st Position

You can play scales many different ways, but in this book you play them the classical guitar way, which requires that you observe a couple of rules. First, you use the correct right-hand approach for playing single-note melodies, because a scale is a type of melody (as opposed to a chord or a bass line). So you proceed using strict alternation of the right-hand fingers (*i-m-i-m* or *m-i-m-i,* and so on). Second, observe the proper left-hand fingers according to the rules of 1st position. In 1st position, the index finger plays the 1st fret, the middle finger plays the 2nd fret, the ring finger plays the 3rd fret, and the little finger plays the 4th fret. In any position, you can play open strings without leaving your current position. Classical guitar pieces take advantage of this, and for this section, you can, too.

Playing scales isn't just about the pitches (frets) and rhythms (eighth notes, for example). You must also approach them using the proper right-hand technique (with alternating fingers), left-hand placement (parallel to the strings), and (don't forget) posture — sitting up straight with your left leg raised or with the guitar raised by means of a support. If you need a refresher on any of these, check out the section "Situating Yourself" in Chapter 2.

The one-octave C major scale

You start off with one of the most basic and widely used scales in music: the C major scale. It's often the first real piece of coherent musical thought that a beginning music student expresses, after he learns the basic operation of his instrument. Figure 6-2 shows the ascending C major scale, beginning on the 5th string and ending on the 2nd string. Be sure to play this using the indicated left- and right-hand fingering or it doesn't count (at least as classical guitar playing, anyway).

Track 14

Figure 6-2:
An ascending C major scale in 1st position.

Usually, you play a complete scale both ascending and descending, so we present all subsequent scales that way. Figure 6-3 shows a C major scale in both directions. Note that your individual right-hand fingers play the same notes on the way down as they do on the way up. For example, because you play the note F with *m* on the ascent, you know that on the descent you'll also play F with *m*. Knowing this helps you memorize which right-hand fingers plays which notes, as you may find that it requires a little more concentration to maintain the correct alternate right-hand pattern on the descent.

Figure 6-3: An ascending and descending C major scale.

The two-octave G major scale

After you have a one-octave ascending and descending scale under your fingers, it's time to expand your horizons. And in this case, you can look beyond a single octave to a two-octave run that incorporates all six strings. The two-octave G major scale in Figure 6-4 starts on the 6th string and runs all the way up to the 1st string before descending. Watch for the F♯ (as indicated in the key signature), which occurs in two places: at the 4th string, 4th fret, and at the 1st string, 2nd fret.

As you did with the one-octave C scale previously, make sure that your individual right-hand fingers play the same notes on the way down as they do on the way up. Going forward, be sure to monitor your right-hand fingers as well as the left-hand ones when playing the scale exercises in this chapter.

If you're ever not sure that you're fretting with the correct left-hand fingers, simply look at the numbers on the tab staff. In 1st position (and 1st position only), the tab numbers, even though they indicate frets, correspond to left-hand fingers.

Figure 6-4: An ascending and descending two-octave G major scale.

The two-octave F major scale

You continue your exploration of two-octave scales in 1st position, turning to the key of F major, which has one flat — B♭. That means that when it's time to play the note between A and C, you play B♭, not B♮, as you do in the keys of C and G. Don't make the mistake of playing B♮ right after you play B♭, either. Figure 6-5 starts on the 6th string, 1st fret and takes you through a two-octave journey in your first brush with a flat-key scale. This scale doesn't use the left-hand fourth finger because it contains no 4th-fret notes. Having just three fingers to keep track of (instead of four) should help you memorize this scale a little quicker, and leaving out the little finger may make it slightly easier on your left hand, too. So try playing this one at a brisk tempo!

Track 14, 0:33

Figure 6-5:
A two-octave F major scale.

The two-octave E major scale

Our next scale is E major, which is another sharp key, like G, but this one contains a whopping four sharps (F♯, C♯, G♯, and D♯), whereas G has only one. This scale pattern uses all four left-hand fingers and gives the fourth (little) finger a healthy workout by requiring it to make an appearance on four of the six strings! Figure 6-6 presents the two-octave E major scale in 16th notes. Because 16th notes are twice as fast as eighth notes (at the same tempo), be sure to count this off at a slower tempo at first.

Try playing a G scale first and then an E scale to see if you can play the correct notes for each scale using just your ear to guide your left-hand fingers to the correct string-and-fret combinations. Because the G major and E major scales are distant relatives as far as their key signatures are concerned (one sharp and four sharps, respectively), alternating between them — using just your ear — can be tricky. But it's a good test to determine how well your ear anticipates the next correct note and how well your fingers successfully fret the note you hear in your head.

Track 14, 0:49

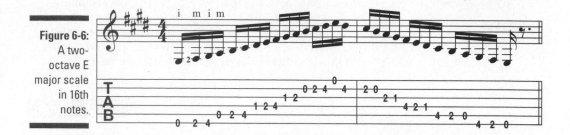

Figure 6-6: A two-octave E major scale in 16th notes.

The two-octave A♭ major scale

From your previous exercise in four sharps, you make a quantum leap, key signature-wise, to play a two-octave major scale in four flats. The A♭ major scale in Figure 6-7 starts with your fourth finger on the 6th string, so you may want to take a little care in placing your finger there in advance, in case you're not used to starting a scale with this normally weaker finger. Note that this scale includes only one open string, the open G.

Track 15

Figure 6-7: A two-octave A♭ major scale.

Playing Minor Scales in 1st Position

You play minor scales just as you do their major-scale counterparts: with alternating right-hand fingers and by using left-hand fingering dictated by the frets in that position. Remember, in 1st position, 1 (index) plays the 1st-fret notes, 2 plays the 2nd fret, 3 plays the 3rd fret, and 4 plays the 4th fret. Use the correct fingering indications in the score to help train your ears to recognize the minor scale as well as you can the major scale (or nearly so).

The one-octave A minor scale

The key of A minor shares a key signature with C major, so the A minor scale (which is based on the name-tone of the key, A) also has no flats or sharps. Figure 6-8 shows a one-octave ascending and descending A minor scale in 1st position using open strings. If you're looking for a simple minor scale to warm up with, this is a good one, because it spans only three strings — the 5th, 4th, and 3rd — and uses only two fingers of the left hand, 2 and 3.

Track 15, 0:16

Figure 6-8:
The A minor scale using open strings.

Every key signature has a major key and a minor key associated with it. For example, the friendly key signature that has no sharps or flats causes many people to instantly think "C major." And they're right. But it's also the key signature of A minor. Though some people often refer to just the major keys when memorizing the key signatures, you should take care to memorize both the major and minor keys associated with each key signature. (For more on key signatures, see Chapter 3.)

The two-octave E minor scale

You adopt the same key signature of Figure 6-4 (the two-octave G major scale) — one sharp (F♯) — to now play in the minor key that goes with it, E minor. The two-octave scale in the following exercise has the same pitches as the one in Fig. 6-4, but it starts and ends on E (not G), so the resulting scale (named similarly for the key) is E minor. Figure 6-9 is a two-octave E minor scale in ascending and descending eighth-note triplets, and even though the rhythm has changed from two notes per beat to three notes per beat, your individual right-hand fingers still play the same notes on the way down as they do on the way up. Use that knowledge to help you maintain the correct right-hand fingering on the descending version of the scale.

Track 15, 0:29

Figure 6-9:
A two-octave E minor scale in triplets.

The two-octave F minor scale

As you do with E minor in the previous exercise, you now play a scale in the relative minor key of a major key you played earlier in the chapter. Figure 6-10 shows a two-octave F minor scale, which, like its relative-major counterpart, A♭ major (refer to Figure 6-7), has four flats, and also starts on the 6th string. The F minor scale contains the same notes as A♭ major, but it starts two steps (three frets) lower. Note that this exercise is in 6/8 time, which arranges the notes together in two groups of three eighth notes each. To help get the feel of 6/8, slightly emphasize (by playing a little louder) the first note in each group of three.

Track 15, 0:46

Figure 6-10:
A two-octave F minor scale in 6/8.

Try playing the F minor and A♭ major scales one right after the other so that your memory of the major scale notes helps you correctly play the same ones in the minor-scale exercise in Figure 6-10.

Playing Scales in 2nd Position

The next logical step up from 1st position is 2nd position. In 2nd position, the first finger plays the 2nd fret, the second finger plays the 3rd fret, the third finger plays the fourth fret, and the 4th finger plays the 5th fret.

The obvious difference between 2nd position and 1st is that 2nd position gives you access to frets and notes that are higher on the neck than those in 1st position. Second position also gives you the opportunity to play what would normally be open strings as fretted ones, increasing your choices for left-hand fingering and tone production (a note played on a fretted string has a different sound than when it's played as an open string, and the fretted-note version is sometimes more desirable). In Chapter 11 you get ample opportunity to explore the higher positions by going up the neck with major and minor scales, using all fretted notes. For now we limit you to 2nd position and the two ways to approach it: using open strings in combination with fretted strings and using just fretted strings.

The D major scale in 2nd position using open strings

The D major scale in Figure 6-11 has a range of one and a half octaves and can be played a number of different ways with regard to fingering. But play it here according to the rules of 2nd position. To do that, place your left hand above the fretboard such that your index finger hovers over the 2nd fret. Check to see that your left hand is relaxed enough that your remaining left-hand fingers (the middle, ring, and little) are poised roughly over the 3rd, 4th, and 5th frets.

However, in the following exercise, your fourth finger gets a break and isn't required to play at all, because the notes that would normally fall on the 5th fret — the fret the fourth finger plays in 2nd position — are either the same pitch as an open string or not part of the scale. So you don't play the 5th fret here, even though it's normally fair game for 2nd-position playing.

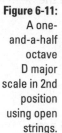

Figure 6-11:
A one-
and-a-half
octave
D major
scale in 2nd
position
using open
strings.

Track 16

The D major scale in 2nd position using all fretted notes

Now here's where the real magic of position playing comes in: In Figure 6-12 you play the same pitches as in Figure 6-11, but instead of using open strings, you substitute the fretted-string versions of the same notes wherever possible. So instead of playing the open 4th string for the starting low D, you play the 5th string at the 5th fret. This means you play the scale using no open strings. The advantage of using all fretted strings is that you can treat this fingering as a fixed pattern that you can move all over the neck to produce a major scale in different keys — just by moving to a new starting note. Try Figure 6-12 now, noting where you play fretted notes that you once played as open strings.

Track 16, 0:13

Figure 6-12:
A D major
scale in 2nd
position
using fretted
strings only.

Memorize the scale pattern in Figure 6-12. (Use your ears to help you hit the right notes when you take your eyes off the page.) Then try moving the pattern up the neck two frets, so that you start the scale with the fourth finger on the 7th fret (which turns your D major scale into an E major scale). You should be able to play the scale perfectly without even thinking about the notes, because you're just executing a memorized pattern. You can apply this pattern to play all 12 keys simply by moving your hand up or down the neck to 12 different starting notes, or positions.

The G major scale in 2nd position using all fretted notes

Now try the following exercise (Figure 6-13), which uses all fretted notes on six strings for a two-octave ascending and descending G major scale in 2nd position. As you play this version of the G scale, keep in mind that you played the same pitches in Figure 6-4 but in a different position and using different fingers. This fingering uses no open strings, and you can move the pattern up and down the neck to create different major scales.

Track 16, 0:26

Figure 6-13: A G major scale in 2nd position using fretted strings only.

The B minor scale in 2nd position using all fretted notes

Minor scales are no different from major scales in that you can play them using open strings or using all fretted notes. For example, you *could* play the B minor scale in Figure 6-14 using open strings, but we arrange it here using all fretted notes, as this prepares you to use this minor scale as a *pattern* — one you can play all over the neck (which you can't do if the scale contains open strings), just as you can with all-fretted major-scale patterns. Additionally, a fretted note gives you the opportunity to apply vibrato to it (by jiggling the left-hand finger; for more on vibrato, see Chapter 10), something you can't do with an open string.

Track 16, 0:41

Figure 6-14:
A B minor
scale in 2nd
position
using fretted
strings only.

Applying Scales in Simple Pieces

In this section you apply your newfound scale savvy to some pieces that incorporate scales and scale segments as part of their melodies. It's rare to find an entire, uninterrupted seven-note scale in a melody, though you may find scales an octave or more in length in some long passages of fast-paced instrumental music. For the most part, though, scale material appears as snippets of three or four notes in the same direction. So these pieces have scale segments as well as some longer lines to allow you to strut your scale stuff!

Following are some insights and tips that will help you better understand and play through the pieces.

✔ **Scale Study in F:** We place the first half of this piece in the upper octave only, which means you don't have to worry about traversing all six strings right away.

Try anchoring your right-hand thumb on the 6th string for greater stability. The second half focuses on the lower octave, so remove your anchored thumb after measure 4.

This piece is in the key of F, which has one flat, B♭, so you never play the open 2nd string, B. If you try to play the F major scale by ear instead of reading it, you may at first make the mistake of playing the open 2nd string because it's so often used in the more guitar-friendly keys of C, G, D, A, and E.

Musical convention dictates that if a piece is in a major key, it's usually referred to by just the key's letter name itself (as in, "Let's play 'Happy Birthday' in F"). But if the key is *minor,* the word "minor" must be used ("Let's play 'Greensleeves' in E minor"). In this book, when we refer to pieces in keys signified by just a letter name, you know they're in a major key.

Note that the second half sounds like the first half. That's because the letter names are identical (at least for the first three bars), but the notes are in different octaves. Real music is often based on repetition, but with variations to keep things interesting.

✔ **Scale Study in B Minor:** This piece is in 2nd position, so to prepare, move your hand up the neck so that your left-hand 1st finger hovers above the 2nd fret. Note that bars 5 through 8 are similar to, but not exactly like, bars 1 through 4. This is the same type of variation device you see in the previous piece, but the second statement takes a little more liberty with the melody. Use the interplay of the open and fretted strings to help create a sustained, *legato* (smooth and connected) sound.

✔ **Scale Study in G:** As in the previous piece, Scale Study in G is in 2nd position. Unlike the previous piece, however, this one contains no open strings — every note is fretted. In bar 6, the low F♯ isn't part of the scale pattern you practice in the exercise in Figure 6-13, but it's easily playable in 2nd position, so you shouldn't have a problem dipping down to the 1st finger to fret it.

Scale Study in F

Scale Study in B Minor

Moderately

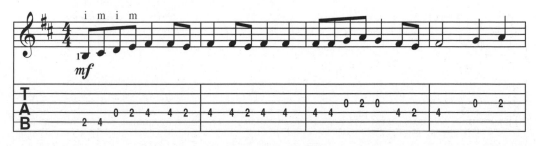

Track 19

Scale Study in G

Moderately

Chapter 7

Exploring Musical Textures

*I*n this chapter the fun begins, because you get to play honest-to-goodness pieces of music. What the pieces we present here have in common is that they're all rather easy to play. Where they differ is in *texture*.

What do we mean when we say the pieces here are easy to play? First, they make use of lots of open strings — and as any guitarist knows, an open string is easier to play than a fretted one. Next, they contain no notes played above the 5th fret. Even though fretting a note at the 6th fret is technically no more difficult than playing a note at the 4th fret, people learning to read music on the guitar customarily begin with the lower frets and find playing music in low positions the easiest. And open strings and low positions naturally go together, because scales and chords played in low positions often include open strings in their very makeup. (The higher you go on the neck, the less likely you are to encounter those easy-to-play open strings.) Finally, the pieces here include no difficult fingering techniques such as barres or slurs (see Chapters 8 and 9 for more on special fingering techniques).

And what do we mean when we say that the pieces here differ in texture? Look at it this way: Lemon sorbet and rice pudding are both desserts, but one is light and smooth while the other is thick and chunky; that is, they have different textures. Musical compositions have texture, too. Some sound light and airy (a flute duet, for example) while others sound heavy and dense (a funeral march played by a full orchestra, for instance). Texture can also refer to how the notes of a composition relate to each other. For example, are they played one at a time or all together? Do they work with each other or against each other? And how densely layered is the piece? Is it written for two instruments or 50? The classical guitar is such a versatile instrument that it can create a myriad of textures all by itself!

One classical guitar texture — arpeggio texture — is so important that we devote an entire chapter to it (see Chapter 5 for exercises and pieces in arpeggio style). In this chapter we focus on the two other main classical guitar textures: counterpoint and melody and accompaniment.

Coordinating Contrapuntal Music: Layered Melodies

Sometimes composers create music by combining individual melodies that are independent of each other yet sound good together. Music containing independent melodies is known as *counterpoint* — or, to use the adjective, *contrapuntal* music. Often (but not always), a contrapuntal piece includes nothing but those melodies; that is, no instrument plays any actual chords. If a chord does occur, it's because the various melodies happen to meet at a certain point and coincidentally (perhaps accidentally) produce one, not because the composer decided to put a chord there.

The simplest contrapuntal music is music that has two parts. That is, it contains just two melodies, usually a high one (often called the *treble,* or *treble part*) and a low one, which can sometimes be thought of as a bass line. J. S. Bach's two-part inventions (which he wrote for the keyboard) are well-known examples of two-part counterpoint. But how can you tell, you may wonder, whether the low melody part is a true bass line or simply a low melody line? One answer is that it makes no difference what you prefer to call it. But perhaps a better answer is that it depends on how the low part sounds. For example, a low part made up of long sustained notes, or of many repeated notes, can be considered a bass line, whereas a low part that moves a lot, as a melody does, can be thought of as part of the contrapuntal fabric (that is, as one of the independent melodies).

In classical guitar music, you always play the low part (whether you choose to call it a bass line or a low melody) with your thumb and the high part(s) of your fingers. By the way, in contrapuntal guitar compositions you rarely see more than two melodies combined, because playing more than two independent parts on the guitar is technically quite difficult. However, the upper melody can often be thickened with double-stops.

Another term for counterpoint is *polyphony,* which comes from the Greek and literally means "many voices." So, contrapuntal music (music containing a number of independent melodies) can also be referred to as *polyphonic* music.

Playing two melodies in sync rhythmically

The easiest way to start playing counterpoint is with music that contains only two lines (melodies) that happen to be in the same rhythm. Now, you can understandably argue that because they're in the same rhythm, the melodies aren't truly independent of each other — and you'd be right. But for now, concentrate on how your fingers and thumb work together to play two melodies without having to worry about executing independent rhythms. The exercise that follows gives your thumb and fingers a workout without taxing your rhythmic sense.

In Figure 7-1, a two-part arrangement of the famous Christmas carol "O Little Town of Bethlehem," play all the low notes with your thumb, and use any comfortable combination of *i* and *m* (see Chapter 3 for an explanation of fingering indications) for the top *voice* (part, or melody). Because the thumb and one of the fingers sometimes must play on adjacent strings (making a rest stroke impossible), use all free strokes on this one.

Pay special attention to places where the thumb and finger play on adjacent strings. That's where the free stroke follow-throughs may cause your thumb and finger to bump into each other. But if you watch your right-hand position (that is, if you keep your right hand perpendicular to the strings), your thumb should extend well to the left of your fingers, and bumping shouldn't be a problem.

Opposing forces: Separating the thumb and fingers rhythmically

Music whose parts are all played in the same rhythm can become boring fast. In this section, your thumb and fingers play melodies that are truly independent; that is, they're independent in rhythm as well as in pitch.

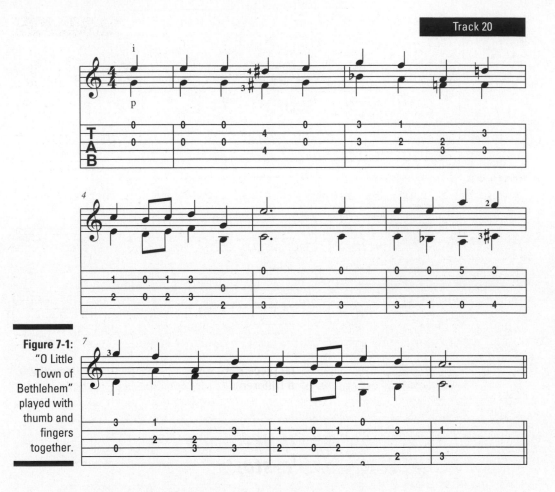

Figure 7-1: "O Little Town of Bethlehem" played with thumb and fingers together.

The tricky part of playing two independent melodies is that you have to keep track of two rhythms at the same time, which, until you get used to it, is sort of like rubbing your stomach and patting your head. Just make sure to count the required number of beats in each measure properly. For example, in 3/4 time, even though you see what may look like six beats (three in the upper part and three in the lower), count the beats simultaneously for a total of three, not six. And keep in mind that if you have trouble counting any of the rhythms, you can listen to the CD for help.

Figure 7-2 comes from a *minuet* (a ballroom dance) by an unknown composer of the late 17th century. This arrangement (adaptation for guitar) is especially easy to play because of the numerous open strings in the bass part. Play this exercise using free strokes and with any comfortable combination of right-hand fingers.

Track 20, 0:23

Figure 7-2:
Minuet in
A Minor
played with
thumb and
fingers
separated
rhythmi-
cally.

To play a two-part contrapuntal piece right now, skip to "Minuet in G" in the section "Playing Easy Pieces in Different Textural Styles," later in this chapter.

Thickening the upper part by adding double-stops

The exercise in the previous section is pretty, but it doesn't sound especially full because it consists of only two single-note parts. In this section, you thicken the texture by adding some *double-stops* (two notes played together) to the upper part. Actually, if you play a double-stop in the upper part along with a bass note, you're playing three notes at once — a chord! And chords help classical guitar pieces sound full. Playing three notes at once isn't especially difficult. Just make sure to keep your right hand relaxed and your fingers nicely aligned. Depending on the strings involved, you can play the top notes of the chords with *i-m, m-a,* or *i-a.*

Figure 7-3 comes from a *gavotte* (a French dance popular in the 18th century) by German-born composer and organist George Frederick Handel (1685–1759), who, along with J. S. Bach, was the giant of music's Baroque era. (See Chapter 15 for more on Handel and the Baroque era.)

This piece is good for practice because it offers a little of everything: single notes, double-stops (pinches), and three-note chords, with a nice variety of string combinations on those chords (that is, sometimes the strings that make up a chord are adjacent or close together; other times they're far apart).

Track 20, 0:43

Figure 7-3: Gavotte in A played in contra-puntal style with texture thickened with chords.

To play a contrapuntal piece with double-stops in the upper part right now, skip to "Air in A Minor" in the section "Playing Easy Pieces in Different Textural Styles," later in this chapter.

Melody and Accompaniment: Using All Your Fingers

The arpeggio pieces you play in Chapter 5 have no real melody. And the contrapuntal pieces you play here have *two* melodies. But don't most musical compositions, you might point out, have just one melody? They do, and in this section you play pieces in which a single melody predominates. What makes this style — which we call *melody and accompaniment* — tricky is that while the melody is nothing but single notes, the accompaniment can take any form at all: full chords, double-stops, or anything that the composer (or an arranger) dreams up. Here you need to contend with, among other things, four-note chords and conflicting rhythms. That's why we've saved this section for last.

The technical term for music with one main melody (and accompaniment) — especially when the melody and accompaniment are in the same rhythm — is *homophony,* which comes from the Greek and literally means "same sound." So you can also refer to music in melody-and-accompaniment style as *homophonic* music.

Matching rhythm between accompaniment and melody

The simplest way to play melody-and-accompaniment style is to play the accompaniment in the same rhythm as the melody — an approach known as *block chord* style, or *block* style. It's simple because it allows you to concentrate on playing chords without concerning yourself with conflicting rhythms (that may exist between the melody and accompaniment).

When playing block style, even though you're playing nothing but chords, bring out the top note of each chord so that the listener hears those top notes as the melody. You can't use rest strokes to bring out the top notes, however, because the lower adjacent string is also being played and needs to ring out. So accentuate the top notes simply by plucking them slightly louder than the other notes of the chord.

Figure 7-4, an arrangement of the famous Christmas carol "O Christmas Tree," combines the melody and accompaniment in a series of simple three-note chords. For the right hand, play all free strokes and use *p-i-m, p-m-a,* or *p-i-a,* depending on the strings involved and on what feels comfortable to you.

Normally in printed classical guitar music, notes taken by the thumb are written with their stems pointing down from the note head (and this arrangement could have been notated that way). However, because the thumb and fingers play in the same rhythm, indicating separate voices (with up and down stems) is unnecessary. Nevertheless, make sure to play the bottom note of each three-note chord with your thumb.

Track 20, 0:59

Figure 7-4: "O Christmas Tree" played in three-note block chord style.

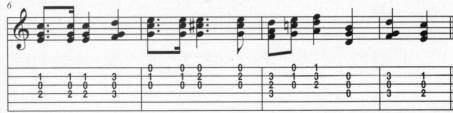

To play a piece in block chord style right now, skip to "America (My Country 'Tis of Thee)" in the section "Playing Easy Pieces in Different Textural Styles," later in this chapter.

Getting creative with the flow: Two parts, two rhythms

Now we break away from block style to examine melody and accompaniment the way it most often appears — with the rhythm of the accompaniment *not* paralleling that of the melody. In other words, the accompaniment has its own rhythm. But whereas in counterpoint a melody is supported by another melody, in melody-and-accompaniment style the melody is supported by, well, an accompaniment — and by that we mean an accompaniment that's mainly chordal in nature. So, in this section you play music that contains melody and chords, but because their rhythms are different, the music seems to nicely flow along.

In melody and accompaniment playing (whether block style or normal, "flowing" style), bring out the top notes so the listener will discern them as a melody.

Figure 7-5 comes from an *andante* (a piece played at a moderately slow tempo) by Spanish guitar composer and virtuoso Fernando Sor (1778–1839). (For more on Sor and his music, see Chapter 14.) Although the melody and accompaniment are in different rhythms, they're rather simple, so you shouldn't have difficulty combining them.

Track 20, 1:18

Figure 7-5:
Andante in E Minor played in flowing, melody-and-accompaniment style.

To play a piece in flowing, melody-and-accompaniment style right now, skip to "Andante in G" in the next section, "Playing Easy Pieces in Different Textural Styles."

Playing Easy Pieces in Different Textural Styles

The four pieces in this section — in different styles and by a variety of composers — sound like what they are: real guitar performance pieces. These are pieces that you can play for your friends (or your parents or your date, as the case may be) and duly impress them with your talent and skill. Here's some useful information about the pieces to help you along:

✔ **Minuet in G:** This minuet (a ballroom dance of the 18th century) by German composer and organist J. S. Bach (1685–1750) wasn't originally written for guitar, but because of its beauty and simplicity, it's performed by guitarists with great frequency. (For more on Bach and his music, check out Chapter 15.) The piece is rather famous, too. As explained by the character Mr. Holland in the 1995 film *Mr. Holland's Opus,* it was used as the basis for the 1965 pop hit "A Lover's Concerto," by the Toys.

Notice that when one voice is rhythmically active (playing eighth notes), the other is relatively inactive (playing longer notes), and that the active part sometimes switches from voice to voice. This type of interplay (with fast notes against slow ones and with the active rhythm moving from voice to voice) is typical of Bach's music and of contrapuntal music in general. And that's a good thing, not only because it makes the music interesting but also because on the guitar it's easier to play one actively moving voice than two. You'll find that as you play this piece, if you focus on the rhythm of the active part, the rhythm of the other part seems to automatically take care of itself.

✔ **Air in A Minor:** *Air* is another word for melody or song, and this one was written by the preeminent English Baroque composer Henry Purcell (1659–1695). The arrangement offers single notes, pinches, and chords — and a nice variety of string combinations on those chords.

Note that in measure 9, beat 3, the upper voice moves so low that it actually converges with the bass. Although that note has stems pointing both up and down, implying that it can be taken by either the thumb or a finger, you'll find it easier to take with the thumb. Also notice that in bars 3 and 4 the fingering is tricky because the first finger must suddenly jump from the 2nd string down to the 6th and then up to the 3rd. You may find it helpful to isolate those two measures for special practice.

✔ **"America (My Country 'Tis of Thee)":** This arrangement uses many four-note chords in block style. When playing four-note chords, keep your hand in a steady but relaxed position and let all the motion come only from the thumb and fingers. But the arrangement also contains three-note chords, and pinches — and a couple of single notes to boot! In other words, a little of everything, so it's a good piece for practice. As always, use the thumb for all notes with stems down. For notes with stems up, use whichever fingers feel most natural (but with four-note chords always fingered *p-i-m-a*).

✔ **Andante in G:** This andante was composed by Fernando Sor, and it offers some nice interplay between melody and accompaniment. Pay special attention to the rests; that is, don't let a note before a rest continue to ring into the beat the rest falls on. If that note happens to be fretted (measure 5, beat 3, for example), simply release the left-hand finger pressure to stop the note from sounding. But if the string is open (measure 13, beat 3, for instance), you need to lightly touch it with a finger (of whichever hand feels more natural) to stop it from sounding. You find that as you become proficient, your hands automatically stop strings from sounding when necessary without even having to think about it.

As usual, take advantage of all guide finger opportunities, as in measures 7, 9, 10, 15, and 16. Measures 15 and 16, in fact, are a guide finger extravaganza. You use two guide fingers at the same time (fingers 1 and 2), making it a "double guide finger," and those fingers guide your hand down the neck twice in a row (from 3rd position to 2nd, then from 2nd position to 1st), making it a "double double guide finger"!

Track 21

Minuet in G

Track 22

Air in A Minor

Moderately

Track 23

America (My Country 'Tis of Thee)

Andante in G

Part III
Improving Your Technique

"This next exercise is designed to stretch my fingers and Mona's patience."

In this part . . .

When you master the basic mechanics of playing notes, you can turn your attention to the special techniques that make your playing richer and more flavorful. And that's what we do in Part III. In Chapter 8 you see how to use half barres and full barres, and in Chapter 9 we show you how to play ascending and descending slurs, as well as trills — the rapid alternation of two notes that's a hallmark of classical music. Chapter 10 offers additional ways to create new sounds, including harmonics, timbre changes, and tremolo. Chapter 11 has you playing all over the neck with major and minor scales. In Chapter 12 you combine arpeggios and melody into one cohesive sound, and in Chapter 13 you get to employ barres and slurs at the higher frets.

Chapter 8

Flat-Fingered Fretting with Barres

Classical guitarists move beyond beginner status when they learn and apply a number of skills and techniques that allow them to play virtually any classical guitar composition or arrangement. Among these skills, which we examine in this chapter and the four chapters that follow, are slurring notes, varying tone quality, playing in the higher positions, and highlighting melody lines from within arpeggios. But perhaps the most basic and essential skill a guitarist (classical or otherwise) needs is the ability to press down more than one string at a time with a single finger; or, to use the technical term for such a technique, the ability to barre.

Discovering How to Play Barres

When a single finger frets (presses down) more than one string at a time (across the neck at the same fret, that is), that finger is called a *barre* (from the French word *barré,* which means "bar"). And that term is appropriate, because when you use a single finger in such a manner, it resembles, well, a bar. And as a verb, to *barre* is to place or use a finger in such a fashion.

Often, the first finger forms a barre, sometimes stretching across all six strings, sometimes encompassing fewer. But you can use other fingers to form barres as well.

Barres (and chords that employ barres) are a bit tricky for beginners to master because notes under them ring out only if you apply sufficient pressure. But after you perfect the technique, barring actually makes playing easier in many situations, such as when fretting each string of a chord with a separate finger is awkward or impossible.

Barres come in two varieties: the *full barre,* which encompasses all six strings, and the *half barre* (also referred to as a *partial barre*), which covers anywhere from two to five strings. We know that two-sixths, four-sixths, and five-sixths don't equal a half, but the term *half barre* is generally used to express all these fractional (partial) barres. In the following sections we look at both types of barres.

Half barre

Take a look at Figure 8-1, in which a first-finger barre covers the top three strings at the 2nd fret. Go ahead and duplicate that half barre on your own guitar. When you have the barre pressed down firmly, pluck the top three strings with your right-hand fingers *p-i-m* (first all at once, as a chord, then one at a time, as an arpeggio). All three notes should ring clearly.

Figure 8-1:
Playing a
half barre.

In case any of the notes under the barre are muffled or buzz, here are some tips for getting all the notes under the barre to sound clearly:

✔ Place your barring finger as close to the fret (metal fret wire) as possible (rather than midway between frets).

✔ Apply counter-pressure with your thumb (from behind the neck) to squeeze your thumb and finger together.

✔ If helpful, rotate your finger slightly in one direction or the other so that you use some of the side of your finger in forming the barre.

✔ Apply downward pressure along the entire length of the barre, not just to the outer strings (unless they're the only ones being played).

Full barre

Though any of your fingers may be called on to form a half barre, only the first finger is used to play a full barre. Take a look at Figure 8-2, which shows a full barre at the 2nd fret, and reproduce that on your own guitar. All the tips listed in the preceding section for successfully forming a half barre apply to the full barre as well, but because all six strings need to be pressed down, even greater strength and pressure are required for the full barre, making it a bit more difficult to master than the half barre.

Pressing down a full barre hard enough to get all the notes to ring out causes tension in the hand, which may lead to cramping (especially for beginners). So take care to give your hand a rest if you begin to experience any pain.

Figure 8-2:
Playing a
full barre.

With the barre firmly in place, strum quickly across all six strings with your thumb. Now play the strings one at a time from low to high (pluck each of the bottom three strings with your thumb, then the top three strings with *i-m-a*). Do all the notes ring out clearly? If not, review the tips provided earlier. Don't become discouraged; getting all the notes under a full barre to ring clearly takes practice. Try forming the full barre at various frets. You may find it easier to get the notes under the barre to ring out around the middle of the neck (at the 5th fret, say) than at the bottom of the neck.

Practicing Barres in a Musical Context

In this section we give you exercises for practicing both half and full barres, and you have an opportunity to play the barred notes as both chords and arpeggios. Note that in standard music notation, the letter C — which can stand for either of the Spanish words *ceja* or *cejilla,* or for the Italian word *capotasto,* all of which roughly mean "bar" — stands for a full barre, and a C with a vertical line through it indicates a half barre (which may encompass two, three, four, or five strings).

Some printed classical guitar editions use the letter B (for the French word *barré*) to indicate a barre, and some editions use a fraction before the letter to indicate exactly how many strings are included in a particular half barre. For example, $^4/_6$B or $^2/_3$B indicates a partial barre (half barre) encompassing exactly four strings.

Half barre

The first half of Figure 8-3 is a simple chord progression that you play first as solid chords (measures 1 through 4) and then as arpeggios (measures 5 through 8) — all *without* the use of barres. The second half (measures 9 through 16) is identical (note-wise) to the first, but here you use half barres to play many of the notes. Playing the same music both with and without barres gives you a chance to see how barring can make playing easier (simply because fewer left-hand fingers are involved). And playing the notes of barred chords both all at once and one at a time (arpeggiated) best allows you to determine if any notes under the barre are muffled (and if so, which ones). In fact, playing Figure 8-3 allows you to practice the half barre in a number of ways — you play two-string barres and three-string barres; you barre sometimes with your first finger and sometimes with your third; and you pluck barred notes on both adjacent and nonadjacent strings.

Because all the barring occurs in measures 9 through 16, you can treat that section as a separate exercise. In other words, after playing the first half of the progression once, play the second half several times, concentrating on getting all barred notes to ring out clearly.

Figure 8-3:
Using the
half barre
in a simple
progression.

Full barre

Full barres and the longer half barres (the four- and five-string variety) are often used to form chords — especially major chords, minor chords, and 7th chords. Figure 8-4 gives you an opportunity to practice playing these types of chords using full barres and five-string half barres. As in Figure 8-3, you first play solid chords, and then you arpeggiate them (which allows you to detect and isolate any muffled notes).

In the first half of the example, you play a chord progression using barres (F-B♭-C7-F) in a major key (F major). This gives you an opportunity to practice major chords with both six- and five-string barres (as well as a 7th chord with a five-string barre). In the second half you play a progression using barres (Fm-B♭m-C7-Fm) in a minor key (F minor). This adds the opportunity for you to practice minor chords with both six- and five-string barres. Play the progression slowly and steadily until you can do so with all barred notes ringing out clearly.

Track 26

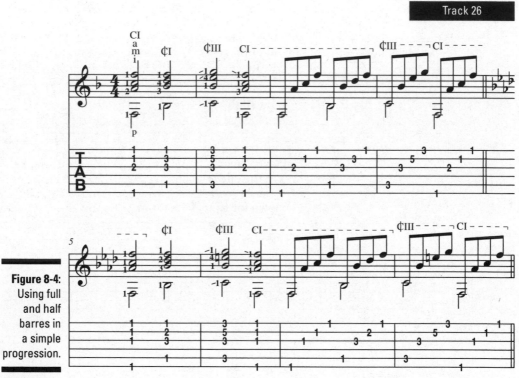

Figure 8-4:
Using full and half barres in a simple progression.

To play actual pieces using half and full barres, skip to the forthcoming section, "Playing Pieces with Barres."

Playing Pieces with Barres

In this section you play pieces that use both half and full barres. Here's some useful information about the pieces to help you along:

- **Minuet in B Minor:** This piece, an arrangement of a minuet by German composer and organist Johann Krieger (1651–1735), gives you an opportunity to practice both half barres (measures 1, 7, 9, and 11 through 14) and full barres (measures 6 and 7). Note that in measure 7, you can apply a full barre for the entire measure (rather than a half barre at beat 1, then a full barre at beat 2). Try it both ways to see which you prefer. Also notice that the notes indicated as barres in measures 9, 11, 13, and 14 can also be played without barres — but you'll probably find that barring them (with a single finger) is easier than playing the notes with separate fingers.

- **"Angels We Have Heard on High":** In this piece you have a chance to practice barres of various length, from two-note barres on adjacent strings all the way up to full (six-string) barres. Note that the last beat of measure 9 normally wouldn't require a barre (each note of the chord is at a different fret); however, because the chords before and after are each played with a barre at the 2nd fret, and because the chord in question includes the 2nd fret (as its lowest fret), you find that it's actually easier to hold the barre down for that chord than to remove it.

Track 27

Minuet in B Minor

Track 28

Angels We Have Heard on High

Chapter 9

Getting a Smooth Sound with Slurs and Trills

In This Chapter

▶ Discovering ascending and descending slurs

▶ Using slurs to produce a trill

▶ Practicing pieces with slurs and trills

Some people consider such techniques as slurring and trilling the fancy stuff of classical guitar, and in a sense they're right. After all, applying what you learn here makes you sound more like an accomplished guitarist. But whether you see these techniques indicated in a musical score or you apply them according to your whim, you use them not to show off but to add finesse (smoothness, refinement, delicacy) to your playing.

The *slur* is a device by which you sound more than one note with a single right-hand pluck, and the *trill* is an ornament with a fluttering sound. Learning these techniques, which we discuss in detail in this chapter, brings your classical guitar playing to the next level.

Connecting Your Notes with Slurs

Sometimes when you sing, you have to vocalize two notes on a single syllable, as when you sing, say, the first word of "O say can you see . . . ." What you're doing there (smoothly connecting two notes, that is) is known as *slurring*. And in music (whether vocal or instrumental), to *slur* notes is simply to connect them smoothly — and, to use the noun, a smooth connection of notes is known as a *slur*. In written music, a slur is a curved line joining two or more notes that indicates that those notes should be connected smoothly in performance.

The Italian word *legato* is used as a directive in musical scores to indicate that you're to connect notes (even those notated without curved lines) in a smooth manner, with no break in sound between them. In the classical guitar world, the Spanish equivalent of *legato,* which is *ligado,* is sometimes used.

When you sing, your voice automatically connects notes smoothly whenever necessary. For example, you would never accidentally sing "O-O say can you see . . . ," but on the guitar, slurring doesn't happen automatically. To achieve a slur on a classical guitar, you pluck only once with a right-hand finger but produce two (or more) consecutive pitches by means of special left-hand techniques.

Hammering and pulling: Exploring slurs

Guitar slurs come in two varieties: *ascending* and *descending.* The ascending slur is equivalent to what non-classical guitarists call a *hammer-on* (or *hammer*); the descending slur is what they call a *pull-off* (or *pull*).

On guitar, when you slur two notes together (whether ascending or descending), playing the first note isn't tricky — you simply pluck it with a right-hand finger. The trick in playing the second note is to use a *left-hand* finger to make it sound — either "hammering" a left-hand finger for the ascending slur or "pulling" a left-hand finger for the descending slur. The following sections explain these techniques.

Ascending slurs

Figure 9-1 shows six types of ascending slurs, one per measure. In each, the curved line tells you to play the notes of the measure with a single pluck of a right-hand finger (*i,* in this case) on the first note only.

Track 29

Figure 9-1:
A variety of ascending slurs.

To play the slur in measure 1 in Figure 9-1:

1. **Start by plucking the open 3rd string.**

2. **To cause the second note (the A at the 2nd fret) to sound, while the open G is still ringing, use the tip of a left-hand finger (1, in this case) — which is poised and waiting about a half inch above the string — to firmly strike down (as a hammer might) just behind the 2nd fret.**

   If you strike with enough force, the A will sound. If it doesn't (or if the sound is too soft), either you waited too long after striking the open G or you didn't strike the 2nd fret hard enough. Try it a few times and experiment with different amounts of force. Not only should the A sound, but the connection between the G and A should be smooth (which is the point of playing a slur).

The slur in measure 1, because it involves only an open string and a single left-hand finger, is the easiest type to play. In measure 2, the slur involves two fretted notes and so is a bit trickier. Strike the A (first finger at the 2nd fret) normally (plucking the note with a right-hand finger), then (while the A is still ringing) hammer down the third finger at the 4th fret, sounding the B.

Slurred notes aren't always adjacent scale steps (notes that are one or two frets apart, that is). In measure 3 you play a one-fingered slur from the open G up to the 4th fret. In measure 5 you play a two-fingered slur from the 2nd fret to the 5th.

Sometimes you slur together more than two consecutive notes. In a case where, say, you slur three notes, you must hammer twice: once for the second note and then again (with a different finger) for the third note. In measure 5, for instance, you pluck the open G, then use your first finger to hammer the 2nd fret, then your third finger to hammer the 4th fret. All three notes should sound smoothly connected. Playing a three-note slur in such a fashion is sometimes called a *double slur* (for obvious reasons), though non-classical guitarists like to call it a *double hammer-on*. In measure 6, because no open string is involved, you must use three fingers (1, 3, and 4, in this case) to achieve the double slur.

Descending slurs

In Figure 9-2 you play six types of descending slurs (which look like upside-down versions of the slurs you play in Figure 9-1), each with a single pluck of a right-hand finger. But whereas in ascending slurs you start by simply plucking the first note, in descending slurs (except when you slur down to an open string) you must prepare all the involved left-hand fingers before you strike the first note, as we explain in the descriptions that follow.

Track 30

Figure 9-2:
A variety of
descending
slurs.

To play the slur in measure 1 in Figure 9-2:

1. **Finger the A (first finger, 2nd fret) and cause it to sound in the normal manner (by plucking the 3rd string with a right-hand finger).**

2. **To sound the open G, while the A is still ringing, pull (or snap) your first finger sideways (toward the 2nd string), causing the open 3rd string to ring (and allowing your first finger to rest against the 2nd string — but making sure it doesn't set the 2nd string in motion, causing an unwanted open B to vibrate).**

   By using this so-called "pull-off" technique, you actually pluck the open G with your left-hand finger (the one that just finished fretting the A above it) rather than with a right-hand finger.

In measure 2, you play a descending slur with two fingers rather than one. The important point here is that when you play any two-fingered descending slur, both left-hand fingers must be in position, pressing down on their respective frets, *before* you pluck the first note (otherwise, when you pull off, the open string will sound instead of the fretted note you want). With your first finger pressing down the 2nd fret and your third finger simultaneously pressing the 4th, pluck the 3rd string with a right-hand finger to sound the note at the 4th fret; then, pull (or snap) your third finger sideways to sound the note at the 2nd fret. The two notes should sound smoothly connected.

Measures 3 and 4 show descending slurs (one-fingered and two-fingered, respectively) that are several frets apart. Use the same pull-off technique to play these that you use in measures 1 and 2.

Measures 5 and 6 show three-note descending slurs (double slurs), with measure 5 requiring only two fingers (because the last note is an open string) and measure 6 requiring three. In both cases, place all applicable fingers on their assigned frets before striking the first note. Pull off the first note to smoothly sound the second, then pull off the second to smoothly sound the third.

Slurring in the context of a larger musical phrase

Before playing pieces with slurs, you should practice playing them in musical contexts. In this section, you practice single and double slurs (both ascending and descending, and both with and without open strings) in scale and arpeggio exercises.

Slurs in scales

Figure 9-3 shows a series of 2nd-position ascending and descending D major scales played in 6/8 time (two beats per measure, three notes per beat). For the scale in measures 1 and 2, you practice single (two-note) slurs. Slur the first two notes of each three-note group together, then strike the third note separately. In measures 3 and 4 you play the scale downward, giving you the opportunity to practice two-note descending slurs. Again, slur the first two notes of each group together, then strike the third note separately.

The second half of the example uses the same scales as the first, but here you play double (three-note) slurs. Strike only the first note of each group and then smoothly produce the next two notes with double hammers (measures 5 and 6) or double pulls (measures 7 and 8).

Track 31

Figure 9-3: Playing ascending and descending slurs in a scale.

Slurs in arpeggios

Figure 9-4 gives you a chance to practice ascending slurs within an arpeggiated figure. Measures 1 and 4 are rather simple because you hammer on from open strings. Don't forget to let all the notes of the arpeggio ring out.

Track 32

Figure 9-4:
Playing ascending slurs in an arpeggiated figure.

Figure 9-5, which is like an upside-down version of the preceding figure, allows you to practice descending slurs within an arpeggiated figure. Measures 1 and 4 are easy because you pull off to open strings. In measure 2, make sure you simultaneously fret both notes on the 1st string before executing the slur (the simplest way to achieve that is to keep the 2nd fret pressed down throughout the measure). Similarly, in measure 3, hold down the 2nd-fret half barre with the first finger throughout the measure.

By the way, if Figure 9-5 sounds familiar to you, that's not surprising. It's the beginning of the well-known Prelude from Bach's *Cello Suite No. 1.*

Track 33

Figure 9-5: Playing descending slurs in an arpeggiated figure.

Fluttering a Note with a Trill

If you play a series of rapidly alternating ascending and descending slurs (back and forth between notes one or two frets apart), you produce a fluttering sound known as a *trill*. Trills aren't generally played in a particular rhythm; rather, you alternate between the notes as quickly as possible. You use trills both to ornament notes and to give them *sustain* (a lasting, rather than decaying, quality). In the notation, the letters *tr* and a wavy horizontal line above a note tell you to play that note as a trill (with the pitch you slur up to shown in parentheses).

Playing trills on their own

Figure 9-6 shows how to play a trill between an open string and a fretted note (measures 1 through 3) and between two fretted notes (measures 4 through 6). To do so, refer to Figure 9-6 and follow these steps:

1. **Play the open G in measure 1.**

2. **Play an ascending slur, then a descending slur, then another ascending slur.**

In other words (to use popular guitar lingo), play the open G, hammer on the 2nd-fret A, then pull off to the open G, then hammer on the 2nd-fret A again. In that measure, the rhythm is not especially fast — eighth notes (or two notes per beat).

 3. **In measure 2 you play a series of eight slurred notes in 16ths (four notes per beat) by hammering and pulling multiple times.**

That rhythm and that number of notes gives you an idea of how a trill works and sounds.

 4. **In measure 3, alternate between G and A (with a continuous series of alternating upward and downward slurs) as quickly as possible (playing even more than four notes per beat).**

Don't even try to count how many notes you play per beat; just alternate between the notes as fast as you can. Now you're playing a trill.

Measures 4 through 6 show a trill between two fretted notes. Keep your first finger firmly planted at the 2nd fret throughout those three measures (so that when you pull off from the 4th fret, the 2nd-fret note will sound). Start slowly with a few notes at a moderate speed (measure 4), then play more notes at a faster clip (measure 5), and finally alternate between the notes as quickly as you can to play a true trill (measure 6).

Track 34

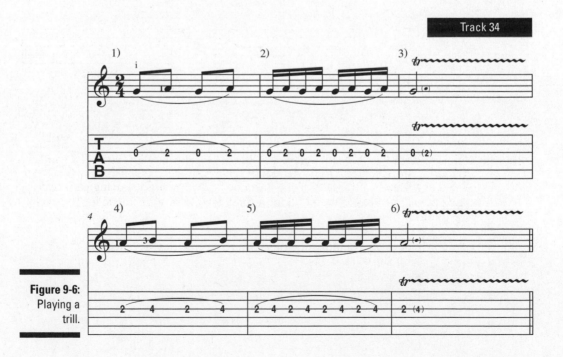

Figure 9-6:
Playing a
trill.

Practicing trills in context

Figure 9-7 allows you to practice trills in context — in musical phrases, that is. The two-measure phrases shown here (which are identical to each other, except in different keys) are typical of the ending portions of longer melodic lines. By the way, endings of musical phrases are often called *cadences*.

The first phrase (cadence) here is in the key of F and allows you to trill between an open string and a fretted note (which means you need to use only one left-hand finger). The second phrase, in the key of G, requires you to trill between two fretted notes with your first and third fingers (so make sure to keep your first finger planted at the 2nd fret throughout the trill). In each phrase, the trill begins on beat 3 and lasts for a beat and a half. Listen to the CD if you have any trouble with the rhythm.

Track 35

Figure 9-7:
Playing trills
in musical
phrases.

Interestingly, while trills generally begin with the lower note (which is considered the "main" note, or the note that's being ornamented or prolonged), most musical scholars insist that trills in music of the Baroque era (1600–1750), such as those in "Passepied in A Minor" later in this chapter, are to be played starting from the upper note. No doubt this viewpoint exists because the great J. S. Bach himself, the giant of the Baroque era, advocated starting trills from the upper note. (See Chapter 15 for a rundown of Baroque music for the classical guitar.)

To play pieces using slurs and trills, skip to the forthcoming section, "Playing Pieces Using Slurs and Trills."

Playing Pieces Using Slurs and Trills

In this section you play pieces that use slurs and trills. Here's some useful information about the pieces to help you along:

- ✔ **Passepied in A Minor:** A *passepied* is a quick dance in triple time, or a piece to accompany such a dance. This one — written by Belgian Baroque guitar composer François Le Cocq — features a nice assortment of slurs, including descending ones to both open and fretted strings and ascending ones from both open and fretted strings. The trills in measures 6 and 17 give a nice ornamental flourish to the phrase endings (as is typical of music of the Baroque era).

- ✔ **Ländler in C:** A *ländler* is an Austrian folk dance in 3/4 time, or a musical composition written to accompany such a dance. In this one — composed by Austrian composer, guitarist, and publisher Anton Diabelli (1781–1858) — you get to play a nice variety of slurs (and some trills, too). Some slurs involve open strings and so require just one finger to execute. Others involve only fretted notes and so require two left-hand fingers.

  Normally, slurs involving notes played at adjacent frets are fingered with adjacent fingers. But check out measures 7 and 13. In those instances, the slur occurring on beat 2 involves the 2nd and 3rd frets, but it must be fingered with non-adjacent fingers 2 and 4 (as 1 and 3 are otherwise occupied). Also note that slurs are normally played with strong fingers (1 and 2, for example). But look at measure 12, where, because of the fingering of the other notes of the measure, the slur must be fingered with the weakest fingers (3 and 4). Finally, note that whereas most slurs start on *accented notes* (the beginnings of beats), as in measure 7, for example, many slurs in this piece begin on *unaccented notes* (notes that fall between the beats), as in measure 3, for instance. Because of the irregularities in slur fingering and rhythm in this piece, you may want to isolate the various measures in question for special practice.

Track 36

Passepied in A Minor

Track 37

Ländler in C

Chapter 10

Coloring Your Sound with Tone-Production Techniques

In This Chapter

▶ Playing harmonics

▶ Producing vibrato

▶ Changing tone

▶ Using tremolo

▶ Putting tone-production techniques into practice

*W*ith the fingering techniques you play in Chapters 8 and 9 (barring, slurring, and trilling) and the tone-production techniques you practice in this chapter, you'll be prepared to tackle almost any classical guitar music.

Special tone-production techniques include harmonics (high, silvery, bell-like tones), vibrato (a wavering sound), timbre changing (making the strings sound brighter or mellower), and tremolo (a shimmering "Spanish" sound). You use these techniques (or composers or arrangers indicate them) to make classical guitar pieces sound more colorful or exciting than they otherwise might.

Creating Tones That Ring like Bells: Harmonics

If you lightly touch a string with a left-hand finger at a point exactly halfway, a third of the way, or a quarter of the way along its length (the distance between the nut and the bridge saddle), and then pluck the string, you hear a high, pretty, bell-like tone known as a *harmonic*. You can produce harmonics by lightly touching a string at other fractional points along its length as well (a fifth, a sixth, and so on), but the aforementioned points — halfway, a third of the way, and a quarter of the way — are the most common and the easiest to achieve.

Why does touching a string that way produce a high tone? When you lightly touch the center point of a string (which is directly over the 12th metal fret wire) and then set it in motion with the right hand, it vibrates in halves rather than along its full length, producing a tone an octave higher than that of the open string. Likewise, when you touch a string at a third of its length (directly above the 7th fret wire), it vibrates in thirds, producing a tone an octave and a 5th above that of the open string. And if you touch a string at a quarter of its length (above the 5th fret), it vibrates in quarters, producing a tone two octaves above that of the open string. It's as if the strings are very good at mathematics and know how to instantly convert fractions into tones.

What happens, you may wonder, if you touch a string a third or quarter of the way along its length from the bridge side rather than from the nut? You produce the exact same harmonics as you do by measuring from the nut (because you're still dividing the string in thirds or quarters). But it's easier and much more common to produce those one-third and one-quarter harmonics from the nut side, over the 7th and 5th frets, respectively, than from the bridge side, where you don't have frets to guide your fingers to the proper spots.

Harmonics produced in the manner explained here are known as *natural* harmonics because they naturally occur when you lightly touch open strings at certain points. Other harmonics, known as *artificial* harmonics, are produced on fretted strings. But because they require the right hand to lightly touch a string with one finger while simultaneously plucking it with another, they're rather difficult to produce — and so beyond the scope of this book. Therefore, in this section we explore natural harmonics only, and only the ones that most frequently occur — namely, those at the 12th, 7th, and 5th frets.

Playing harmonics

Figure 10-1 shows how to produce a natural harmonic. Use the pad of a left-hand finger (the fleshy part between the fingertip and the first knuckle) to lightly touch a string directly over a certain fret (rather than to press the string all the way down to the fingerboard); then pluck the string with a right-hand finger. Important: Instead of placing your finger between the frets (as you would when fretting normally), place it directly over the metal fret wire (as shown in the photo); that's where the dividing point is located along the string. Try playing a harmonic at each fret (12th, 7th, and 5th) on each string, taking care not to press too hard on the string. Experiment to see exactly how hard you need to press to achieve the strongest-sounding harmonics.

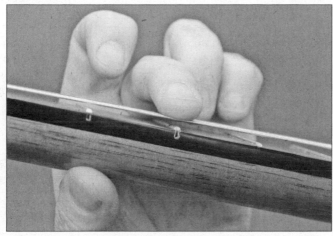

Figure 10-1:
Playing a harmonic.

Practicing harmonics in context

Figure 10-2 is both an exercise and a reference chart. In measures 1 through 6 you play harmonics from low to high according to their position on the neck, from 6th string, 5th fret, all the way up to 1st string, 12th fret. In measures 7 through 12 you play from low to high according to the harmonics' sounding pitches, from E above middle C (written) to three octaves above that. Note that you can produce certain harmonics at more than one string/fret combination. In fingering this exercise, you can use whichever fingers from each hand feel most comfortable.

The symbol *8va* stands for *ottava* (the Italian word for *octave*) and means that the notes indicated sound an octave higher than written.

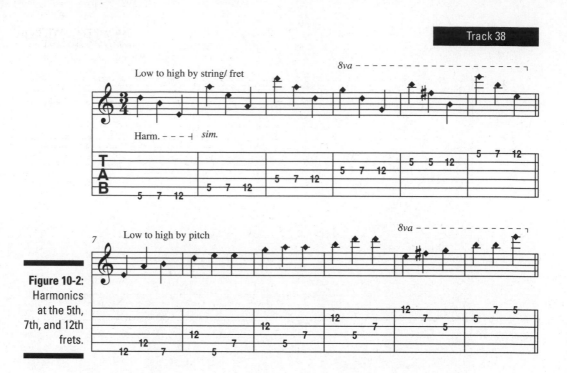

Track 38

Figure 10-2: Harmonics at the 5th, 7th, and 12th frets.

Harmonics are used rather sparingly in compositions to add color and excitement. But here, for the sake of practice, and to hear harmonics in a musical context, you play a melody — the well-known bugle call "Taps" — entirely in harmonics (see Figure 10-3).

Varying the Tone with Vibrato

The word *vibrato* comes from an Italian word meaning *vibrate*. And that's fitting, because when you apply vibrato to a note (whether vocally or on an instrument), you cause it to vibrate — or to shake, or waver. Opera singers employ liberal amounts of vibrato, and some well-known pop singers — Johnny Mathis and Willie Nelson, for example — are also known for their vibrato technique. Imagine either of those stars holding a long note, and you get a good idea of what vibrato sounds like.

Classical guitarists generally apply vibrato to notes for one of two reasons: to make them more expressive or to make them sound richer. (Notes played normally on classical guitar tend to fade or decay quickly, but applying vibrato causes them to continue ringing.)

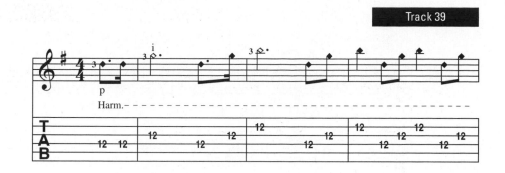

Track 39

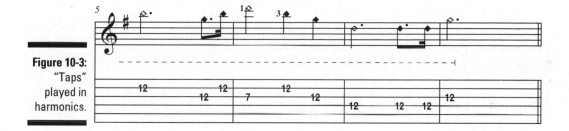

Figure 10-3:
"Taps"
played in
harmonics.

Vibrato generally isn't written into musical scores. Rather, performers take it upon themselves to decide if and when to apply it and to what degree (that is, is the vibrato slight or intense?).

Playing vibrato

Classical guitarists achieve vibrato differently from rock and blues guitarists. Rockers and blues players "shake" a note back and forth *across the neck,* parallel to the frets; or, to put it another way, they bend and release a note to a slight degree over and over again very quickly. This causes subtle changes in pitch, which causes the wavering sound. But classical guitarists play vibrato by very quickly sliding a left-hand finger up and down *along the length of a string,* but within a given fret (see Figure 10-4).

You may wonder how sliding along the length of the string within a fret causes a wavering sound if the string in question is vibrating only between the bridge and the metal fret bar just above your finger. The answer is that even though your finger moves back and forth along the length of the string, that motion, without your realizing it, also causes the string to be very slightly bent and released. And, technically speaking, these slight variations in pitch create the wavering effect of vibrato.

Figure 10-4:
Playing
vibrato.

Practicing vibrato in context

Achieving a strong vibrato is a little easier on the inside strings than the outer ones, and it's a little easier on the higher frets than the lower ones. Figure 10-5, the first phrase of the song "Londonderry Air" (also known as "Danny Boy"), gives you an opportunity to practice vibrato at the 2nd string, 5th fret (an easy one) with the third finger, and at the 3rd string, 2nd fret (a more difficult one) with the first finger. As is typical, you apply the effect to the phrase's longest notes. What's untypical (but occurs here for instructional purposes) is the appearance of the indication *vib.* in the score (normally, as we state earlier, vibrato is not indicated and is left to the performer's discretion).

Track 40

Figure 10-5:
"London-
derry Air"
with vibrato.

Use your whole hand to help move the finger back and forth within the fret. And if you have trouble hearing the vibrato effect, try pressing down your left-hand fretting finger a little harder than normal while executing the rapid back-and-forth slide. Pressing hard usually makes the vibrato effect "read" a little better.

Brightening or Darkening Your Sound by Changing Timbre

With many musical instruments (such as the piano), you have no way of changing their *timbre* (tone quality, or brightness or mellowness of sound) as you play; it is what it is. Sometimes the most you can do, assuming you'd like some variety of sound, is play the notes either louder or softer. Not so with classical guitar, where your right-hand placement actually affects the instrument's tone quality.

Implementing tonal changes

You can make your guitar's strings sound either brighter or mellower than normal simply by placing your right hand (and striking the strings) either higher or lower along the strings. And you can achieve a muted, muffled sound by placing the side of your right hand along the bridge.

Bright and metallic, or soft and mellow: Sul ponticello and sul tasto

In Figure 10-6, the photo on the left (Figure 10-6a) shows a normal right-hand position (with the fingers just above the sound hole and the thumb over it), which produces a normal tone.

The middle photo (Figure 10-6b) shows the right hand close to the bridge, a position known as *sul ponticello* (an Italian phrase that literally means "on the bridge"). When you play *sul ponticello,* you produce a sound that's thin but bright and metallic.

The photo on the right (Figure 10-6c) shows the right hand moved toward the fingerboard. This position is known as *sul tasto* (an Italian phrase that means "on the fingerboard"). Playing *sul tasto* produces a tone that's soft and mellow. By the way, the terms *sul ponticello* and *sul tasto* are also used in music for such stringed instruments as violin and cello; they tell the performer where to bow the string (either near the bridge or over the fingerboard).

Figure 10-6:
Placing the
right hand
near the
sound hole,
near the
bridge *(sul
ponticello),*
and close to
the finger-
board *(sul
tasto).*

You may wonder why changing your right-hand placement changes a string's tone. A full explanation would require complex mathematical formulas, but suffice it to say that when you pluck a string, you set it in motion in two directions at once — from your plucking finger to the top endpoint (the bridge) and from your finger to the bottom endpoint (the nut or a fretted note). As you move your right-hand finger to different points along the string, you change the distance between it and those endpoints. And that changes how the string's two vibrating portions interact with each other, which changes the tone.

You also may wonder why you should change tone in the first place. Classical guitarists often play *sul ponticello* or *sul tasto* to add variety and interest to their music. For example, if a composition includes a repeat, a guitarist may think to himself, "Gee, I just played that section. If I play it again the listener may become bored, even though the composer called for a repeat. I think I'll change the tone on the repeat to make it sound a little different." By the way, tonal changes are rarely indicated in written music for classical guitar — rather, they're left to the performer's discretion.

Go ahead and play a few notes or chords of your choice with your right hand first near the sound hole, then near the bridge, and then over the finger-board, and see if you can hear the difference in tone.

Short and muted: Pizzicato

In music for violin and cello (and other bowed string instruments), the directive *pizzicato* (an Italian word meaning "pinched") tells players to pluck the strings with their fingers rather than use the bow. But in classical guitar music, the term has a different meaning (after all, on guitar you normally pluck with the fingers). When you see *pizzicato* (usually abbreviated *pizz.*) in written guitar music, that tells you to imitate the sound of string *pizzicato* by causing the notes to sound short, muted, and muffled. You do that by placing the side of your right hand (the side toward the little finger) along the bridge as you play (see Figure 10-7). By the way, this is the same technique popular guitarists call *palm muting.*

Figure 10-7: To achieve a *pizzicato* (muted) sound, place the side of your right hand along the bridge.

Now, if you place your right hand against the bridge, you can't maintain proper right-hand position (with the fingers properly angled, relative to the strings). That's why *pizzicato* playing is virtually limited to the thumb. Even arpeggios are generally played all with the thumb when *pizzicato* is called for.

In playing *pizzicato,* you can place the side of your right hand on the bridge, up against the bridge's side, or merely close to the bridge. The closer to the bridge you are, the more muted the notes sound. You can even make them so muted (by placing your hand on top of the bridge) that their pitches can't be discerned — they just sound like thuds. Play a few low single notes of your choice and experiment with various right-hand placements to find just the right spot for the amount of muting you want.

Practicing changing tone in context

In this section you have a chance to practice changing tone by means of right-hand placement. Figure 10-8 is an exercise made up of a two-measure phrase (containing both single notes and a chord) played three times in a row. The tone gets progressively brighter as you move through the exercise. That is, you start out *sul tasto* (with a mellow tone), then you play normally, and finally you play *sul ponticello* (with a bright tone).

Figure 10-8: Changing tone by means of right-hand placement (relative to the sound hole).

Figure 10-9 gives you a chance to practice *pizzicato* playing (palm muting). First you play a simple phrase (based on an E minor scale) normally; then you place the side of your right hand against or very near the bridge to play the same phrase *pizzicato*. Remember to use your thumb to play all the notes.

Figure 10-9: Changing tone with the *pizzicato* (palm mute) technique.

To play a piece using harmonic technique, vibrato technique, *sul tasto, sul ponticello,* and *pizzicato,* skip to "In the Hall of the Mountain King" in the section "Playing Pieces Using Tone-Production Techniques," later in this chapter.

Tremolo: The Classical Guitar Machine Gun of Sorts

Some classical guitar pieces feature a right-hand technique — often used by flamenco guitarists — that produces a sustained, shimmering, "Spanish" sound. When you hear it, the notes sometimes sound as if they're being played faster than humanly possible. This technique is known as *tremolo,* and it is humanly possible to execute — if you know the trick behind it.

Playing tremolo

In playing tremolo, the thumb alternates with the fingers in a particular scheme. The thumb first plays a bass note, and then the fingers play a single treble note three times in a row, very quickly — first with *a,* then with *m,* then with *i.* So you use four fingers (thumb, ring, middle, index) to play just two pitches, like this: low-high-high-high.

Tremolo sounds authentic only if you can play the rhythm very steadily and evenly (normally, each thumb note and each of the finger notes is a 16th note) and if you can play the passage at a fast tempo. If you can do that, the thumb notes, coming at the beginning of each beat, provide the basic pulse, and the finger notes (all struck lightly with free strokes) provide the "shimmer" mentioned earlier.

Figure 10-10 gives you an opportunity to play the tremolo technique on a simple D minor chord. Hold down the notes with your left hand before striking any strings. In measures 1 through 4 you play the tremolo finger pattern using quarter notes, which allows you to play them rather slowly at first (just to get your fingers working in the proper manner). In measures 5 and 6 you play the same thing but in eighth notes, which starts to give you an idea of how tremolo actually sounds. Then in measure 7 you play in 16ths, which is how tremolo is truly played.

Track 43

Figure 10-10: Tremolo technique on a D minor chord.

Practicing tremolo in context

Figure 10-11 is an exercise that uses the tremolo technique on a series of basic chords. In each measure, hold down the entire chord with your left hand before playing the notes. Think of the bass notes as the melody — that's the part that provides the motion.

To get a handle on this technique, you must start slowly and gradually increase your speed. Working with a metronome is a good idea. Start out at a tempo slow enough to allow yourself to play *p-a-m-i* (on the two appropriate strings) in a perfectly steady rhythm. Then, gradually increase the speed, maintaining a perfectly even rhythm at whatever tempo you choose.

In counting notes and beats in tremolo playing, think of the thumb notes as the beats. For example, if you have four beats and four thumb notes in a measure, count "1-2-3-4" along with the thumb strokes. Don't even try to count or think about the "in between" finger notes; they're merely providing that shimmer.

Figure 10-11:
Tremolo
exercise in
D minor.

To play a piece using the tremolo technique, skip to "Tremolo Study in A Minor" in the next section, "Playing Pieces Using Tone-Production Techniques."

Playing Pieces Using Tone-Production Techniques

In this section you play pieces that use harmonics, employ changes in timbre, use *pizzicato,* and use the tremolo technique. Here's some useful information about the pieces to help you along:

✔ **"In the Hall of the Mountain King":** You probably recognize this piece by its melody, if not by its title. It was written by Norwegian composer Edvard Grieg (1843–1907) as incidental music for Norwegian playwright Henrik Ibsen's play *Peer Gynt.* As indicated in the score, play the first four measures *pizzicato*, the next four normally, the next four *sul tasto*, and the next four *sul ponticello*. Pay special attention to the dynamic markings — in this arrangement, as the tone changes, the volume level does, too. Harmonic technique and vibrato technique punctuate the phrase endings.

✔ **Tremolo Study in A Minor:** In this tremolo study, written by Hungarian composer and guitar virtuoso Johann Mertz (1806–1856), your left hand (as well as your right) has some work to do. That is, you can't always just hold down a chord and leave it there for the duration of each measure, because the bass line sometimes plays an actual melody (consisting of stepwise motion). Though you can sometimes hold down your left hand as a chord throughout a measure (measure 2, for example), in measures 1, 3, and 5, pay special attention to the thumb notes (and the fingering necessary to play them) as they move from note to note. The good news is that in the spots where the thumb does move melodically, the treble notes are open strings, so you can devote all your attention to the fingering of the thumb.

In the Hall of the Mountain King

Track 46

Tremolo Study in A Minor

Chapter 11

Scaling the Musical Ladder beyond Second Position

*I*n this chapter, you concentrate on doing two things: playing notes up the neck and playing scales (you know, those *do-re-mi* type things that melodies are based on). But to make things simple, we combine the two tasks into one by playing scales up the neck. This provides the most efficient way to get to know the notes in the higher positions — that is, to know the letter name of each string/fret combination above the 5th fret, as well as each note's location on the music staff. This, combined with the study of the lower frets (1 through 5) in Chapter 4, completes your knowledge of the fretboard. The added benefit is that by practicing scales, you strengthen your fingers and make the playing of actual pieces, which are based on scales, more automatic. (For more on scales and their benefits, see Chapter 6, as well as our companion publication, *Guitar Exercises For Dummies.*)

An Introduction to the Scales and Skills in This Chapter

Real classical guitar pieces usually involve notes along most of the neck. To play those pieces, you need to be able to read and play notes in the higher positions, and you also need to know how to play those notes both within one position (that is, by moving *across* the neck in a given position) and among several positions (by moving *up and down* the neck with position shifts).

The first half of this chapter helps you play scales that stay in either 5th position (frets 5 through 8) or 9th position (frets 9 through 12). In the second half of the chapter, you practice shifting among positions while playing scales up the neck.

The fingering of a scale — whether you play it across the neck or up and down the neck — never changes how a scale sounds (for example, a major scale always has the familiar *do-re-mi-fa-sol-la-ti-do* sound); the fingering only changes where and how you play the scale.

Getting to know the higher positions

By *higher positions,* we mean positions that include notes above the 5th fret, especially positions that *begin* at or above the 5th fret (in other words, positions where your first finger covers the 5th fret or higher). Here we focus on scales in 5th position (frets 5, 6, 7, and 8) and 9th position (frets 9, 10, 11, and 12) because those two positions, taken together, cover all the higher frets (that is, frets 5 through 12).

You rarely play above the 12th fret, because the guitar's body gets in the way of your left hand and the frets are difficult to finger. Therefore, the scales in this chapter don't go above the 12th fret. But figuring out the letter names of the higher frets is easy: Frets 13 through 19 have exactly the same names as frets 1 through 7, but they sound an octave higher. For example, on the 1st string, the letter names of frets 1 through 3 are F, F♯, and G; likewise, the letter names of frets 13 through 15 are F, F♯, and G (but an octave higher).

Even though the many different scales in this chapter give you an opportunity to play all pitches between the 5th and 12th frets, any one particular major or minor scale doesn't require you to play at every single fret. But as you play scales up the neck (noting the letter names of the notes you play), be aware of the pitches of the in-between frets — the frets you don't play. That is, if you play, say, a D at the 7th fret of the 3rd string, realize that the note a fret below is a D♭ (also known as C♯), and the note a fret above is a D♯ (also known as E♭). Doing so helps you learn the entire fretboard — string by string and fret by fret — rather than merely the locations of the notes that happen to make up a given scale. For more on sharps and flats, see Chapter 3.

To see the neck and staff positions of all the notes on the guitar (up through the 12th fret) at a glance, check out the guitar neck diagram, also in Chapter 3.

Strengthening your technical skill with practice variations

Scales are versatile things: They get you ready to play real-life melodies, help you learn the letter names of the various string/fret combinations of the fretboard, and help you develop your technique. After you learn the scales we present in this chapter, you can vary them in a few simple ways to increase the dexterity of both hands, as the following list explains:

- ✔ **Vary your right-hand stroking pattern.** You typically practice scales by alternating *i-m-i-m,* and so on (with free strokes). But to increase your right-hand dexterity and strength, practice the scales with a variety of finger combinations: *i* and *m* (both *i-m-i-m* and *m-i-m-i*), *m* and *a* (both *m-a-m-a* and *a-m-a-m*), and *i* and *a* (both *i-a-i-a* and *a-i-a-i*).

- ✔ **Move scale patterns up or down the neck.** Because the distance between the frets gets progressively narrower as they go higher, each position on the guitar has its own unique left-hand "feel" (because you use your hand and finger muscles a little differently to play at wide frets compared to narrow ones). To get you used to playing in any and all positions on the neck, the scales we present in this chapter don't use open strings, which means they're *movable;* that is, you can instantly change, say, a B♭ major scale into a B major scale simply by moving your whole hand up one fret and then playing the same pattern. (Of course, only scales consisting entirely of fretted notes are movable because open strings retain their pitch no matter what position of the neck your hand may be in.) So after learning a scale in one position, move it (its left-hand fingering pattern, that is) up and down the neck to other positions.

The letter name of the scale you're playing in the new position (or any position) is the same as the letter name of the first note of the pattern. If you need help determining the name of that first note, see the guitar neck diagram in Chapter 3.

- ✔ **Mix up the order of notes by varying scale sequence patterns.** A good way to strengthen your fingers and have them simultaneously "memorize" a scale pattern is by playing what are known as *scale sequences.* When you play a scale sequence, you start by taking a few notes of a scale (sometimes consecutive, sometimes not) and playing them from a given pitch, often starting from the scale's *tonic* (the note the scale is named after). Those few notes make up a short musical phrase, which often has more in common with actual music than a straight scale does. Then you play that same phrase over and over, with each repetition starting from a new pitch. For example, if you number the notes of a major scale 1-2-3-4-5-6-7, you might play, as a scale sequence, 1-2-3, 2-3-4, 3-4-5, 4-5-6, and so on.

Literally hundreds (even thousands or millions!) of possible scale sequence patterns exist. You can make up more by yourself (by ear or even by picking a few numbers from 1 through 7 from a hat), or you can enter the phrase "scale sequences" in any online search engine to locate many, many possibilities. The point is that, in order to memorize scales and develop your technique, you should practice scales as well as scale sequences. We provide an example of varying sequence patterns in the section "The F major scale," but be sure to play and practice similar scale sequences for all the across-the-neck scales we present in this chapter.

You don't usually play scales requiring position shifts as scale sequences, because the fingering you use to play such a scale in its entirety (with position shifts) is different from the fingering you use to play just a portion of the scale (which may not require a position shift).

In the sections that follow, we present scales (both major and minor) from a variety of starting notes, in a variety of directions (up, down, across the neck, along the neck), and with a variety of fingering patterns. Practice these scales by playing them multiple times, keeping an eye on the notes you play (in other words, be aware of their letter names, their neck positions, and their locations on the music staff). After you're comfortable with each scale, practice it with the variations we describe in the preceding list. Don't worry about which technique variation — changing your right-hand fingering, moving a scale up or down the neck, playing scale sequence patterns — to apply first (or second, or third). They're all equally important, and you can apply them in any order, or in any combination, as you see fit.

Scales That Stay in 5th Position

Certain keys and scales are associated with certain positions because all (or most) of their notes happen to fall comfortably within the four-fret span of that position. For example, F and B♭ are two scales normally associated with 5th position. By knowing those 5th position scales, you're able to play and read the notes between the 5th and 8th frets.

Composers write in major keys more often than in minor, so here we give you two different ways, or fingering patterns, to play a major scale in position — one starting from the 5th string and one from the 6th. At the end of this section we give you one minor scale fingering pattern to play.

The F major scale

The scale shown in Figure 11-1 is an F major scale in 5th position in an eighth-note rhythm. Because they move along at a nice, comfortable clip (not too fast or slow), eighth notes are often used to present and play scales.

The general scale pattern

Note that the scale begins with the F at the 8th fret of the 5th string. Though some notes of the F scale exist in 5th position below that note (beginning as low as the A at the 5th fret of the 6th string), we start this scale on F simply because starting on any other note would make the scale sound like something other than an F scale. For example, if you start on the low A, the scale sounds like some kind of A scale. On the other hand, at the high end of the scale pattern, because the sound of the F scale is already established, we take you to the top of the position (8th fret) so that you have an opportunity to play and practice as many notes as possible in 5th position.

Note that this scale pattern begins with the fourth finger, as indicated in the music (the numeral *4* appears next to the first note head). Of course, because when you play in position each finger is assigned to a certain fret (with the fingers covering a four-fret span and with the position named after the fret the first finger plays), any note on the 8th fret (in 5th position) is played by the fourth finger.

Track 47

Figure 11-1:
The F major
scale in 5th
position.

The scale with varying sequence patterns

Figure 11-2 shows the beginnings of six scale sequences based on the F major scale in 5th position (the first three ascending, the last three descending). Some are based on four-note phrases (numbers 1, 2, 4, and 5) and some on three-note phrases (numbers 3 and 6). Some phrases flow in one direction only (numbers 2, 3, 5, and 6) and some change direction within the phrase (numbers 1 and 4). For each of the six sequences, play the measure as written, and then continue the established pattern all the way across the neck. For example, in number 1, play (as written) scale degrees 1-2-3-1 and 2-3-4-2, and then continue (without the help of written music) with 3-4-5-3, 4-5-6-4, and so on, all the way across the neck.

Track 48

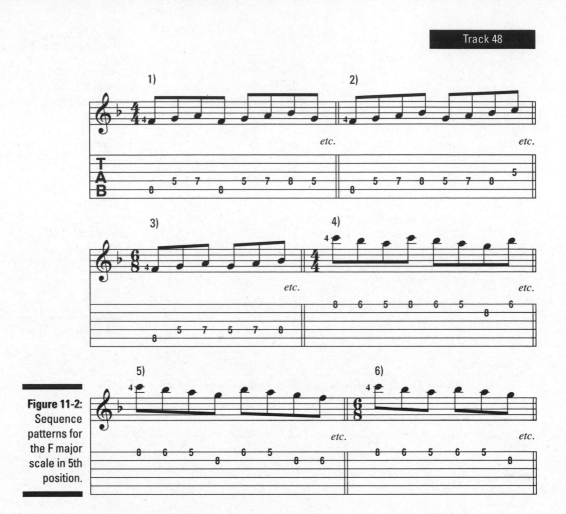

Figure 11-2:
Sequence patterns for the F major scale in 5th position.

The B♭ major scale

Figure 11-3 shows a B♭ major scale in 5th position. Whereas the F scale in this position starts on the 5th string with the fourth finger and covers a span of only about an octave and a half, this scale, employing a different fingering pattern (that is, using its own unique combination of left-hand fingers), begins on the 6th string with the second finger and covers two full octaves.

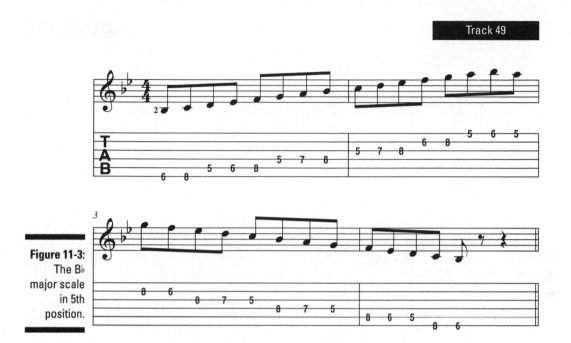

Figure 11-3: The B♭ major scale in 5th position.

The D minor scale

Like major scales, minor scales are associated with certain positions (because their notes also happen to fall comfortably within the four-fret span of those positions). D minor (D-E-F-G-A-B♭-C-D) is a scale closely associated with 5th position.

The D minor scale shown in Figure 11-4 begins on the 5th string and extends nearly two octaves. The final high D is omitted because it's out of range (that is, it would be played at the 10th fret, which is beyond the span of 5th position). As always, be mindful of the letter names you play and where they're located on the neck and on the music staff.

Figure 11-4: The D minor scale in 5th position.

Scales That Stay in 9th Position

When you play in 9th position, you familiarize yourself with the notes between the 9th and 12th frets. Two major scales closely associated with 9th position are A and D, which we present in the sections that follow.

Because less music is based on minor scales than major, in this section we give you just one minor scale fingering pattern to play (rather than two, as with the major scale).

The A major scale

The scale shown in Figure 11-5 uses the same fingering pattern (combination of left-hand fingers) as the 5th position F major scale, which we cover earlier in this chapter. However, because A is four half steps above F, it's played four frets higher. You already know the fingering pattern for this scale (the pattern that begins with the fourth finger on the 5th string, then proceeds with fingers 1, 3, and 4 on the 4th string, and so on), so concentrate on the letter names of the notes you play (A, B, C♯, and so on) and on where they occur — both on the guitar neck (at which string/fret location) and on the music staff (on which line or space).

Track 51

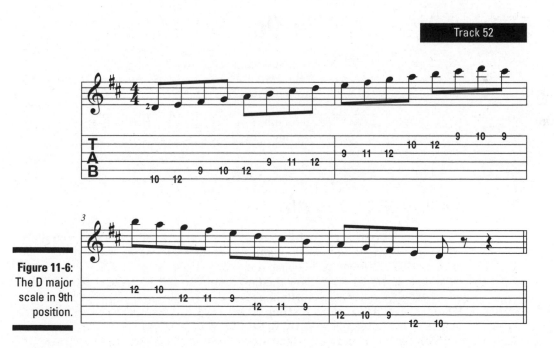

Figure 11-5:
The A major scale in 9th position.

The D major scale

The scale shown in Figure 11-6 uses the same fingering pattern (left-hand fingering) as the B♭ scale you play in 5th position (refer to Figure 11-3), but here you play four frets higher. Again, because you already know this fingering pattern (the one starting with the second finger on the 6th string and covering two full octaves), concentrate on the letter names you play (D, E, F♯, and so on) — and on their locations on both the neck and music staff.

Track 52

Figure 11-6:
The D major scale in 9th position.

The F♯ minor scale

The F♯ minor scale (F♯-G♯-A-B-C♯-D-E-F♯) is closely associated with 9th position. As shown in Figure 11-7, it uses the same fingering pattern as the D minor scale you play in 5th position (fingers 1, 3, and 4 on the 5th and 4th strings, then 1 and 3 on the 3rd string, and so on), but because F♯ is four half steps above D, you play it four frets higher. Playing this scale in 9th position helps you get to know the names of the notes between the 9th and 12th frets.

Track 53

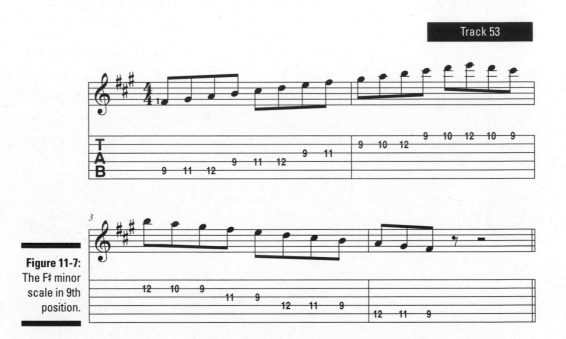

Figure 11-7:
The F♯ minor
scale in 9th
position.

Scales That Require Shifting Positions

In this section you play two major scales and two minor scales. One major scale requires one position shift (from 6th position to 9th and back again) and the other requires two (from 1st position to 5th to 8th and back again). One minor scale requires one position shift (from 4th position to 7th and back again) and the other requires two (from 1st position to 4th to 9th and back again).

Of course, playing in 4th, 6th, 7th, and 8th positions is technically no different from playing in other positions — in 4th position your left hand covers frets 4 through 7, and in 6th position it covers frets 6 through 9, and so on. The good news is that playing scale passages in various positions improves your note-reading skills — assuming, of course, that you pay attention to the letter names and positions (on the fretboard and the music staff) of the notes you play.

To shift positions, simply slide your hand up or down into the new position, following the exact fingering given in the notation. The trick is to make the shift imperceptible to a listener; that is, someone listening to you play the scale (including yourself!) shouldn't be able to hear that you've executed a position shift. The notes of the scale should sound smooth, even, and steady, with no squeaking.

How do you accomplish that? It takes practice, but one thing you can do is keep your left hand as close to the strings as possible (even touching them sometimes) while smoothly gliding it into the new position. Make sure that if you maintain contact as you slide your hand along a string, your pressure is light enough that you don't produce any sound.

For practice, it's a good idea to isolate a short passage containing the shift (starting from a note or two before it and ending a note or two after it) and to practice that passage over and over in both its ascending and descending forms. That way, when you play the full scale, the shift will be effortless (as it should be).

The E major scale — one position shift

Figure 11-8 shows an E major scale with one position shift, starting with the second finger on the 5th string. Note that in the music notation, as a reading aid, we indicate exactly where the position shifts occur. We also indicate which left-hand fingers to use for the last note of the old position and the first note of the new position. The range is two full octaves, going all the way up to the high E at the 12th fret of the 1st string. Play the scale up and down several times.

Track 54

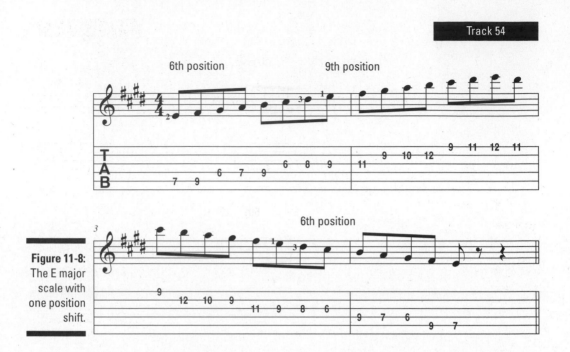

Figure 11-8:
The E major scale with one position shift.

The A♭ major scale — two position shifts

In this A♭ major scale (see Figure 11-9), you really stretch out, going all the way from the 1st fret (in 1st position) up to the 11th fret (in 8th position). Here you have two position shifts (labeled in the score) to contend with, and each should sound seamless — so isolate a short passage around each one and practice just the shifts (both ascending and descending) separately before playing the scale in its entirely.

The C♯ minor scale — one position shift

The C♯ minor scale you play in Figure 11-10 requires one position shift, from 4th position to 7th (labeled in the score). By playing in the 4th and 7th positions — as well as in all the aforementioned positions in this chapter — you complete your study of all the upper positions on the guitar. And that prepares you to play and read any classical guitar music you may encounter.

Track 55

1st position   5th position   8th position

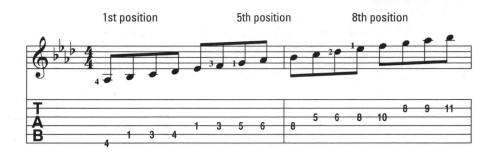

Figure 11-9:
The A♭ major scale with two position shifts.

Track 56

4th position   7th position

Figure 11-10:
The C♯ minor scale with one position shift.

The G♯ minor scale — two position shifts

The along-the-neck G♯ minor scale (see Figure 11-11) has a range of about two and a half octaves and requires two position shifts (labeled in the score). Here you play in 1st, 4th, and 9th positions, which reinforces your knowledge of the note names in those positions.

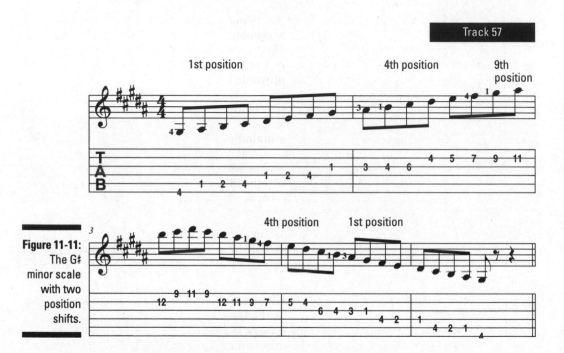

Figure 11-11: The G♯ minor scale with two position shifts.

Playing Some Pieces Using Scales up the Neck

This section is your reward for diligently practicing your scales and for getting to know the letter names of all the frets on all the strings (and for figuring out which music staff locations those notes correspond to). So here we give you actual pieces to play that utilize the scales you practice in the previous sections — one piece based on the A major scale in 9th position and the other piece based on the D minor scale in 5th position.

When we say that these pieces utilize the scales you practice, we mean that their melodies consist of nothing but notes from the scales (often in step-wise, scale-like motion) and that you finger the notes according to the actual fingering pattern you practice. But playing a single melody isn't much of a reward, so we incorporate the low open strings as bass notes (which you play with your thumb) to make these songs sound like real classical guitar pieces.

The two songs we present are Christmas carols, and we present them not because we imagine that you're reading this in December but because Christmas carols are both well-known and beautiful. These pieces don't just give you something nice to play; they also give you an additional opportunity to practice your scales in an enjoyable way.

Here's some useful information to help you along:

- **"Silent Night":** The serene-sounding melody to "Silent Night" uses the scale shown in Figure 11-5 — A major in 9th position (if necessary, review that scale before playing the piece). If you have trouble combining the open bass notes with the 9th-position melody, try playing the melody alone a few times. Then, when you're comfortable with that, try adding the bass notes.

  The last measure uses harmonics for an ornamental ending (see Chapter 10 for more on harmonics). For the very last note of the piece (the high A harmonic), you need to move your left hand out of 9th position (down to 5th position).

- **"God Rest Ye Merry, Gentlemen":** The jaunty melody to "God Rest Ye Merry, Gentlemen" uses the D minor scale as shown in Figure 11-4. Again, we include open-string bass notes for fullness, and you can play the melody alone a few times before adding the bass notes.

  Note that your left hand stays in 5th position throughout, except in measures 8 and 15, where you play a high D at the 10th fret of the 1st string. As the notation indicates, use your fourth finger (which just played the preceding C at the 8th fret) to slide up to grab that D (but without making an audible sliding sound).

Track 58

Silent Night

Track 59

God Rest Ye Merry, Gentlemen

Chapter 12

Combining Arpeggios and Melody

In This Chapter

▶ Understanding how arpeggios combine with melodies

▶ Combining arpeggios with melodies in the bass and in the treble

▶ Shifting the melody between the thumb and fingers

▶ Practicing pieces with arpeggios and melodies

*P*erhaps nothing is more satisfying to a classical guitarist than a composition that deftly combines arpeggios and melodies. And the reason is simple: To a listener, the piece sounds intricate and advanced (sometimes even virtuosic), yet typically, it's not very difficult to play. So, with such pieces, you can amaze (or at least impress) your friends — without being a Segovia.

In this chapter, we show you how melody and arpeggios work together quite simply to create beautiful pieces, and we show you how to play them with ease. If you need to brush up on arpeggio technique before you begin, review Chapter 5.

Grasping the Combination in Context

Combining a melody with an arpeggio is often a matter of simply playing the notes you're already fingering (rather than having to play additional notes) — the melody's notes are usually contained within the arpeggio itself. Also, when you play an arpeggio, all or many of the chord's notes are either open strings or are already held down (as a chord) by your left hand. Your right-hand fingers, too, are already in position — each resting in preparedness against its respective string. In other words, your hands hardly move for the duration of each chord!

How, you may wonder, can you simultaneously play notes with various values (that is, quarter notes, whole notes, eighth-notes, and so on) and keep them from sounding like a blur of overlapping pitches while also letting them all ring out as long as possible in each measure? The answer is that you actually play the notes at different levels of loudness — or, perhaps, different levels of emphasis. You do that by giving more *oomph* to some notes than to others.

The human touch (your touch, as determined by your understanding of the notes' roles and interactions) imparts the proper textural feel to the listener — and that's what makes playing such pieces so exciting. If you give the right amount of emphasis to the respective notes (even merely psychologically), the effect comes across to the listener, who hears the music not as just a blur of overlapping pitches but as a melody, an accompaniment, and a bass line. The technique for doing that varies, depending on whether you play the melody with your thumb or fingers.

As always when playing arpeggios, hold down your left-hand fingers as a chord whenever possible and for as long as possible. And keep the motion of your right hand to a minimum by resting your fingers ahead of time against the strings they need to play in each arpeggio. For example, before playing an A minor arpeggio (as in measure 1 in Figure 12-1), your thumb should be resting against the 5th string, your index finger against the 3rd string, and your middle finger against the 2nd string. While playing each arpeggio, your right hand itself doesn't move; only your fingers and thumb move as they strike their respective strings.

In the sections that follow, we present exercises that allow you to combine arpeggios with melodies in the bass (played by the thumb) and the treble (played by the fingers), and we explore ways to draw the melody out of the background and into the limelight, where it belongs.

Going Downtown: Melody in the Bass

The melody of a classical guitar piece, though usually played by the fingers on the high strings (in the treble), is sometimes played by the thumb on the low strings (in the bass). (This concept applies to the piano, too, by the way. The right hand plays the melody of most pieces, though for a different effect, the melody can be placed in the left hand.)

You may find it easier to combine arpeggios with a melody played by your thumb than by your fingers. For one thing, your thumb usually plays *on* the beat (rather than between the beats, as the fingers do). For another, you have no decisions to make about *which* finger plays the melody; that is, your thumb, acting alone, plays nothing but the melody notes while your fingers play nothing but the accompaniment (the higher notes of each arpeggio).

Don't worry about having to hunt down the melody in a piece. The melody usually reveals itself soon enough when you start to play, just in the way the composer or arranger wrote the notes. (Sometimes the written music itself even offers clues, such as giving the melody its own stem direction.) After you're able to hear where the melody falls, you can work to bring it out further, using slightly stronger strokes on the melody notes themselves. Or, if the piece has no melody at all (which sometimes happens in short passages between melodic phrases), you hear that, too, and give no emphasis to any particular notes.

Playing a bass melody within arpeggios

How do you bring out the notes when the melody is in the bass line? Just play them a little louder (striking them a little harder) than the other notes, and make sure the other notes are consistent with each other in loudness.

Figure 12-1 is an exercise that offers you an opportunity to practice the basic technique of combining arpeggios with a bass melody without having to worry about any of the complicated rhythms or unusual left-hand fingerings that real-life pieces may contain.

Note that the first note of each triplet group has a downward stem (in addition to an upward stem). Those downward stems tell you not only to play those notes with your thumb but also to play them as quarter notes; in other words, to let them ring throughout the beat.

Now, alert reader that you are, you may point out that one of the rules of arpeggio playing is that all the notes of an arpeggio should ring out (rather than be stopped short) — so all those bass notes would sound as quarter notes anyway. And you're right. So in reality, those downward stems on the first note of each triplet group tell you not only to play them with the thumb and to let them ring out but also to bring out those thumb notes so that a listener hears them as an independent melody.

Measure 2 presents an interesting right-hand fingering dilemma. Normal, or typical, right-hand position has the index finger assigned to the 3rd string, the middle finger to the 2nd, and the ring finger to the 1st. Also, you generally try not to move the right hand itself, if at all possible. For those reasons, you'd expect to use fingers *m* and *a* to play the top two notes of the D minor arpeggio.

But another rule of arpeggio playing says that you should use the strongest fingers whenever possible — and the combination of *i* and *m* is stronger than that of *m* and *a*. So, according to that rule, you should use *i* and *m* for the top two strings (even though you have to move your right hand across the neck a bit). Hence the dilemma.

The important point is that when you have a situation in which those right-hand fingering rules conflict, the "strong fingers" rule takes precedence over the "minimize motion" rule, and thus we indicate in measure 2 that you play the top two notes of the D minor arpeggio with *i* and *m*.

Figure 12-1 presents no technical difficulties, but for best results, follow the left-hand fingering carefully, and keep the rhythm as steady and even as possible.

Track 60

Figure 12-1:
Arpeggio
exercise
with melody
in bass.

Practicing making a bass melody stand out

Figure 12-2 is taken from a study by early 19th-century Spanish guitar virtuoso Dionisio Aguado. It features a single right-hand pattern throughout (*p-i-
m-i*) and a uniform rhythm. That's what makes it easy to play. But at the same
time, the study is somewhat challenging for a few reasons.

First, the notes are 16ths, which means that they move along rather briskly.
So start out by practicing slowly, then gradually increase the tempo. Second,
the bass notes — because they're all chord tones that occur at the beginning
of each four-note group — have a tendency to sound like nothing more than
simply the first note of each arpeggio. So it's your job to make them especially
melodic; that is, bring them out forcefully — but smoothly and sweetly — so
that a listener hears a "tune" in the bass. Finally, you play some of the notes on
strings you may not expect. Check out measure 2, beat 4, for example, where,
in order to preserve the right-hand pattern (and flow), you play the C on the
3rd string, and the repeated E's alternate between the 2nd and 1st strings.

For ease of playing, pay special attention to the left-hand fingering (and especially to the guide finger indications). And for an effective performance, keep
the rhythm as even as possible.

Track 61

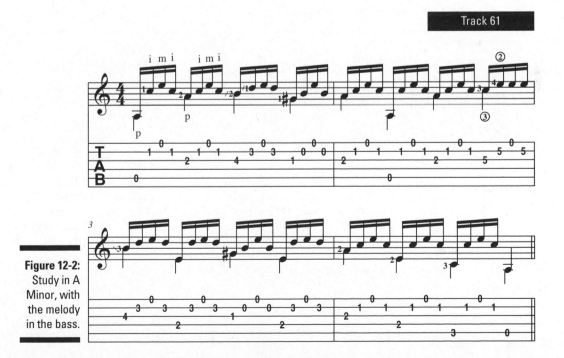

Figure 12-2:
Study in A
Minor, with
the melody
in the bass.

To play an actual piece featuring arpeggios with a melody in the bass right now, skip to "Ländler in D" in the section "Playing Pieces That Combine Arpeggios and Melodies," later in this chapter.

Moving Uptown: Melody in the Treble

In this chapter you start with melodies in the bass because, as we explain earlier, they're a bit easier to combine with arpeggios than are melodies in the treble. However, arpeggio pieces with melodies in the treble are actually more common than those with melodies in the bass, and in this section we look at the technique you use to play such pieces.

Playing arpeggios with the melody in the treble rather than the bass can be a bit trickier for a few reasons, as the following list explains:

- ✔ **Question of fingering:** Technically, any given melody note can be taken with any available finger — *i, m,* or *a* — and it's often up to you to decide which to use (see Chapter 3 for explanations of these finger labels).

- ✔ **Use of the ring finger:** Because the *i* and *m* fingers usually play accompaniment notes on the inner strings, the *a* finger takes many melody notes. The problem is that the melody notes must be emphasized, but the ring finger is the weakest.

- ✔ **Question of right-hand technique:** As explained in the sections that follow, you have more than one way to bring out a treble melody from an arpeggio, and it's up to you to decide which technique to use.

- ✔ **Use of rest strokes:** Whereas you play arpeggios with a melody in the bass with free strokes only, you generally combine rest strokes and free strokes when you play arpeggios with a melody in the treble.

- ✔ **Complexity of notation:** Standard music notation for arpeggio pieces with a melody in the treble often requires the indication of three separate parts, or *voices* — one each for the melody, the accompaniment (usually filler notes on the inner strings), and the bass. Normally, stem directions tell you which notes belong to which part (for example, notes with stems up are melody and notes with stems down are bass). Depending on the musical context (or sometimes simply on the amount of available space), the accompaniment notes may be stemmed either down (sometimes making them hard to distinguish from bass notes) or up (sometimes making them hard to distinguish from melody notes).

Sometimes, at the whim of a composer or arranger, the melody and accompaniment notes are combined into a single voice (as a continuous flow of upstemmed eighth notes, for example), and it's up to you, using your ear, to discover the real melody.

Although the aforementioned potential complications may cause you concern, remember that most arpeggiated pieces — even those with the melody in the treble — aren't difficult to play. That's because, as stated, in such pieces, the left hand generally holds down a chord, and the melody notes themselves are often contained within that chord.

To bring out the melody in the treble, you have to make it either louder than, or different in tone from, the other notes. You can do this simply by

- ✔ Making the melody notes sound stronger than the others by playing them with rest strokes (and the accompaniment notes with free strokes). You can also try the techniques in the following bullets, but this technique — the use of rest strokes for melody notes — is generally used by classical guitarists, and it's the one you should strive to perfect.

- ✔ Striking the melody notes harder than the others (as you do when you bring out a bass melody with the thumb).

- ✔ Making the melody notes brighter-sounding than the others by using more nail when you strike them (that is, if you play with a combination of flesh and nail, use more nail than flesh on the melody notes, and more flesh than nail on the accompaniment notes).

Playing a treble melody within arpeggios

Figure 12-3 is an exercise that allows you to combine a treble melody with a series of arpeggios. Note that you play the melody in quarter notes (indicated by upward quarter-note stems), that the bass notes are whole notes (and thus must ring throughout each measure), and that the accompaniment notes are eighth-note triplets, which, though they're written as short notes, should also ring out (according to the general rules of arpeggio playing).

Practice Figure 12-3 using rest strokes on all the melody notes. Start out playing slowly (but evenly), then gradually increase your speed. Follow the left-hand fingerings to ensure that you can hold down each chord with your left hand for as long as possible. If necessary, listen to the CD to hear how the piece works rhythmically and how the separate voices interact.

Figure 12-3: Arpeggio exercise with melody in treble.

Practicing making a treble melody stand out

Figure 12-4 comes from a study by late 19th-century Spanish guitar virtuoso Francisco Tárrega. It employs a consistent right-hand pattern throughout: *p-i-m, a-m-i, a-m-i, a-m-i.* Play all the melody notes as rest strokes with the ring finger.

Note that the bass notes sustain throughout each arpeggio, but in measure 3, fingering requirements force you to stop the bass from ringing one beat early (as the finger that plays the bass note, the first finger, is suddenly needed on the 1st string to play the last melody note of the measure).

To play a piece right now that combines arpeggios with a melody in the treble, skip to "Romanza" in the section "Playing Pieces That Combine Arpeggios and Melodies," later in this chapter.

Figure 12-4:
Study in C, with the melody in the treble.

Mixing Up Your Melodic Moves: The Thumb and Fingers Take Turns

Not all arpeggiated passages are as straightforward as those you encounter earlier in this chapter — where the melody occurs consistently in either the treble or bass part. In some cases the melody moves back and forth between the treble and bass, and in others the treble and bass parts contain melodic motion simultaneously. Fortunately, the playing of such pieces requires no new techniques, but it does require a heightened awareness (on your part) of where the melody is and how to bring it out.

Playing a shifting treble-and-bass melody within arpeggios

In Figure 12-5, from measure to measure, the melody alternates between the treble and bass. In the odd-numbered measures, which have the melody in the treble, bring out the melody (the upstemmed notes) with rest strokes. For the even-numbered measures, which have the melody in the bass, bring out the melody (the downstemmed notes) by giving the first note of each triplet a little more *oomph* than the other notes.

Note that the melody note that occurs on the third beat of each measure is a *dissonance* (that is, it's not a member of the chord being arpeggiated), but that it passes smoothly from one chord tone to another. For example, in measure 1, in which an E minor chord (made up of the notes E, G, and B) is arpeggiated, the F♯ on beat 3 functions as a *passing tone* (a dissonance that, in stepwise motion, passes between, and thus fills the gap between, two chord tones — in this case, G and E). Also note, as a point of interest, that each bass melody is a repetition, but two octaves lower, of the treble melody that precedes it. Repetition imparts structural unity and thus a sense of balance to a composition.

Track 64

Figure 12-5: Arpeggio exercise with melody alternating between treble and bass.

Practicing making a shifting melody stand out

Figure 12-6 is an excerpt from a waltz from the guitar method of early 19th-century Italian guitar composer and virtuoso Ferdinando Carulli. A glance at the music reveals that the melody begins in the bass (measures 1 and 2) and moves to the treble (measures 3 through 5).

In measures 3 and 4, note that in the written notation, for the sake of simplicity, the composer combined the melody (the upstemmed notes on the beats: F♯-G-F♯, G-F♯-G) and the accompaniment notes (the open B's) into a single voice. What you need to realize is that although the melody notes are written as eighths, you render them in performance as quarters.

In Figure 12-5 you play a dissonance known as a *passing tone*. In Figure 12-6, Waltz in E Minor presents another type of dissonance: the *neighboring tone*. A neighboring tone is a non-chord tone that, in stepwise motion, follows a chord tone and then returns to it (with the word "neighboring" obviously coming from the idea that, being just one step away from the chord tone, the dissonant note is like the chord tone's next-door neighbor). For example, in measure 3 you arpeggiate a B chord (B-D♯-F♯), and the G on beat 2 follows and then returns to the chord tone F♯. Because G is above F♯ in the scale, it's called, specifically, an *upper neighbor*. In the following measure you arpeggiate an E minor chord (E-G-B), and the F♯ on beat 2 (following and then returning to G) is a *lower neighbor*.

To play a piece right now that combines arpeggios with a melody that appears in both the treble and bass, skip to "Andante in C" in the forthcoming section, "Playing Pieces That Combine Arpeggios and Melodies."

Track 65

Figure 12-6:
Waltz in E
Minor, with
the melody
alternating
between the
bass and
treble.

Playing Pieces That Combine Arpeggios and Melodies

Unlike simple arpeggio-and-melody practice exercises, which generally feature easy left-hand fingerings or consistent right-hand patterns, real-life pieces often contain complications in the form of some not-so-easy fingerings and not-so-consistent patterns. In this section we offer, for your practice and enjoyment, pieces by classical guitar masters that combine arpeggios with melodies — one with the melody in the bass, one with the melody in the treble, and one with a melody that moves between the treble and bass.

Here's some information to help you with the pieces:

✔ **Ländler in D:** A *ländler* is an Austrian folk dance in 3/4 time (or a musical piece to accompany such a dance), and this one was composed by 19th-century Hungarian guitar virtuoso Johann Kaspar Mertz.

Play notes with stems both up and down (generally on beats 1 and 3 in the first section and on each beat in the second) with the thumb, and bring them out as a melody (and remember to hold down all the notes of each measure as a chord whenever possible).

In measures 13 through 20, you play only a single note after each bass note, and so the patterns aren't true arpeggios. That is, an arpeggio is a "broken chord," and a chord, by definition, contains three or more notes. However, in that section, if you think of each beat as a two-note "chord," then you can see that you're still playing in arpeggio style (meaning that the thumb and fingers alternate).

In two-note arpeggio figures (as in measures 13 through 20), your thumb, of course, plays all the bass notes. You play the treble notes, if they change pitch from beat to beat, by alternating between *i* and *m*. But if the pitch of the treble notes remains constant, as in this instance, you usually play the notes with just one finger — either *i* or *m* (depending on which strings your thumb plays and how close they are to the treble string in question). Try measures 13 through 20 first using *i* for all the open E's and then using *m*, and see which fingering you prefer.

✔ **"Romanza":** This is one of the all-time most famous classical guitar pieces; virtually every classical guitarist encounters it and plays it at some time or another. It is known by several titles, including "Romanza," "Romance," "Spanish Romance," and "Romance d'Amour." In most collections that include it, the composer is said to be anonymous, which may lead you to believe that the piece was written hundreds of years ago. Actually, the piece isn't nearly that old, and the identity of the composer isn't so much unknown as it is in *doubt,* or in *dispute;* a number of composers have claimed authorship of this piece.

As indicated, play all the melody notes with the *a* (ring) finger, and bring them out by emphasizing, or accenting, them slightly. Even though *a* may be the weakest finger, it's charged with the important work of carrying the melody here; that's why in Chapter 5 we give you an exercise to strengthen your right-hand ring finger.

What makes this piece relatively easy is the great number of open strings (as is typically the case with pieces in the key of E minor). What makes it difficult (besides the many barre chords) are the left-hand stretches in measures 10, 27, and 28. Isolate those measures and practice them separately, if necessary. And what makes the piece interesting (besides its inherent beauty) is the shift from the minor to the major key in the second section (at measure 17), and then the return to the minor key after measure 32. Note the double-sharp (x) in measure 20, which tells you to play the note two frets higher than the natural version.

✔ **Andante in C:** Just as Carulli did with Waltz in E Minor in Figure 12-6, so too did early 19th-century Italian guitar virtuoso Matteo Carcassi combine the melody and accompaniment notes into a single part. But whereas in the Carulli piece it's obvious which notes are melody and which are accompaniment, this piece has a certain amount of ambiguity. Sometimes, as in the first two full measures, it's easy to discern the melody: It's made up of the notes that occur at beats 1, 2, and 4 (and which you should render in performance as a quarter note, a half note, and a quarter). But in the next measure, is the A on beat 4 melody or accompaniment? And in the measure after, are the final three notes (G, F, and D) melody or accompaniment? Only Carcassi could answer definitively, but because you can't ask him, it's up to you, the performer, to answer such questions by bringing out (or not bringing out) those ambiguous notes accordingly.

If you look at the piece's second section (measures 10 through 17), you see that the upper voice contains a melody (albeit intermingled with accompaniment notes in the same voice) and that the bass part also moves melodically. This really gives you an opportunity to practice your melody/arpeggio chops (or to display them, as the case may be). All at once you have to decide which of the upstemmed notes you consider the real melody notes, to bring out those notes from the notes that function merely as accompaniment, and to also bring out the separate melody that occurs in the bass!

Because Carcassi's notation leaves some unanswered questions, you may wonder why he didn't employ three separate voices in his notation — one for the upper melody, one for the filler (accompaniment) notes, and one for the bass line. He could have, and some pieces are so notated. However, the risk is that the notation is so complicated that it's counterproductive. That's why Carcassi chose to notate the piece as he did. But that doesn't mean a different composer may have notated it as three separate voices.

(continued)

Ländler in D

(continued)

D.C. al Fine

Romanza

(continued)

Andante in C

D.S. al Fine

Chapter 13

Combining Left-Hand Techniques While Playing up the Neck

*I*n this chapter we introduce you to playing pieces as they most often appear in the real world — you know, authentic, grown-up, classical guitar music! When you can successfully apply barres, slurs, and up-the-neck playing to the three main textures of classical guitar — arpeggios, counterpoint, and melody and accompaniment — you're equipped to handle just about any piece that hits your music stand. Previous chapters cover those techniques; this chapter shows you how to put them all together.

The arpeggio technique and the combining of arpeggios and melodies are such important topics that we devote an entire chapter to them (Chapter 12, which includes exercises and pieces in which you not only combine arpeggios and melodies but also play up the neck with barres and slurs). To combine up-the-neck playing and left-hand techniques (barres and slurs) in counterpoint and melody-and-accompaniment styles, read on!

Layering Melodies and Using Barres up the Neck: Counterpoint

Being able to play all over the neck using left-hand techniques widens the range of available contrapuntal material you can play; you're no longer limited to simplistic music in the lower positions. Remember, *counterpoint* is music in which two or more melodies are combined, with the idea being that the melodies are independent of each other yet sound good together. (For more on counterpoint, see Chapter 7.)

Figure 13-1 is a contrapuntal exercise that includes both barres and notes that you play above the 5th fret. Make sure to follow the left-hand fingering very carefully, as the passage is virtually unplayable with any other combination of fingers. (For a refresher on how to play barres, see Chapter 8.)

Note that, as is typical in contrapuntal music, when one *voice* (melody) is rhythmically active, the other is relatively inactive. This type of interplay makes the music both more manageable for the performer and more interesting for the listener.

Track 69

Figure 13-1: Counterpoint up the neck with barre chords.

Figure 13-2, a passage from Baroque composer/guitarist Robert de Visée's Prelude in D Minor, gives you a chance to practice counterpoint up the neck with barres in context before playing a full contrapuntal piece (also by de Visée) later in this chapter.

In this passage, which starts up the neck and gradually moves down, you play a number of two-string barres with the first finger (measures 2 and 3) before playing a five-string barre (measure 4). Note de Visée's colorful use of *chromaticism* (the use of notes out of the key, especially as employed in a passage that moves by half steps, or fret by fret) in measures 2 and 3, as the notes on the 3rd string descend from C (5th fret) to B (4th fret) to B♭ (3rd fret) to A (2nd fret).

Figure 13-2: Prelude in D Minor by de Visée.

To play a complete up-the-neck contrapuntal piece featuring left-hand techniques right now, skip to "Allemande in D Minor" in the section "Playing Pieces up the Neck with Left-Hand Techniques," later in this chapter.

Combining Melody and Accompaniment with Barres and Slurs up the Neck

In this section you have a chance to play in melody-and-accompaniment style using left-hand techniques in the higher positions. Remember, many classical guitar pieces are neither arpeggiated nor contrapuntal; instead, they feature one predominant melody with a (non-arpeggiated) chordal accompaniment. That style has no universally agreed upon official name, but in this book we say that those pieces are in *melody-and-accompaniment* style.

Figure 13-3 is an up-the-neck exercise in melody-and-accompaniment style that features both barres and slurs. (For a refresher on how to play slurs, see Chapter 9.) As with all melody-and-accompaniment pieces, bring out the melody (the top voice); that is, make it "sing" (after all, it *is* the melody!).

The challenges of this exercise are threefold:

- ✔ You hold down barres in every measure, so your left hand gets no chance to rest (fortunately, the passage is short).

- ✔ You must add slurs to the mix (so now you're executing two left-hand techniques at the same time — barres and slurs).

- ✔ You must deal with three separate voices (melody, bass, and chord tones in the middle), each with its own rhythm, requiring you to give just the right amount of emphasis to each part — that is, you need to give the most emphasis to the melody, a moderate amount of emphasis to the bass, and the least emphasis to the chord tones in the middle.

Track 71

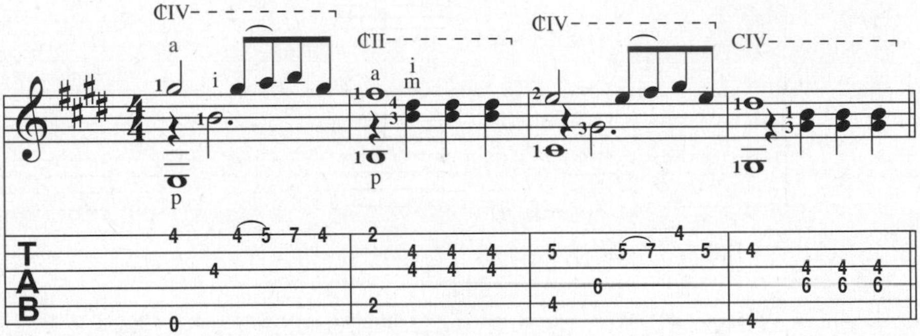

Figure 13-3:
Melody and accompaniment up the neck with barres and slurs.

Figure 13-4, a passage from Waltz in A Minor by American composer/guitarist J. E. Agnew, is an exercise that features melody-and-accompaniment playing — with barres and upper-position notes — in context.

In this waltz, as in the previous exercise, make sure to emphasize the melody and, to a lesser extent, the bass (with the chords in the middle sounding like they're slightly in the background).

This passage allows you to play melody and accompaniment all over the fingerboard — from the 1st fret all the way up to the 12th. Note that although you use barre chords for the A minor chords in measures 7 and 8 and 11 and 12, you play the same A minor chord in measure 2 without a barre (owing to the fingering of the previous and following measures). However, you can try playing measure 2 with a barre (with the third or fourth finger) to see which way you prefer.

Track 72

Figure 13-4:
Waltz in A
Minor by
Agnew.

To play a complete melody-and-accompaniment piece featuring barres and notes in the higher positions right now, skip to "Study in F" in the next section, "Playing Pieces up the Neck with Left-Hand Techniques."

Playing Pieces up the Neck with Left-Hand Techniques

In this section you play two full-length pieces, one each in counterpoint style and melody-and-accompaniment style. Here's some useful information about the pieces to help you along:

✔ **Allemande in D Minor:** An *allemande* is a dance that was popular in Germany in the 16th century — or it's the music that accompanies such a dance. This one, along with Prelude in D Minor, excerpted earlier in the chapter, comes from a Baroque *dance suite* (a set of dance-based compositions in a certain order) by guitarist/composer Robert de Visée (1650–1725), who often performed for French King Louis XIV. (For more on Baroque dance suites, see the sidebar "The Baroque dance suite" in Chapter 15.)

This piece gives you a chance to play in contrapuntal style using notes up the neck, barres, and slurs aplenty (see measures 2, 4, 11, 13, 15, 18, 19, 20, 27, and 28!). Pay careful attention to the string indications in measures 21 and 22, where, owing to fingering requirements, you must play some notes on strings you may not expect.

The piece also contains a few expression and articulation techniques. The *mp* in measure 14 stands for *mezzo piano* and indicates that the volume level changes to moderately soft (from the opening volume level of *mf*, which stands for *mezzo forte* and means moderately loud). The wedge-shaped symbol in measure 18 is a *crescendo* (gradual increase in volume) that returns you to the original volume level *(mf)*. The *rit.* (short for *ritardando*) in measure 28 indicates a gradual slowing down. The dots above and below the notes in measure 16 are *staccato* dots, which indicate that you play the notes in a short and detached manner. (For a full explanation of these and other terms, see Chapter 3.)

Compositionally, this piece contains a couple of interesting devices. For instance, rather than striking many of the bass notes anew at each measure, you sustain them (with ties) over the bar line (as in measures 2–3, 7–8, and 8–9), giving the music a *syncopated* effect — an off-kilter feeling in which it's hard to tell the strong beats from the weak ones. Also note that the bass line in measure 23 is the same as that in measure 22, but down a step. The two measures make up what's known as a *sequence* (or, more specifically, a *melodic sequence*), which is the repetition of a given phrase but from a different starting point.

✔ **Study in F:** This is "Study No. 16" from the well-known *25 Studies* (op. 60) of master Italian guitar composer and educator Matteo Carcassi (for more on Carcassi, see Chapter 14). In one way this piece is somewhat easier than many other melody-and-accompaniment pieces in that it contains no bass line. So instead of having three parts to deal with, you have only two: the melody, which of course you should emphasize, and the double-stop chord tones that fall in between the melody notes. What makes it somewhat difficult, though, is its key, F major, which, owing to the lack of open strings in chords normally used in that key, is less guitar-friendly than many other major keys (namely, E, A, D, G, and C).

Because the piece contains no bass line, use your thumb for the bottom notes of all the double-stops (and your index finger for all the upper notes). For the melody notes (all of which you play on the 1st string), use either *m* or *a,* depending on which string your index finger plays. That is, if your index finger plays the 2nd string (measure 1, for example), use *m* (putting adjacent fingers *m* and *i* on adjacent strings 1 and 2); and if your index finger plays the 3rd string (measure 5, for example), use *a* (putting nonadjacent fingers *a* and *i* on nonadjacent strings 1 and 3).

Like de Visée, Carcassi uses chromaticism — as in measures 16 through 18, where the melody moves down in half steps (fret by fret) from C (8th fret) to B (7th fret) to B♭ (6th fret) to A (5th fret). He also uses a type of *dissonance* (lack of harmony) known as a *suspension*. In a suspension, a note that is a chord tone (a member of the chord being played) is held over (suspended) when the original chord changes to a new chord that doesn't happen to include that suspended tone (thus creating the dissonance). The suspended tone then moves down a step to properly (harmoniously) blend in with the new chord. For example, the melody note F in measure 1 is part of that measure's chord, F major. Then in measure 2, when the chord changes to C7, the F (which is not part of a C7 chord) is suspended (held over) for two beats; it then resolves down to E (which is part of a C7 chord). Carcassi repeats the device in measures 4 and 6, giving the passage a sense of structural unity.

Track 73

Allemande in D Minor

Track 74

Study in F

Moderately slow

Part IV
Mastering Classical Guitar Repertoire

The 5th Wave   By Rich Tennant

ON JULY 9th 1983, ANDRES SEGOVIA
INEXPLICABLY BEGAN DUCK WALKING
THROUGH THE ADAGIO SECTION OF
BACH'S SUITE FOR GUITAR.

In this part . . .

One of the best things about classical guitar is that you get to play the greatest composed music of the ages. In fact, it's required! In Part IV we present pieces we think you'll enjoy playing that are well-known and found in many guitarists' *repertoire* (the body of pieces a musician has mastered and can play from memory). We devote Chapter 14 to what we call the "great guitar composers" — Carcassi, Sor, Giuliani, and Tárrega — because they wrote specifically for the guitar. Chapters 15 and 16 cover the main historical eras in music (Renaissance, Baroque, Classical, Romantic, and Modern), where you sample guitar arrangements of the music of Dowland, Bach, Handel, Mozart, Beethoven, Brahms, and Debussy.

Chapter 14

Playing Pieces by the Guitar Greats

The world's most famous composers — Bach, Mozart, and Beethoven, for example — never wrote for the guitar, though Bach wrote for the lute, which is a very close relative of the guitar. But in the early 1800s, soon after Beethoven achieved renown, a group of guitarist/composers arose, mainly in Spain and Italy (the leading guitar centers of Europe), who wrote music especially for the guitar.

Some of these composers, like Spain's Dionisio Aguado and Italy's Ferdinando Carulli, wrote pieces that were more instructional than musical in nature; that is, a guitarist would more likely play their pieces as exercises to develop technique than to delight listeners with the beauty of their melodies (although some of these exercise pieces are actually quite beautiful). You might say that these composers put the guitar first and the music second.

Other guitarist/composers, however, put the music first, and their pieces have stood the test of time and are played by guitarists the world over. In this chapter we take a look at four such composers — Fernando Sor and Francisco Tárrega of Spain, and Mauro Giuliani and Matteo Carcassi of Italy.

Getting Acquainted with the Master Guitar Composers

Because less music had been written for guitar than for keyboard and orchestral instruments, the guitar for a long time suffered from a lack of regard. Sor, Tárrega, Guiliani, and Carcassi were four guitar composers who strove to elevate the classical guitar to the same status as any popular solo recital instrument. They did this by combining pretty melodies and harmonies with textures and techniques that demonstrated exactly what could be achieved on the instrument — by turning the guitar into (as Beethoven called it) a miniature orchestra. Table 14-1 describes each composer's style and indicates what he's best known for.

Table 14-1	Profiles of the Four Master Guitar Composers	
Composer	*Style*	*Known For*
Fernando Sor (Spain)	Wrote with the harmonic vocabulary of Mozart and Haydn, but with the spontaneity and freedom of expression of Schubert and Beethoven.	*Method for Guitar,* which explains every aspect of classical guitar technique, and his 97 studies covering all aspects of guitar playing and technique.
Francisco Tárrega (Spain)	Wrote melodic and expressive music with a Spanish flavor.	The premier tremolo-style piece, *Recuerdos de la Alhambra,* and expert transcriptions for guitar of pieces written for other instruments by other composers, including Beethoven, Chopin, Mendelssohn, and Albéniz.
Mauro Giuliani (Italy)	Often wrote in a theme-and-variations form, in which a theme is stated simply and then repeated several times with variations. Also tended to write notes on the open G string that rhythmically come in between pinches played on other strings.	Three concertos for guitar and an instructional method that begins with his well-known 120 exercises for the right hand.
Matteo Carcassi (Italy)	Wrote pieces that display the performer's skill and the instrument's versatility but that also feature appealing melodies and harmonies.	Instructional method, which is still used today and is more comprehensive than most, covering the basics of reading music and music theory as well as guitar technique.

Music by the Spanish Composers

Before the classical guitar existed in its present form, Spaniards wrote for instruments that were similar (though typically smaller and with fewer strings), with Baroque composer Gaspar Sanz (1640–1710) perhaps the best known. The group that flourished during the 1800s includes the aforementioned Dionisiso Aguado (1784–1849), Julián Arcas (1832–1882), and José Ferrer (1835–1916). But the two standouts were Fernando Sor (1778–1839) and Francisco Tárrega (1852–1909).

Saying hello to Sor

Sor excelled at all compositional techniques for the guitar, but perhaps none more than the blending of pretty melodies with intricate arpeggios, a technique he used in many of his well-known studies.

Figure 14-1 is an excerpt from Sor's Study in E Minor, which is in arpeggio style with the melody on top. Note the three levels of notation — melody (notes with stems up), bass (long notes with stems down), and middle part (eighth notes with stems down) — and emphasize or accentuate them properly; that is, bring out the melody and make it sing (by striking the notes a little harder or using more nail in the attack), and keep the middle part in the background. (For more on bringing out melodies from within arpeggios, see Chapter 12.)

To play a complete study by Sor right now, skip to "Study in B Minor" in the section "Playing Pieces by All the Master Guitar Composers," later in the chapter.

The back story: Fernando Sor

Fernando Sor first fell in love with music as a boy, when his father introduced him to opera. It was Sor's father, too, who introduced him to the guitar, and by the time the young Sor was 8, he was an accomplished guitarist. But Sor also studied piano, violin, and harmony, and by the time he finished school, he was a well-rounded musician and composer writing not only guitar pieces but also operas, ballets, symphonies, and piano pieces. Sor's technical skill on guitar was unmatched in his day, and he traveled throughout Europe delighting audiences and heads of state with his virtuosity.

Figure 14-1:
Study in E Minor by Sor.

Tackling Tárrega

Tárrega was greatly influenced by the music of his native Spain, and his compositions often have a flamenco or Spanish folk song flavor.

Figure 14-2 is an excerpt from a *mazurka* (a dance in 3/4 time) entitled *Adelita,* which is one of Tárrega's best-known compositions. It's in melody-and-accompaniment style, so be sure to bring out the melody (that is, accentuate the melody by means of rest strokes or greater volume). (For more on melody-and-accompaniment style, see Chapters 7 and 13.)

Each of the first three measures in Figure 14-2 begins with a descending slur, but the fourth measure begins with a quick double slur (ascending and descending). The double slur's notes are written smaller than normal to show that they're *grace notes* (embellishing notes that you play quickly just before the main note and that take virtually no time of their own).

Note also that in measure 4, you play the passage with some unusual string combinations, so follow the string number indications (or tab) carefully. You can play the final E minor chord on open strings, but coming as it does after the last chord of measure 3, its tone sounds more balanced if you play it on the fretted inside strings, as indicated.

Figure 14-2:
Adelita by
Tárrega.

To play a complete piece by Tárrega right now, skip to "Lagrima" in the section "Playing Pieces by All the Master Guitar Composers," later in the chapter.

The back story: Francisco Tárrega

As a boy, Francisco Tárrega was fascinated by his father's guitar and would grab it and experiment with it whenever he could get his hands on it. But one day young Francisco, running from a babysitter, fell into an irrigation canal whose water was impure and contracted an eye infection that impaired his vision. Because his family feared that he may become blind, they enrolled him in guitar and piano courses with the idea that he'd be able to earn a living as a musician, even if blind. In fact, his first two music teachers were blind themselves. When he was only 10, Francisco ran away from home and began his career by playing in small coffee houses and restaurants in Barcelona (in Spain's northeast corner). After he was found and returned to his father, who continued to try to advance the boy's musical education, he ran away again at 13 and joined a band of gypsies! He was returned home again, only to run away once more, this time to Valencia (in the middle of Spain's eastern coast). At the age of 21, Tárrega, having settled down, entered the Madrid Conservatory, where he studied composition and focused on guitar (abandoning his idea of a career as a pianist). After leaving school, he taught guitar and performed as a virtuoso throughout Spain as well as in France, England, and Italy. He was even invited to perform for a queen — Spain's Isabel II.

Music by the Italian Composers

Like Spain, Italy produced composers who wrote for early guitar-like instruments before the modern classical guitar was developed, with Baroque composer Francesco Corbetta (1615–1681) perhaps the best known. Then, starting around 1800, a group of Italian guitarist/composers came to notice for both their technical and compositional abilities. These include the aforementioned Ferdinando Carulli (1770–1841), Francesco Molino (1775–1847), and Giulio Regondi (1822–1878). But the two most famous were Mauro Giuliani (1781–1829) and Matteo Carcassi (1792–1853).

Gelling with Giuliani

Giuliani tended to write in a style that isn't strictly arpeggio, counterpoint, or melody and accompaniment; rather, it's like all three styles blended into one!

Figure 14-3 comes from a *maestoso* (a piece you play in a majestic manner) in theme-and-variations form, and this excerpt is from the first variation, which, as is typical for Giuliani, is in eighth notes. (By the way, note the open Gs between the pinches.) In measure 4, beat 4, you need to flatten your first finger (which is already fretting the 6th string) into a full barre to fret the note on the 2nd string. Such a barre, in which a finger already fretting a string flattens out to cover additional strings, is sometimes informally called a *hinge barre*.

Figure 14-3: Maestoso in C by Giuliani.

To play a complete piece by Giuliani right now, skip to "Andante in C" in the section "Playing Pieces by All the Master Guitar Composers," later in the chapter.

The back story: Mauro Giuliani

As we say in Chapter 1, Beethoven once referred to the classical guitar as a "miniature orchestra in itself." And what, you may wonder, prompted that description? He'd heard a performance by guitar virtuoso and composer Mauro Giuliani. As a boy, Giuliani studied cello, violin, and harmony, but on the instrument for which he is celebrated — the guitar — he was self-taught! When he was 25, he moved from Italy to Vienna, the European capital of classical music. There he hobnobbed with such notables as opera composer Gioachino Rossini *(The Barber of Seville)* and the great Beethoven himself (seven years later, Giuliani even performed as a cellist in the premiere of Beethoven's Symphony No. 7!). As a performer, Giuliani toured most of Europe, and everywhere he went, he astonished people with his virtuosity. As a composer, he preferred to write in a classical style (not unlike that of Mozart and Haydn).

Cozying Up to Carcassi

Like Sor, Carcassi excelled at combining melodies and arpeggios in an interesting, intricate manner. For color, he often employed a stationary bass note under a series of moving chords.

Figure 14-4, an excerpt from Carcassi's Study in E Minor, is in arpeggio style with the melody in the treble, so make sure to bring out the uppermost voice. To keep things interesting and to give the *a* finger a rest every so often, Carcassi alternates melodically active measures (the odd-numbered bars) with melodically static ones (the even-numbered bars). Measure 7 requires you to play a half barre, but you can form the barre a measure sooner if you like, as the notes in measure 6 are all playable with that barre already in place.

Carcassi uses a technique known as *pedal point* (or *pedal*), in which a tone (usually a bass note) is sustained while various chords (especially chords that don't contain that sustained tone) move above it (or against it), causing a *dissonance* (lack of harmony) between the sustained tone and some of the moving chords. Generally, the final chord in the series does contain the note in question so that the dissonance is resolved. The thumb here plays an open low E throughout, while the chords above it move from E minor to a series of diminished chords (that don't contain an E) and back to E minor again.

To play a complete piece by Carcassi right now, skip to "Study in A" in the section "Playing Pieces by All the Master Guitar Composers," later in the chapter.

The back story: Matteo Carcassi

Not much is known about Matteo Carcassi's life, but it is known that as a boy he learned to play the piano before turning to the guitar. When he was 18 he moved to Germany, where he found success as a virtuoso performer. Soon after, he gave a concert tour in Europe, playing in London, Paris, and Florence (his birthplace). But for most of his adult life, Carcassi lived and worked in Paris; in fact, France was his favorite country, and he even served in the French army.

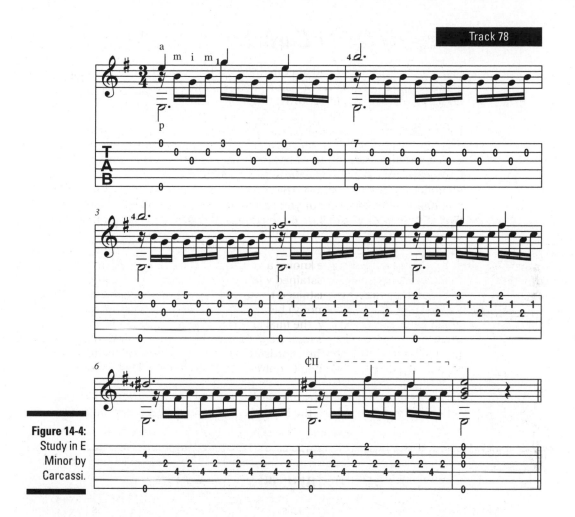

Track 78

Figure 14-4:
Study in E
Minor by
Carcassi.

Playing Pieces by All the Master Guitar Composers

This section gives you an opportunity to play complete pieces by the four master guitar composers we discuss in this chapter. Here's some useful information about the pieces to help you along:

✔ **Study in B Minor (Sor):** The simple and charming Study in B Minor is perhaps Sor's best-known piece, and it's played by guitarists (and guitar students) the world over. It's in arpeggio style, so hold down each chord with the left hand as long as possible and let all the notes ring out. Although the melody is in the treble, you need to bring out (emphasize) certain thumb notes as well, as Sor indicates with half notes (with stems down) on beat 2 of most measures. This double accentuation (finger and thumb on successive beats) gives the piece a sense of rhythmic intensity.

Most of the piece is in 2nd position, but toward the end (measures 41 through 44), you move through 4th position into 5th position, creating a high point, or climax, just when you also play an interesting combination of open and fretted strings (as indicated in the score). We've taken some editorial license and indicated a *crescendo* (a score direction that tells you to get gradually louder) in that passage.

✔ **"Lagrima" (Tárrega):** Tárrega performed in London, but he didn't like the weather or the language there. After a concert one evening, people saw that he looked sad and asked him if perhaps he missed his home and family, and they suggested that he capture his sadness in music. He did so with "Lagrima," which means *tears*. So when you play this piece, make sure to give it an appropriately mournful quality.

"Lagrima" is in melody-and-accompaniment style but with a bit of an arpeggiated feel. It has lots of guide finger indications, so be sure to follow them for ease of performance. (For more on guide fingers, see "Fingering indications for the right and left hands in Chapter 3.)

Compositionally, in measures 1 through 6 and again in measure 13, Tárrega uses a device known as *parallel motion,* in which two voices (in this case the melody and bass) move in the same rhythm at a fixed interval from each other (in this case the interval of a 10th, which is an octave plus a 3rd).

The piece's form is a three-part structure that we can describe as ABA. Here, the first section (A) is in E major, and the second section (B) is in E minor. The piece closes with a return to the first section (A), again in E major. By the way, this is exactly the reverse of the key scheme of "Romanza" (see Chapter 12), whose ABA form takes you from E minor to E major and then back to E minor.

✔ **Andante in C (Giuliani):** As with the Giuliani excerpt you play earlier in this chapter (refer to Figure 14-3), this piece is a mixture of arpeggio, counterpoint, and melody-and-accompaniment styles (Giuliani seems to have had a penchant for that kind of writing!). And like the earlier example, this piece employs another favorite Giuliani device — open Gs placed between pinches (see measures 6 through 9). Compositionally, to give the piece some flavor, Giuliani adds some colorful *chromaticism* (notes outside the key) in measures 9 through 12.

✔ **Study in A (Carcassi):** Like Sor's Study in B Minor, Carcassi's Study in A is extremely popular with guitarists all over the world. It's in arpeggio style with the melody in the treble, so bring out the top voice with rest strokes. Follow the fingering indications carefully, because some passages are unplayable except with the fingering given.

Note how Carcassi imparts structural unity with the shape of his melody. In each measure, beat 2 is a *dissonance* (a non-chord tone) that resolves down a step to a *consonance* (a chord tone) on beat 3. This gives the piece a nice balance of tension and release.

For harmonic interest, Carcassi *modulates* (changes key) within the piece. Though Study in A starts in the key of A, it gradually moves to the key of E by measure 9, then gradually returns to the key of A by measure 17. And to heighten the sense of tension and release produced by the melody, Carcassi uses the pedal point technique in the bass in measures 17 through 20 (as he did in the excerpt in Figure 14-4 you play earlier in the chapter). In that four-bar passage, the repeated A bass note is a chord tone in measure 17, then a non-chord tone in measures 18 and 19 (adding to the tension already created by the melody), then a chord tone again in measure 20 (providing the much-desired release).

Track 79

Study in B Minor

2

(continued)

Lagrima

Track 81

Andante in C

(continued)

Chapter 15

Early Guitar Music from the Renaissance and Baroque Eras

. . . .

In This Chapter

▶ Getting acquainted with the musical styles of the Renaissance and Baroque eras

▶ Looking at some key Renaissance composers

▶ Discovering the major Baroque composers

▶ Practicing pieces from both eras

. . . .

Music historians like to divide the history of music into well-defined periods, or eras. Music from before around 1450 — the *Middle Ages,* or *medieval period* — was mainly sung in church, and today it sounds so primitive that it's hardly ever played on guitar. The next period, from about 1450 to 1600, is known as the *Renaissance* era, and the following period, from around 1600 to 1750, is the *Baroque* era — and the music of those eras does work well on guitar. (Of course, terms like medieval, Renaissance, and Baroque are used to delimit eras not only of music but also of other artistic endeavors, such as painting, sculpture, and architecture.)

In this chapter you take a look at what typifies Renaissance and Baroque music and you play arrangements of pieces by composers of those early times.

An Overview of the Styles

If you want to hear some relaxing music, you couldn't do better than choosing pieces from the Renaissance or Baroque era. That's because music of those eras often has a peaceful, flowing sound that's free of the boldness and drama that sometimes characterizes music of later eras. In the sections that follow we take a look at exactly what makes music of those early periods tick.

The Renaissance

Because the Renaissance directly followed the Middle Ages, composers of the late 1400s and 1500s were influenced by the earlier era's music — namely, vocal music performed in church. To show respect for God, such music contained nothing ugly or jarring. So Renaissance melodies, like the tunes of the earlier period, tend to be rather simple (containing more stepwise motion than wide leaps), and the harmonies tend to be mostly pure and simple (three-note major and minor chords). Of course, Renaissance composers also wrote instrumental and secular (nonreligious) music, and there they pushed the limits of what had gone before.

Renaissance music differs from music of other eras in the scales, instruments, and textures it uses. Our modern ears are used to hearing songs and classical pieces in major and minor keys (keys based on major and minor scales), but in the Renaissance era, the system of major and minor keys had not yet been developed. Instead, music was based on special scales called *modes,* which is why Renaissance pieces sound somewhat strange and exotic to us.

If you play only the white notes of a piano keyboard step by step, from C to C, you get a major scale, and if you play from A to A you get a minor scale. But if you play from any of the other five white keys (for example, from D to D or from F to F), you get a unique-sounding scale — a mode — that's neither major nor minor. During the Renaissance, composers wrote pieces based on those unique scales as well as on major and minor scales. (But to a Renaissance composer, the major and minor scales were nothing special; they were simply two of the seven possible modes.)

Today we're used to hearing music played on instruments like the piano, guitar, and violin, but those weren't fully developed during the Renaissance. Instead, music was played on instruments like the harpsichord, lute (a predecessor of the guitar with a rounded back), recorder, and viol (an early cello-like instrument with frets).

The Baroque era

If you ask a casual music listener what his favorite kind of classical music is, he's likely to answer Baroque. And that's not surprising, because Baroque music — exemplified by such composers as Bach, Handel, Vivaldi, Scarlatti, and Telemann — has quite a bit in common with modern-day popular music. For one thing, Baroque music, like popular music, is based on major and minor keys and the chords (and chord progressions) derived from those keys. For another, Baroque pieces often feature one instrument playing melody (a violin, for example), another playing chords (a harpsichord, for instance), and another playing a bass line (a cello, for example) — not unlike today's pop group with a singer, guitarist, and bassist! Also like today's pop music, Baroque music is known for its regular, steady rhythm.

The Baroque dance suite

You may wonder why many Baroque pieces have unusual names, like Bourrée, Allemande, Courante, and Sarabande. What these words have in common is that they're all names of dances (or names of pieces written to accompany these dances). During the Baroque era, composers liked to write a set of dance pieces (often for a solo instrument) in a particular order. Such a set is called a *suite* (or *partita*). The idea was that the suite would have a certain unity because each piece would be written in the same key (thus, you'd have a set of pieces called, say, Suite in D Minor). But at the same time, the suite would have variety because each dance would have its own distinctive rhythm and feel. Usually a *freestyle* introductory piece (that is, a non-dance piece in any style of the composer's choosing), called a *prelude,* would begin a suite. The list that follows gives the dances, in order, that were typically contained in a Baroque dance suite and briefly describes each dance:

- ✔ **Allemande:** A stately dance of German origin in 4/4 time.

- ✔ **Courante:** A lively dance of French origin in triple time.

- ✔ **Sarabande:** A slow dance of Spanish origin in triple time.

- ✔ **Gigue:** A quick dance of Scandinavian origin in 6/8 time.

In addition to these four dances, a number of optional dances, all of French origin, were often inserted between the Sarabande and Gigue. These include the *minuet* (a slow dance in triple time), the *passepied* (a quick dance in triple time), the *bourrée,* and the *gavotte* (both of which are quick dances in double time).

But Baroque music is different from today's popular music in many ways, too, and not just because it sounds like, well, classical music. Baroque music often employs *imitative counterpoint,* in which a melody played in one voice is repeated a few beats later (usually from a different starting pitch) in another voice. Also, whereas popular music employs simple song structures that are usually made up of two or three short sections that sometimes repeat, Baroque music uses all sorts of complex, extended forms, such as concertos, suites, operas, and cantatas. And whereas today's popular music can be played by amateurs and professionals alike, much Baroque music was written for virtuoso performers who often added their own highly complex ornamentation — quick trills and turns, for example — as they played.

Renaissance Composers

Two types of Renaissance music often played on classical guitar are arrangements of traditional 16th-century melodies and arrangements of pieces originally written for the lute. We explore both of these in the sections that follow.

Traditional 16th-century melodies by anonymous composers

The Renaissance — the time of William Shakespeare, Christopher Columbus, and Leonardo da Vinci — happened so long ago that the authorship of many of that era's musical works is unknown. In such cases, the composer is considered *anonymous* (not known), or the piece in question is *traditional*. Some anonymous melodies from that era are well-known today because musicians throughout the ages have continued to arrange and perform them. Such songs include "Greensleeves" (also known as "What Child Is This?"), "Scarborough Fair," "Coventry Carol," and "The Three Ravens."

"Greensleeves" has been recorded by countless modern artists, from the Chipmunks to Frank Sinatra, from Lawrence Welk to Elvis Presley, from Jeff Beck to Julian Bream. But Figure 15-1 shows how a Renaissance musician — Francis Cutting (c. 1550–1596) — arranged the song for lute (here adapted for guitar). The melody and chords may sound a little different from how you're used to hearing them, but that's understandable when you consider that this arrangement was written more than 400 years ago!

The song sounds like it's in the key of A minor, but the F♯ in measure 6 tells you that the piece is actually based on one of the Renaissance modes (in this case the so-called *Dorian* mode, which sounds minor-ish but whose 6th degree is a half step higher than that of a normal minor scale). Also note the sudden change in harmony to A major (as opposed to A minor) in the final measure. Such sudden shifts between major and minor harmonies are typical in Renaissance music.

Track 83

Figure 15-1: "Greensleeves."

To play a complete piece based on a traditional Renaissance melody right now, skip to "The Three Ravens" in the section "Playing Pieces from the Renaissance and Baroque Eras," later in this chapter.

John Dowland and other great lutenists

During the Renaissance, lute composer/performers flourished in England, France, and Italy, but the English lutenists — including Thomas Campion, Francis Cutting, and Philip Rosseter — are best known today. The most famous of all is Englishman John Dowland (1563–1626), who, in his later years, served as court lutenist for King James I.

Dowland is known for both his solo lute pieces and his *lute songs,* which consist of a vocal part (a poem set to music and sung) and a lute accompaniment. But the accompaniment was generally of such intricacy that the lute part was more or less equal to the vocal part (rather than subordinate to it), and a lute song was really more like a duet (between voice and lute) than a simple melody and accompaniment.

In writing a lute song, a composer tried to reflect in his music the mood or emotion of the poem (lyric) being sung. Because many of the poems Dowland set to music concern grief and sorrow ("Flow My Tears" and "In Darkness Let Me Dwell," for example), he has a reputation for being melancholy. In fact, Figure 15-2, an example of Dowland's writing, is an excerpt from a solo lute piece he titled "Melancholy Galliard"! (A *galliard* is a dance in 3/4 time — or music written for such a dance — popular in Europe in the 1600s.)

As a compositional device, Dowland here employs the *suspension,* in which a consonant tone becomes dissonant when the chord behind it changes (see beat 2 of measures 2, 4, and 8). Also note that Dowland — and Renaissance composers in general — gives an important role to the inner voice (in this case, the one featuring the aforementioned suspensions); in music of most other eras the melody and bass predominate, with the inner voices relegated to second-class status.

Track 84

Figure 15-2: "Melancholy Galliard" by Dowland.

To play a complete Dowland piece right now, skip to "Tarleton's Resurrection" in the section "Playing Pieces from the Renaissance and Baroque Eras," later in this chapter.

A bit about the lute

During the Renaissance, the most popular instrument was the lute. It resembles a modern classical guitar in that it has a body and a neck with frets, strings, and tuning pegs, but it differs from a guitar in a number of ways, as we describe in the list that follows:

✔ The lute has a rounded back rather than a flat one. To get an idea of what a lute's body looks like, think of half a watermelon that's been cut lengthwise.

✔ The lute's neck is shorter than a classical guitar's, and the lute's body typically meets the fretboard at the 9th fret (rather than at the 12th fret, as on a modern guitar).

✔ The neck is also wider because the lute typically has more strings than a guitar. A lute can have more than six strings (seven, eight, or more), and most of the strings — all but the highest one or two — are actually sets of *double* strings (but plucked together as if a single string, as on a modern

12-string guitar). A single high string or a set of double strings — whether tuned in unison, as with the middle strings, or tuned in octaves, as with the low strings — is called a *course*, so you may hear of a six-course lute or an eight-course lute (rather than a six- or eight-*string* lute).

✔ A lute is typically tuned a little differently from a guitar. In a six-course lute (a common configuration), the 3rd course, which corresponds to the open G string on a guitar, is tuned a major 3rd above the 4th course (the guitar's open D string), rather than a perfect 4th above it, as on a guitar. That's why music originally written for lute must be adapted (rearranged or refingered) for the guitar (unless the modern guitarist tunes his 3rd string down a half step to F♯).

✔ The lute's headstock (the part with the tuning pegs) is angled back from the neck perpendicularly rather than being in line with the neck, as on a modern guitar.

Baroque Composers

Two composers who brought Baroque music to its peak are Johann Sebastian Bach (1685–1750) and George Frideric Handel (1685–1759). In the following sections we take a look at classical guitar music based on their compositions.

Back to Bach

Bach's music is known for its almost paradoxical combination of intricate structure and strong passion. In a way, it sounds as though it was put together mathematically, and in another way, it sounds as though it came purely intuitively, or from the heart. One of Bach's most famous pieces, popularly titled "Jesu, Joy of Man's Desiring," comes from one of his many church *cantatas* (pieces for vocal soloists, chorus, and orchestra that form part of a church service). The piece's beauty and elegance has made it a popular wedding processional (even though that wasn't what Bach intended when he wrote it), and it's performed routinely by classical guitarists.

Figure 15-3 is an excerpt from "Jesu, Joy of Man's Desiring," and you can hear that the music is both logical and beautiful at the same time. It's in a style known as *strict counterpoint,* which means that each note of one voice is played against a strictly set number of notes in another voice (in this case, for each bass note there are exactly three treble notes).

Track 85

Figure 15-3: "Jesu, Joy of Man's Desiring," by J. S. Bach.

Although today Bach is the most famous Baroque composer (and among the most famous composers of all time), during his lifetime in his native Germany he was celebrated as a virtuoso organist rather than as a composer because his original works were considered too complex (and it was the simpler pieces of fellow German composer Georg Philipp Telemann that were held in the highest regard). In fact, it wasn't until 79 years after his death — when 20-year-old German composer Felix Mendelssohn produced and conducted a performance of the *St. Matthew Passion* in Berlin — that Bach's music began to receive the acclaim it deserved.

To play a complete piece by Bach right now, skip to "Bourrée in E Minor" in the section "Playing Pieces from the Renaissance and Baroque Eras," later in this chapter.

Getting a handle on Handel

Along with J. S. Bach, G. F. Handel was the giant of the Baroque era. Handel is well-known for two of his orchestral suites, *Water Music* and *Royal Fireworks,* but he's probably best known for his large-scale work for orchestra, chorus, and soloists that's now performed every Christmas — the *Messiah* (even though he originally wrote that oratorio to celebrate Easter!). And the most famous section of the *Messiah* is the one that audiences customarily stand up for, the "Hallelujah Chorus." (Legend has it that at the first performance of the *Messiah,* England's King George II was so roused by the music that he suddenly rose to his feet — and when the king rose, everyone in his presence was required to rise. Since then, audiences have always stood for that section of the performance.)

Figure 15-4 is an excerpt from Handel's "Hallelujah Chorus," arranged for guitar (don't worry; it's not necessary to stand as you play this). The piece starts with some simple major chords played in a strong, distinctive rhythm, but a suspension in measure 4 changes the mood with a bit of tension.

In this excerpt Handel uses a common compositional device known as *modulation,* in which a piece begins in one key but changes to a different key. (For more on keys and key signatures, see Chapters 3 and 6.) In this case the passage begins in E major (measures 1 through 4) but ends in B major (measures 5 through 8).

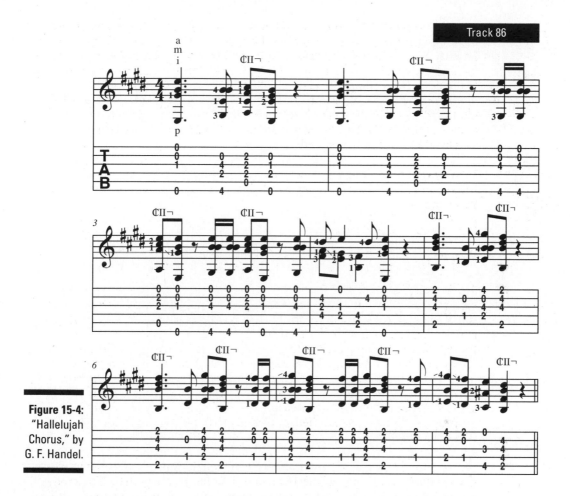

Figure 15-4: "Hallelujah Chorus," by G. F. Handel.

Handel is also known for composing the Christmas carol "Joy to the World." To play a guitar arrangement of the complete song right now, skip to that title in the forthcoming section, "Playing Pieces from the Renaissance and Baroque Eras."

Parallel (and not-so-parallel) lives

Coincidentally, Bach and Handel were born in the same year (1685) in the same country (Germany). Each began to lose his eyesight in his later years, each was treated by the same eye doctor, and each died not long after being treated by that doctor! But Bach and Handel differed in their personal lives. Whereas Bach had 20 children (7 with his first wife, who was his cousin, and 13 with his second), Handel had none (he never married). And whereas Bach lived his life in Germany, Handel lived most of his adult life in England (he became a British citizen in 1727).

Playing Pieces from the Renaissance and Baroque Eras

Even though Renaissance and Baroque composers didn't typically write for guitar, the music of those eras is often arranged for guitar and performed on guitar. In this section you play arrangements of two full Renaissance pieces and two full Baroque pieces. Here's some useful information to help you along:

✔ **"The Three Ravens":** This song first appeared in print in a 1611 collection of anonymous British folk songs compiled by English composer and editor Thomas Ravenscroft. It's still performed today, most notably by legendary folk trio Peter, Paul & Mary.

This arrangement is in melody-and-accompaniment style, so make sure to bring out the top line. The arpeggiated inner voice, which has an eighth-note feel, gives the arrangement some movement. In measure 9, each successive melody note is played on a different string, which allows you to let the melody notes ring out and overlap a bit, creating an interesting effect. The vertical wavy lines in measures 8 and 15 indicate quickly played arpeggios, so "roll" those chords by playing them quickly from bottom to top rather than by plucking all the notes at once.

- **"Tarleton's Resurrection":** This piece, originally for lute, was written by John Dowland in memory of Richard Tarleton, a well-known actor/comedian/clown of Shakespeare's time who had recently passed away.

  The key sounds sort of like A major, but because it's actually modal, it contains a number of tones (and chords) foreign to that key. As a unifying device, the piece employs a rhythmic *motif* (a recurring pattern) consisting of a dotted eighth followed by a 16th followed by an eighth. For color and tension, in measures 10 and 14 Dowland uses suspensions in the inner voice (as in "Melancholy Galliard," earlier in this chapter).

- **Bourrée in E Minor:** This is probably the most-played piece by Bach among classical guitarists (and it's so popular that rock and pop guitarists tend to play it, too!). It comes from Bach's Lute Suite in E Minor. Because Bach was not a lutenist, he didn't indicate fingerings, as real lute composers did; he simply wrote out the notes and left it to the lutenist to figure out how to play it.

  The piece is in a semi-strict contrapuntal style, with quarter notes in the bass played against alternating eighths and quarters in the treble (which produces a very regular, predictable rhythmic pattern). The piece also features a device known as *contrary motion,* in which the treble and bass move away from or toward each other (that is, as one voice moves in an upward direction, the other moves in a downward direction, and vice versa).

  The melody (treble part) illustrates a form of the minor scale known as the *melodic* minor, which contains raised 6th and 7th degrees on the way up (see the C♯ and D♯ on beat 2 of the second full measure) and unraised 6th and 7th degrees on the way down (see D♮ and C♮ on beat 4 of the same measure). The treble part also illustrates *melodic sequence,* in which a particular phrase is repeated but from a different starting note (see measures 10 and 11, 14 and 15, 18 and 19, and 22 and 23).

- **"Joy to the World":** This arrangement of Handel's famous Christmas carol is rather easy to play because all the bass notes are open strings. But to make it pretty — and somewhat challenging — we arrange the melody in double-stops (sometimes on adjacent strings and sometimes on non-adjacent strings). The final note is an appropriately Christmas-like *harmonic* (a high, silvery, bell-like sound). (For more on harmonics, see Chapter 10.)

Track 87

The Three Ravens

Track 88

Tarleton's Resurrection

Track 89

Bourée in E Minor

Track 90

Joy to the World

Chapter 16

The Guitar Comes of Age: The Classical, Romantic, and Modern Eras

*I*n its way, the music of the Baroque era — the period that immediately preceded the Classical era — was rather complex. Bach's counterpoint was sometimes intricate to the extreme, as were many of the instrumental ornaments (trills, turns, and so on) that were written into the music and improvised by the era's virtuoso performers. After the death of Bach (1750), as a reaction against the showy aspect of Baroque (which means "ornate") music, composers began to write pieces that were more formal, sedate, elegant, and graceful. This ushered in music's Classical era (1750–1820).

Toward the end of the Classical era, composers started to feel restrained by that formality and began to use a musical vocabulary that better expressed their innermost feelings, yearnings, and desires. This led to music's Romantic era (1820–1900).

By the end of the 1800s, every aspect of traditional harmony, melody, and rhythm had been explored and employed, and composers began to experiment with new kinds of scales, chords, and rhythms. The result was the Modern era (after 1900), whose music sounds nothing like anything that had gone before it.

Though most of the famous composers of the Classical, Romantic, and Modern eras didn't write for the guitar, some of their works, arranged for guitar by others, have found their way into the classical guitar repertoire.

The Classical Era: Mozart's Muse

Immersing yourself in music of the Classical era is a bit like accompanying your aunt to a formal tea party. Everything is proper and elegant — and perhaps a bit dainty — and everyone is on his or her best behavior. Or, to put it another way, strict rules are followed.

The two most prominent composers of the Classical era were Austrians Franz Joseph Haydn (1732–1809), who wrote more than 100 symphonies and who established the symphony as a musical form, and Wolfgang Amadeus Mozart (1756–1791), with Mozart ultimately becoming the true giant of the era.

What set Mozart apart from many other composers was his ability to write a great melody — a pretty tune. Some composers concentrate on rhythm, harmony, or texture; others create melody by taking short fragments and piecing them together. But nothing lends appeal to a composition as much as a good melody. And Mozart was particularly aware of this. In fact, he once explained, "Melody is the essence of music. A good melody writer is like a fine racehorse, but a counterpoint writer is like a horse that carries the mail."

Because Mozart's melodies are so tuneful, his music can be a delight to play on classical guitar. Figure 16-1 is an arrangement of an excerpt from an *aria* (song) from Mozart's 1787 opera *Don Giovanni.* As you play it (or listen to it on the accompanying CD), you hear that the melody is simple, playful, and quite childlike. Mozart's playfulness is another quality that sets him apart from other Classical-era composers.

Note that Mozart puts the chords on the offbeats rather than on the beats, giving the song a secondary accent (or a kind of backbeat, not unlike that found in today's pop music!). Also note that the piece consists of two four-bar phrases. The three double-stops that connect those phrases (at the end of measure 4) aren't part of the aria's vocal melody, and you should play them very smoothly. In contrast, you should play the two notes that finish the second phrase (also not part of the vocal melody) very short (as indicated by the *staccato* dots).

A secondary accent is similar to, but a little different from, syncopation. A *secondary accent* is a normal, natural part of a meter. For example, in 2/2 time, beat 1 gets the primary accent, and beat 2 gets a secondary accent; that is normal and expected. In *syncopation,* notes are accented in unexpected places — places that conflict with, that go against, a given meter.

Mozart: The incomparable prodigy

Mozart's music is so divine that people get the idea that he didn't have to work at it — that he somehow received it in its complete form directly from heaven. In fact, the great physicist Albert Einstein (who was an accomplished violinist) once declared, "Mozart is the greatest composer of all. His music is of such purity and beauty that one feels he merely found it — that it has always existed as part of the inner beauty of the universe waiting to be revealed."

What most people know about Mozart is that he was a child prodigy who, as a young boy, enchanted the kings and queens of Europe with his harpsichord virtuosity, and that he died very young (at the age of only 35). But he was perhaps the most precocious of all prodigies. Not only did he write two operas at the age of 12, a symphony at the age of 8, and keyboard minuets at the age of 5, but, as legend has it, he revealed his ability to identify any pitch by ear at the age of only 2, when he recognized the squeal of a pig as a G-sharp!

Track 91

Figure 16-1: Aria from *Don Giovanni*, by Mozart.

To play a complete piece by Mozart right now, skip to "Theme from *The Magic Flute*" in the section "Playing Pieces from the Classical, Romantic, and Modern Eras," later in this chapter.

Getting in Touch with Beethoven, the Classical Hopeless Romantic

Starting in the early 1800s, certain composers who'd previously written in a Classical style began to make their music more emotional and colorful. This began a transition from the formality of the Classical era to the passion and intensity of the Romantic era. One such composer was Austrian Franz Schubert, who wrote more than 600 songs for voice and piano and is credited with perfecting the German art song. But by far the most important of these transition-era composers was Ludwig van Beethoven (1770–1827) of Germany.

Beethoven was a pretty emotional guy — so emotional, in fact, that he had to invent a whole new style of music to express his feelings. And for that he's generally credited with initiating music's Romantic era.

At the beginning of his career, Beethoven wrote in a style similar to that of Haydn and Mozart, but by his 30s he was breaking free of his predecessors. He expanded the traditional harmonic, rhythmic, and textural vocabulary by lengthening musical forms (adding extra movements, or sections, to pieces), and by adding more instruments to his orchestral scores (such as brass and percussion).

Figure 16-2 is an arrangement of an excerpt from the second movement of Beethoven's Piano Sonata No. 8 (the *Pathétique Sonata*), written in 1798. Though the first movement is fiery and emotional, the second movement, often played by guitarists, is in a straightforward Classical style.

Beethoven's roots

As a boy, Beethoven, like Mozart, was a prodigy. Legend has it that young Ludwig's father, thinking he could turn his son's talent to profit (by exhibiting the boy's virtuosity throughout Europe, as Mozart's father had done with young Wolfgang), often dragged Ludwig out of bed at night and forced him to practice for hours on end.

In his 20s Beethoven started to experience serious health problems (probably as a result of accidental lead poisoning) and began to lose his hearing. Over time, his health grew increasingly worse and he lost his hearing completely (but he was still able to compose because he could hear tones in his head).

In his 40s Beethoven became the guardian of his nephew Karl after the boy's father (Beethoven's brother) died. But Karl gave Beethoven nothing but worries. After a number of years, uncle and nephew were so unhappy with each other that Karl (unsuccessfully) attempted suicide by shooting himself in the head.

It's understandable, then, that Beethoven, with all these problems and worries, would need to express himself musically without the restraints and niceties of Classicism.

The piece features a pretty melody supported by arpeggios, so make sure to bring out the top line and to allow the notes of the arpeggios to ring out as long as possible.

Note that although the harmony consists of simple major, minor, and seventh chords, notes other than the chords' roots often serve as the bass notes. For example, in measure 2, the first chord, C major, has an E (rather than a C) in the bass, and the second chord, G7, has a B (rather than a G) in the bass. A chord that has a tone other than the root (namely, the 3rd, 5th, or 7th) as the bass note is said to be in *inversion.* Composers use inversions to add harmonic interest to their compositions — as Beethoven does here.

Figure 16-2:
*Pathétique
Sonata,* by
Beethoven.

To play a complete piece by Beethoven right now, skip to "Für Elise" in the section "Playing Pieces from the Classical, Romantic, and Modern Eras," later in this chapter.

Letting the Inside Out with the Romantics: Brahms

As the 1800s proceeded, composers of concert music strayed farther and farther from the formal, controlled style of the Classical era. Partly, they were influenced by the new musical style of Beethoven. But they were also influenced by music that was being composed for the opera, where stories of myth and legend required bold new sounds. And they were influenced, too, by traditional tunes from their native countries (as were, for example, Hungarian Franz Liszt and Polish-born Frederic Chopin). And, like Beethoven, Romantic-era composers felt a need to express their inner feelings.

Many composers of the Romantic era are well-known today — including the aforementioned Schubert, Liszt, and Chopin, as well as Germany's Felix Mendelssohn, Robert Schumann, and Richard Wagner; France's Hector Berlioz; and Russia's Peter Ilich Tchaikovsky. But perhaps the most famous of all is Germany's Johannes Brahms (1833–1897).

Though Brahms used the complex musical vocabulary of the Romantic era, he differed from many of his contemporaries in that he wrote *absolute* music (music that exists for its own sake, as pure music) rather than *program* music (music that's meant to tell a story, evoke a mood, depict a scene, and so on).

Next to Brahms' famous "Lullaby," his rhythmically intense "Hungarian Dance No. 5" (composed in 1868 for piano duet as part of a set of 21 Hungarian dances) is probably his best-known work. Though you may not know it by name, you're sure to recognize it when you hear it, as it has been used in countless movies and cartoons.

Figure 16-3 is an arrangement of an excerpt from "Hungarian Dance No. 5." The colorful dissonance (lack of harmony) in measure 3 (a G♯ melody note against a D minor chord) is a Romantic-era harmonic touch; in earlier eras, such a dissonance would have been immediately resolved to a consonance (that is, the unharmonious tone would have been moved up or down to a tone that did blend with the background chord).

A bit of back story on Brahms

Like Mozart and Beethoven before him, Brahms was a child prodigy at the piano, performing at the age of 10. But unlike his predecessors, Brahms decided (at the early age of 16) that he wanted to give up performing to focus all his attention on composing. And that's what he did.

Brahms was known for being a perfectionist in his work. In fact, his first symphony, which

he intended to be the next great symphony after Beethoven's monumental nine symphonies, took him 22 years to complete! But in his personal habits he was anything but a perfectionist. Legend has it that he devoted so much time to composing that he sometimes forgot to attach his suspenders. Then, while conducting, he'd have to use one hand to conduct and the other to hold up his pants!

Track 93

Figure 16-3: "Hungarian Dance No. 5," by Brahms.

To play a complete piece by Brahms right now, skip to "Lullaby" in the section "Playing Pieces from the Classical, Romantic, and Modern Eras," later in this chapter.

Dreaming with Debussy: Music Becomes Modern

Music at the end of the 1800s was very different from, and more complex than, music at the beginning of the century — harmonically, rhythmically, and texturally. Beginning around 1900, some composers who were influenced by innovative ideas in poetry and painting — specifically, so-called *symbolist* ideas, in which reality is rejected and symbols (indirect suggestions) are used to express ideas — threw out the old rules of music and began expressing themselves using a whole new musical language. At first listeners were shocked by what they heard, but eventually, they began to find some of the work quite expressive and beautiful.

The most famous of the aforementioned symbolist-influenced composers, Claude Debussy (1862–1918), developed a new musical language at the end of the Romantic era to express his feelings and ideas. His style of music, like the style of such painters as Claude Monet and Pierre Auguste Renoir, is known as *impressionism.* Impressionistic works, whether of painting or music, are meant to evoke indistinct sensory impressions rather than to convey realism. Or, as Debussy himself explained it: "Every sound perceived by the acute ear in the rhythm of the world about us can be represented musically. Some people wish above all to conform to the rules; I wish only to render what I can hear."

Debussy liked to stir his listeners' imaginations by painting a mood or suggesting beautiful images of nature. He did this by employing unusual scales (the whole tone scale, for example, in which all tones are separated by a whole step), unusual chords (extended chords of the 9th, 11th, and 13th, for example), parallel intervals (such as parallel 4ths or 5ths, which earlier composers eschewed), nebulous rhythms (in which it's sometimes not clear what the basic pulse is or how it's subdivided), and ambiguous tonalities (where you can't tell what key, if any, a piece is in).

Although he was a contemporary of other late-Romantic/early-Modern composers such as Maurice Ravel (with whom he is often compared), Debussy's music was truly revolutionary in that it sounded nothing like anything heard before. It was his rejection of the traditional approach to harmony, his complete departure from the aesthetic of his forebears, and his forward-looking approach that challenged the very idea of tonality itself that paved the way for 20th-century composers such as Béla Bartók and Igor Stravinsky and the Modern era of classical music.

Because of their often complex harmonies, many of Debussy's compositions are difficult to play on guitar; however, a few, notably his most famous work, "Clair de lune," have found their way into the classical guitar repertoire. Figures 16-4 and 16-5 show short passages from two other Debussy works (originally for piano) that guitarists sometimes play.

Debussy the young deviant

Like Mozart, Beethoven, and Brahms, Debussy was a piano prodigy, and he was admitted to music college, the famed Paris Conservatory, at the age of 11. But his teachers there were appalled by young Claude's disregard of the rules of traditional composition (such as that music should sound like it's in a certain key and meter, and that dissonances should be resolved). One irate teacher threatened that any student found in possession of one of Debussy's manuscripts would be kicked out of school — and one student was actually expelled for carrying one of the forbidden scores to class!

In the first passage, from "The Little Shepherd" (a section of 1908's *Children's Corner Suite*), note how dissonant chords exist in their own right, with no need for resolution, and note the lack of a tonal center. (See Figure 16-4.)

Track 94

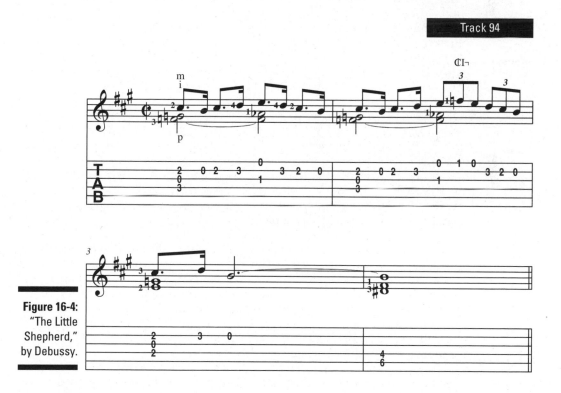

Figure 16-4: "The Little Shepherd," by Debussy.

The second passage is from Debussy's 1910 prelude "The Girl with the Flaxen Hair." (See Figure 16-5.) Note how in the first two measures he uses the interval of a *tritone* (an interval three whole steps in distance, as C to F♯ or D to G♯) to obscure the key center but how in the last three measures he changes the mood by firmly establishing the key of D (the original piano version is in G♭).

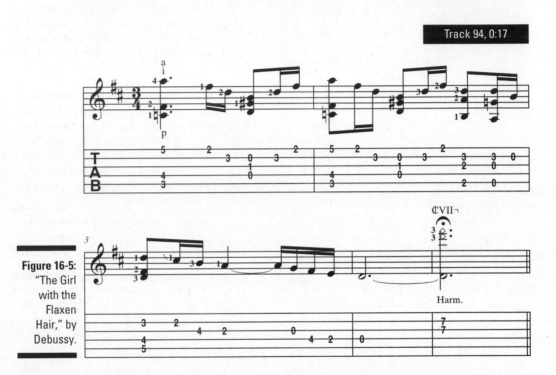

Track 94, 0:17

Figure 16-5: "The Girl with the Flaxen Hair," by Debussy.

To play a complete piece by Debussy right now, skip to "Clair de lune" in the forthcoming section, "Playing Pieces from the Classical, Romantic, and Modern Eras."

Playing Pieces from the Classical, Romantic, and Modern Eras

When not playing pieces originally written for their instrument, classical guitarists tend to play music from the Baroque era more than any other. But many lovely pieces from subsequent eras are in the guitar repertoire, and here we present four of the best known. Following is some useful information about the pieces to help you along:

✔ **Theme from** *The Magic Flute:* One of Mozart's best-known works is his 1791 opera *The Magic Flute.* The simple, childlike melody of one of its arias, "Das klinget so herrlich" (which roughly translated from the German means, "That sounds so glorious"), was used as the basis of Fernando Sor's guitar composition "Variations on a Theme by Mozart." But we find Mozart's orchestral introduction and accompaniment to this aria — which contain playful tunes of their own — much more interesting melodically, and that's what we've arranged here.

We've said that Mozart's music is often simple and childlike. Here, the chord progression is so basic that it's virtually identical (in the first eight measures) to that of the children's folk song "Jimmy Crack Corn"!

What makes this piece different from most other classical guitar pieces is that the melody consists of arpeggio figures; ordinarily, it's the accompaniment of a piece that's arpeggiated. In the second half of the piece, to build excitement, Mozart increases the melody's rhythmic activity (using eighth notes instead of quarters). The chord "punches" (on beats 1 and 4 of most measures) also add to the excitement.

✔ **"Für Elise":** Along with his *Moonlight Sonata,* Beethoven's most famous and popular piece for piano is his 1810 Bagatelle in A Minor, popularly titled "Für Elise" (a *bagatelle* is a short, light piece for piano). But Beethoven never knew how popular the piece would become because it wasn't published until 38 years after his death!

In most measures, the first three notes are written with stems down and the last three with stems up in order to separate the melody (stems up) from the accompaniment (rather than to show which notes to play with the thumb and which to play with the fingers). (For right-hand fingering, use whatever feels comfortable to you in this piece.) In the original piano version, the accompaniment notes and melody notes are played as six consecutively ascending tones (three notes with each hand), with no change of direction.

Because the limitations of the guitar require a direction change here, be extra careful to separate the melody notes from the accompaniment notes by bringing them out (and by keeping the accompaniment notes a bit in the background).

Beethoven provides some nice contrast in the second section of the piece (starting at measure 10) by changing the key from A minor to its relative major (C major) and by changing the contour of the melody from mainly arpeggiated to mainly stepwise.

✔ **"Lullaby":** Brahms' most famous piece is his "Lullaby" (also known as "Brahms' Lullaby" or "Cradle Song," or by its German name, "Wiegenlied"), written in 1868 to celebrate the birth of his friend's son.

Because this song is usually played for children, it's generally arranged in a simple format, as we've done here. The original version, for piano and voice, however, is rhythmically and harmonically more complex. To make it extra sweet on guitar (in case you want to play this for a child or baby), we've arranged the melody mostly in pretty-sounding 3rds.

✔ **"Clair de lune":** Debussy's most famous piece is "Clair de lune," from his 1903 *Suite bergamasque* for piano. Like Brahms' "Hungarian Rhapsody No. 5," even if you don't know this piece by name, you'll recognize it when you hear it, as it has been featured in many motion pictures.

The piece features some metrical ambiguity in spite of the 3/4 time signature. Most of the beats are divided into three parts, but some are divided into two. And sometimes a division into three parts occurs not over a single beat but over half a measure (see measures 19, 21, and 23, for example).

In the first few bars, Debussy harmonizes the melody mostly in 3rds to make the piece pretty (after all, the title means "moonlight," which is one of nature's beauties). Unlike some of his pieces, which are tonally ambiguous, Debussy plants this one firmly in a major key (D♭ in the original piano version, but here arranged in D to take advantage of the guitar's open strings).

The wavy lines in the last few measures indicate that the chords are to be arpeggiated; that is, you should roll the strings quickly from bottom to top (rather than plucking them all at once).

Theme from The Magic Flute

(continued)

Track 96

Für Elise

Track 97

Lullaby

Track 98

Clair de lune

Moderately slow, expressively

(continued)

Part V
The Part of Tens

The 5th Wave   By Rich Tennant

"Why can't you play guitar like everyone else?"

In this part . . .

The Part of Tens is the section of the book where we act like late-night TV talk-show hosts and give you a condensed view of the classical guitar world in easy-to-digest top-ten lists. Chapter 17 is our pick of ten important guitarists who not only play wonderfully but also have been key personalities in shaping the classical guitar world as it exists today. If you're in the market for a new instrument, you don't want to go into a music store (or online) without first going over our list in Chapter 18 of ten important things to consider when shopping for a classical guitar.

Chapter 17

Ten (Or So) Classical Guitarists You Should Know

In This Chapter

▶ Discovering some of the classical guitar masters

▶ Listening to some of the essential classical guitar albums

Check out the following list of classical guitarists (presented chronologically by birth year) who are important and influential, and whose music will inspire you to practice and bring pleasure to your ears!

Andrés Segovia (1893–1987)

No discussion of the progression of classical guitar would be complete — or even possible — without acknowledging one of its greatest practitioners and champions: Andrés Segovia. Many people consider Segovia to be the greatest classical guitarist who ever lived. Segovia changed the landscape of the classical guitar on multiple fronts. As a performer, his virtuosity remains unparalleled, and you can still discover new things from his audio recordings and live performance films.

But he was also successful in many other areas that helped get the classical guitar out of the parlor and salon and onto the world concert stage. As a tireless booster for classical guitar, he brought his art to concert audiences all around the world — a world that had never seen a guitar in a concert hall. He established the Segovia method, which includes the adoption of such techniques as using the fingernails of the right hand in combination with the flesh (breaking ranks with other famous guitarists on the matter), refining the established practices of keeping the right hand at a perpendicular angle to the strings, employing the rest stroke (see Chapter 2 for a definition of the rest stroke), and much more.

Segovia also had several pieces commissioned for him by famous composers — not because the composers were necessarily enthusiastic about the guitar, but because they were so taken with Segovia himself and his prodigious talents! Several of his transcriptions are part of the standard repertoire, including the works of J. S. Bach. Many of Segovia's students became world famous, including Julian Bream, John Williams, Christopher Parkening, and Sharon Isbin (all of whom you can read about in this chapter). That the classical guitar is recognized today as a serious pursuit and a legitimate academic discipline is a recent phenomenon (Juilliard didn't institute its classical guitar performance program until 1989). And it's Segovia — who, amazingly, was self-taught — who's most responsible for bringing serious study of the classical guitar into the mainstream. **Essential listening:** *The Best of Andrés Segovia: The Millennium Collection* (Deutsche Grammophon, 2004).

Julian Bream (b. 1933)

Englishman Julian Bream was something of a child prodigy, starting out playing cello and piano before switching to guitar and making his national debut at age 13. Though he knew Segovia, Bream doesn't profess to have studied with him formally. A passionate and expressive player, Bream always imbues his playing with a wide range of tonal colors. He's also an accomplished lutenist, which gives him particular insight into the fretted-string music of the Renaissance. Bream has had many pieces written for him by such composers as Richard Rodney Bennett, Leo Brouwer, Hans Werner Henze, Michael Tippett, and William Walton. Probably Bream's most famous commission is Benjamin Britten's *Nocturnal,* which is part of the standard repertoire for classical guitarists. He has won four Grammy Awards. **Essential listening:** *Baroque Guitar* (works of Bach, Sanz, Weiss, and others) (RCA, 1966).

Oscar Ghiglia (b. 1938)

Italian guitarist Oscar Ghiglia is the son of artistic parents (his mother was a painter and his father a pianist). He won several important international competitions immediately following his graduation from Rome's Santa Cecilia Conservatory. While still a conservatory student in Siena, he got to attend a Segovia master class. So impressed with the young Ghiglia was Segovia that the Spanish maestro invited him to be his assistant for the master classes at the University of California at Berkeley in 1964, when Ghiglia was only 25. Ghiglia is not only one of the world's top performers but also is known for being a generous and influential teacher, a visiting professor at numerous universities and conservatories, and the founder of the guitar department at the Aspen Music Festival. **Essential listening:** *The Spanish Guitar of Oscar Ghiglia* (Angel, 1973).

John Williams (b. 1941)

Australian-born John Williams (not to be confused with the American film composer of the same name) moved to England as a teenager and quickly established himself as the best classical guitarist to come along since Julian Bream (whom he ended up collaborating with extensively). Where Bream was known for his expressiveness, Williams distinguished himself with his phenomenal technique and precision, which bordered on perfection. In later years, Williams expanded into many musical directions, including jazz, rock, and experimental. He's often held up with Bream as being one of the two titans of classical guitar immediately under Segovia. **Essential listening:** *John Williams Plays Bach and Scarlatti* (Decca, 1977).

Pepe Romero and Angel Romero (b. 1944, 1946)

The Romero family of Spain, or "Los Romeros," is considered to be classical guitar's first family. Originally a quartet of six-stringers made up of father Celedonio (1918–1980) and sons Pepe, Angel, and Celin, the Romeros dazzled audiences all over the world with their fiery arrangements of classical and Spanish pieces and established new precedents for guitar ensemble playing. Pepe and Angel, the two most famous Romero brothers, are soloists in their own right, each having separate careers and having played with major orchestras throughout the world. For the authentic Spanish sound and heart, nothing beats the playing of the Romero brothers. **Essential Pepe listening:** *Guitar Solos* (Philips, 1993). **Essential Angel listening:** *A Touch of Romance* (Telarc, 1989).

Christopher Parkening (b. 1947)

American guitarist Christopher Parkening was born in Los Angeles and first heard Segovia records when he was 11. He enrolled at the University of Southern California's Thornton School of Music, and by age 19 he was already winning international contests and gaining recognition as a world-class talent. Segovia himself proclaimed Parkening "a great artist" and "one of the most brilliant guitarists in the world." In the early 1970s, just after he released his landmark *Parkening Plays Bach,* he pretty much stood alone as the heir to the Segovia mantle, after Bream and Williams. A triple threat of flawless technique, gorgeous tone, and rock-solid musicianship, Parkening did more to inspire classical guitarists of the time than perhaps any other performer. **Essential listening:** *Parkening Plays Bach* (Angel, 1969).

David Starobin (b. 1951)

Born in New York City, where he's still based, David Starobin studied guitar with famed instructor and author Aaron Shearer at the Peabody Conservatory in Baltimore. Starobin has always been a champion of new music and has many of the 20th century's best composers writing pieces for him, including Milton Babbitt, Elliott Carter, George Crumb, Mario Davidovsky, Poul Ruders, and Gunther Schuller. In 1981, he founded Bridge Records, where he produced recordings that have garnered 17 Grammy nominations and 3 Grammy Awards. He has performed with the New York Philharmonic and the National Symphony, and he's on the faculty of the Manhattan School of Music. **Essential listening:** *New Music with Guitar, Vols. 1-3* (Bridge, 1993).

Manuel Barrueco (b. 1952)

Manuel Barrueco was born in Cuba and received conservatory training there before immigrating to the U.S. when he was still a teenager. He completed his studies at the Peabody Conservatory, where he now teaches. Barrueco made his Carnegie Hall debut at age 22 and has gone on to play the world's major concert venues, both as a solo artist and with major orchestras, including the Los Angeles Philharmonic, Boston Symphony, and Philadelphia Orchestra. Equally at home in traditional and modern music, Barrueco made what is perhaps the definitive recording of the best-known concerto for guitar and orchestra — *The Concierto de Aranjuez,* by Joaquin Rodrígo — and he was the choice to premiere Toru Takemitsu's *To the Edge of a Dream.* Barrueco has also collaborated with such top-flight jazz and rock guitarists as Al Di Meola, Steve Morse, and Andy Summers. **Essential listening:** *¡Cuba!* (EMI Classics, 1999).

Eliot Fisk (b. 1954)

Born in Philadelphia, Eliot Fisk studied with Oscar Ghiglia, Alirio Diaz, and Segovia. He attended Yale, later founding its guitar department, and he now teaches at the Salzburg Mozarteum in Austria as well as at the New England Conservatory of Music in Boston. Though other artists have near-flawless technique (such as Williams), Fisk brought the concept of classical guitar virtuosity to new levels with his landmark recordings and live performances of Scarlatti and Paganini. Fisk has also tirelessly supported new music, both classical and popular, in collaborations with such performers as flamenco master Paco Peña and jazz guitar legend Joe Pass, as well as with composers Leonardo Balada, Robert Beaser, Luciano Berio, Wiliam Bolcom, Nicholas Maw, Xavier Montsalvatge, George Rochberg, and Kurt Schwertsik. **Essential listening:** *Paganini — 24 Caprices* (Music Masters Classics, 1993).

Benjamin Verdery (b. 1955)

A prolific composer as well as a guitarist, Ben Verdery grew up in Connecticut and came to classical guitar at the relatively late age of 18, having played rock and listened to jazz in his youth. He studied with Phillip de Fremery and Leo Brouwer and cites Jimi Hendrix and Julian Bream as major musical influences. Verdery made his New York debut in 1980, and since 1985 he has been the head of the guitar department at Yale University. He has made a significant effort to bring the classical guitar to new and different settings, having collaborated with such diverse artists as Leo Kottke, Anthony Newman, Paco Peña, Andy Summers, and John Williams. Verdery's compositions have been performed and recorded by Williams, the Los Angeles Guitar Quartet, and guitarists and orchestras all over the world. **Essential listening:** *Branches* (Mushkatweek, 2006).

Sharon Isbin (b. 1956)

Minneapolis-born Sharon Isbin began studying classical guitar at age 9 and went on to study with Oscar Ghiglia and Segovia. She received both her bachelor's and master of music degrees from Yale University and later founded the classical guitar department at the Juilliard School in New York. Isbin has either commissioned or had written for her more works by notable composers than perhaps any other guitarist. Composers she has collaborated with include Leo Brouwer, John Corigliano, David Diamond, Lukas Foss, Aaron Jay Kernis, Ned Rorem, Joseph Schwantner, and Joan Tower. In 2001 she won a Grammy Award for her recording *Dreams of a World: Folk-Inspired Music for Guitar*, the first Grammy in 28 years to be awarded to a classical guitarist. **Essential listening:** *Greatest Hits* (EMI Classics, 2002).

Chapter 18

Ten Things to Do When Shopping for a Classical Guitar

In This Chapter

▶ Shopping strategies

▶ Evaluating guitars for quality, playability, and sound

Shopping for a guitar is fun and exciting, because it gives you an excuse to sample all the great instruments in the store and then pick the one that's perfect for you. But striding through the door of a music store without having done any research can quickly take the wind out of your sails as you come face to face with a bewildering number of instruments to choose from. And having energetic salespeople firing a bunch of questions at you doesn't make things any easier — especially if you're not sure of the answers! So in this chapter, we try to help you sort out the most important considerations when buying a classical guitar. By simply heeding the following ten bits of advice, you can take much of the uncertainty out of the shopping experience, spend your time efficiently, and really have fun with it!

Go Retail if You Aren't 100 Percent Sure What You Want

Buying online often gets you a competitive price, with the assurance that you can return the instrument for a full refund or exchange. So if you know the exact make and model you want, purchasing online is a great way to go.

But the disadvantage is that you don't get to try out a bunch of instruments right there on the spot, the way you can in a well-stocked store. And if you think you may need ongoing, after-purchase support, buying from your local brick-and-mortar retailer has the edge in providing a more personal touch.

The technical staff can provide helpful advice and service, and even perform small tweaks on your instrument when necessary — often at no additional charge. A good music store is concerned with keeping you as a long-term customer, and most will be glad to help you.

Bring a Friend Along

It's always good to have someone accompany you when you're making an important purchase, and for a guitar it helps to have another guitarist along — preferably one who has more experience than you. Your guitar-shopping buddy will not only have your best interests in mind (rather than the store's), but he can also help keep you focused, ask questions of you and the salesperson, offer opinions, and play the guitar while you stand back and listen. Just be sure to treat him to lunch afterward!

Decide on a Price Range Before You Go

Your budget determines which guitars are eligible for consideration and which are out of reach (at least for now). It's no use trying out a $5,000 guitar if your budget only goes up to $500. (Okay, it may be fun to try that five-grand guitar just *once*.) If you figure out what you can afford before you even leave the house (or go online), you can stay focused on your spending limit when you're at the music store getting swept away by all the choices. In general, the more you pay, the better guitar your money buys you. A decent beginning guitar costs between $200 and $250. A better guitar, of medium quality, with a solid top (see the next section, "Know Your Materials"), starts at about $300. Be sure to ask if the price includes the case (some guitars come with cases; some don't). If it doesn't, you might negotiate for a discount — getting the combined package for less than the total price of the two items separately. And as with any purchase, make sure you know the store's policy on returning the instrument (exchange, refund, restocking fee, and so on).

Know Your Materials

A guitar is made mostly of wood, and the types of woods used offer a clue to its quality and price. The guitar's top is usually made of spruce or cedar, either as an all-solid piece or a veneer (a thin, decorative piece on the outside, with several glued-together layers of inexpensive wood underneath).

The guitar's back and sides can be rosewood, mahogany, cypress, sycamore, ovangkol, bubinga, or nato, with rosewood being the preferred (and pricier) choice. The fingerboard is almost always either ebony or rosewood, with ebony being the favorite, as it's harder and smoother-feeling to the fingers. Naturally, it's more expensive.

Solid-top guitars are more expensive than veneer-top guitars, but they have better tone and improve with age. Veneer tops hold up but don't improve over time. The standard configuration of a high-quality classical guitar is a solid-spruce-top guitar (or cedar) with rosewood back and sides and an ebony fingerboard. Prices start around $500 for a new instrument (slightly less for a used instrument in very good to excellent condition).

Evaluate the Construction and Workmanship

Manufacturing standards, even for inexpensive guitars made in Asia, are quite good overall these days, so it's rare to see any really inferior products that make it all the way to the store showrooms. Still, you should eyeball a potential purchase carefully, and go through the following steps:

- ✔ Check the top, back, and sides for cracks, dull spots, or blemishes in the finish (the protective gloss applied to the wood) or to the wood itself. Check the joint where the neck heel meets the body to see that it has no gaps or glue spots.

- ✔ Peer inside the guitar (through the sound hole) to check the *bracing* (the wooden sticks glued to the back and underside of the top), *kerfing* (the slotted, wooden edging material that helps bind the sides to the back), and other joints. Look for glue gobs and rough spots that haven't been sanded properly.

- ✔ Look at all the frets to make sure they're embedded in their slots all the way and that the ends are smooth to the touch (indicating care has been taken to file them down correctly).

- ✔ Wind the tuning machines. They should operate smoothly, with no feeling of looseness or slippage. You should see no visual signs of wear, corrosion, or other damage.

- ✔ Play every note on the guitar — the six open strings and all 12 frets on each string — listening to the sound as you play. Check that you hear no fret buzz or rattling from within the guitar (indicating loose hardware or a loosened brace or glue joint that failed).

Get a Feel for the Guitar

The thickness of the neck, tension of the strings, and *action* (distance of the strings to the fretboard) all affect a guitar's feel, or *playability*. Often, the best way to make judgments about playability is to compare two or more guitars and see which one plays the easiest. Then go about examining the action, neck thickness, and so on to see what contributes to the differences among the various models. Check that the action is low enough that you can play barre chords comfortably but not so low that the strings buzz against the frets. Action is somewhat a matter of taste: High action is harder to play but creates a good sound, whereas low action is easy to play but can sometimes buzz when the strings are played hard.

If you suspect a guitar is more difficult to play than it should be, ask a friend or the salesperson to make sure the action isn't too high. If it is, the guitar may be perfectly playable after an adjustment, and the store is usually happy to make this adjustment for free if you buy the guitar.

If you're of small stature (say, 5 feet tall or under), have small hands, or are shopping for a guitar for a child, you may want to consider a *short-scale* guitar. These are slightly easier to play because the string tension is lower and the frets are a little closer together (meaning you don't have to stretch your left-hand fingers as far to fret the notes). Short-scale guitars are a good choice for children under 10 and for any player having a hard time fretting normal-sized guitars. But they're sometimes hard to find, so be sure to inquire with the sales staff to see if the store carries a variety of short-scale models.

Check the Intonation

Intonation is how well a string plays in tune when fretted. A neck that's built correctly (and hasn't warped since it left the factory) allows a string to fret perfectly in tune. Intonation has nothing to do with the tuners holding the strings at pitch (though that's important, too, and reflects the quality of the tuners) or whether the strings are in tune with one another (that's your job!) — it has to do with whether the frets produce the right pitches. To test a guitar's intonation, play a 12th-fret harmonic on each string and listen to how closely it matches the fretted version of that note. It should be perfectly in tune. If it's not, several things may be wrong, some of which are fixable (such as having old strings, which can be replaced) but none of which you should inherit when buying the guitar. (For more on playing harmonics, see Chapter 10.)

Listen to the Sound

The normal way to listen to a guitar is to play it and see if you like the sound. But you can also have someone else play it to hear how the guitar really sounds to listeners or an audience (see "Bring a Friend Along," earlier in this chapter).

The process of evaluating tone is subjective and requires a lot of experience, but you can often easily tell the differences between a $4,000 guitar and a $150 model just by playing and listening, even if you can't describe the differences in words. So try both high-quality and lower-quality instruments as a way to train your ears in the ways of tone. In general, better guitars project more than lesser guitars — meaning they sound louder. High-quality guitars also have a warmer, richer tone with sweet, full treble notes and punchy bass tones.

After trying guitars in different price ranges, try to play several guitars in the same price range and make observations about their different tonal qualities. Then have a friend or salesperson play to see if the results are consistent. And be sure to realize that a guitar's sound is distinct from its playability and should be evaluated independently. Some of the best sounding guitars aren't necessarily the easiest ones to play.

Judge the Aesthetics

You certainly don't find the range of wild colors and bold designs among classical guitars that you do with electric guitars, but you're still allowed to decide what you like (and don't like) in a guitar's appearance. You may like the look of the darker, reddish color of cedar versus the lighter, yellow color of spruce. A more ornate design in the rosette (the decorative ring around the sound hole) drives the cost up and doesn't improve the tone or play-ability, but it may be a thing of beauty, and that's as good a reason as any to choose a guitar, all other things being equal.

Determine a Guitar's Growth Potential

Always consider how far into the future an instrument will carry you. The better instrument you acquire now, the longer it will take you to outgrow it. A veneer-top guitar may be cheaper than a solid-top guitar, but as you improve your technique, you may find your guitar's tonal capabilities aren't keeping up. On the other hand, it's perfectly acceptable and prudent to buy a low-cost guitar to see if this "classical guitar thing" sticks. And if you find you're ready for a new guitar in a year or two, you'll always have your first purchase as a backup.

Part VI
Appendixes

The 5th Wave   By Rich Tennant

"I had to improvise replacing the D string, but it should be all right. You can keep the lure. No charge."

In this part . . .

Although changing your strings doesn't make you a better player, it's one sure way to improve your sound. Appendix A takes you through the process of changing each of the guitar's six strings, and we include photos to help you along. We also include a section on how to keep your guitar healthy, both at home and on the road, and what to do when it's in need of some TLC. Appendix B gives suggestions for the best way to use the CD that accompanies this book and provides a track list that contains the track number, corresponding figure number in the text, and brief description for each of the 99 tracks on the CD.

Appendix A

Basic Guitar Care and Maintenance

. . . .

A classical guitar doesn't need much at all in the way of care. If you don't mistreat it or subject it to harsh environmental extremes, it will last indefinitely. In fact, a good guitar with a solid, high-quality top actually improves over time, producing a richer, warmer, and more balanced sound as the wood ages. The only thing you should do — though it won't hurt the guitar if you don't — is change the strings every once in a while.

If your guitar never leaves its climate-controlled room and you never drop or bump it, you literally don't have to do anything except change the strings. But that would be an unusually uneventful life for a musical instrument, especially a guitar! The reality is that your guitar is subject to changing environments, bumps and shocks, and the chemicals and forces of your own body — all of which cause wear and tear. In this appendix, we look at the ways to keep your guitar healthy and happy, showing you what to do when things don't go perfectly. We also show you the right way to change your strings.

Keeping Your Guitar Comfortable

A guitar is just like a person, in that it likes to be comfortable. And what's generally comfortable for a human suits a guitar just fine, too. For the woods, finish (the thin protective coating on the wood), and glues that hold your guitar together, the two environmental conditions that are most important for guitar comfort are temperature and humidity. Staying within a certain range regarding these two factors prevents the guitar's materials from expanding and contracting too much or too quickly.

Temperature

Keep your guitar in an environment that's between about 60 and 85 degrees Fahrenheit. That's a range that well encompasses most indoor living spaces, so keep the guitar in your home's living areas (as opposed to dank basements and sweltering attics). That goes for traveling, too. Try to keep your instrument with you — meaning inside the passenger compartment of a car or in the overhead bin of an airplane. If you must put the guitar in the trunk, position it toward the front of the car, up against the back seat.

Your guitar may sometimes get cold or hot, and if it does, try not to let it experience a sudden change. If the guitar has been in the trunk of a cold car for a couple of hours, don't open the case immediately when you get inside. Leave the case closed for as long as you can, which allows the guitar inside to warm up gradually.

Humidity

Wood is a porous substance that reacts to changes in humidity by absorbing and releasing moisture. If your guitar is in an environment that's very dry and it stays there for a long period of time — say, a few weeks — the wood can shrink enough to cause the frets to pop up out of their slots, or to crack the finish. Similarly, a guitar kept in a steamy jungle will swell and bloat, straining the joints, frets, and finish, and causing the strings to buzz.

Keep your guitar at a relative humidity of between 45 and 55 percent (that's a good range for humans, too, by the way). You can buy an inexpensive hygrometer from the hardware store and keep it in the room where the guitar lives. If the humidity drops below 45 percent, get a humidifier. If the humidity goes above 55 percent, get a dehumidifier. Simple, isn't it?

You can even keep a hygrometer inside your guitar case, along with a specially made instrument humidifier (such as those made by Planet Waves; www.planetwaves.com) or a desiccant (such as a packet of silica gel) to control the humidity in your guitar case away from home.

Protection, both at home and on the road

When your guitar is in the comfort of your home, you don't really have to do anything special — aside from heeding the aforementioned points about temperature and humidity — to keep it safe from the elements.

When you're not playing it, put the guitar in a safe place (that is, out of collision danger), such as hanging from a wall (using a special guitar hanger you can buy at a music store) or on a guitar stand in the corner. (But don't rest your guitar right next to or in front of a radiator, duct, or window.) You don't necessarily have to keep the guitar in its case when you're not playing it, but if you store the guitar in a closet or under a bed — or otherwise leave it unplayed for a long period of time — then the case is the best place for it. If nothing else, you'll keep your guitar protected from dust and other airborne irritants.

If you take your guitar on the road, the best thing you can do is buy a hard-shell case, which costs about $50. A hard-shell case is bigger and heavier than a nylon or leather gig bag that slings easily over the shoulder, but it protects the guitar much more from bumps, collisions, and even falls to the floor. It also allows you to put the guitar in the trunk of a car or the back of a truck and stack things on top of it. If you travel with a gig bag, your guitar always has to be at the top of the pile — not the most versatile arrangement, especially considering that you may not be there to control the stacking order.

If you're traveling by air, you face a real dilemma. You can't get the guitar in the overhead bin in a hard-shell case, as it's too bulky. But if you show up at the airport with just a shoulder bag, you paint yourself into a corner, as the *only* place the guitar is safe is in the overhead bin. And what if the bin has no room, or the airline personnel say no? You're stuck.

When traveling by air, find out what kind of aircraft you'll be flying on. Research the overhead bin size on the Web, and call the airline to find out its policy for overhead storage. If you think the airline personnel will make you check your guitar, put it in a hard-shell case. And obviously, you must do all this before you leave for the airport.

Even if the airline allows guitars overhead (most do), remember that overhead bins can fill up. So if you have your guitar in hand in a gig bag, stand near the gate to be at the front of the line when it's your turn to board.

Cleaning Your Guitar

Your guitar doesn't need cleaning the same way your car does, because it's never subjected to that kind of assault of dirt (we hope!). In fact, you should never, ever let water in any form (a stream, a spray, or a mist) come in contact with any part of your guitar. Most often, cleaning a guitar just means removing dust. Think of your guitar like furniture — very delicate furniture. Most of the time you just wipe down a tabletop, and that's as far as you need to go to restore it to its original luster. So it is with a guitar. You should dust it as often as necessary, and take care when doing so, as a really thick layer of dust can actually scratch your guitar if you press too hard. So dust lightly using a non-abrasive cloth — your guitar will appreciate it.

Occasionally, the wood of your guitar, like your dining room table, can build up with grime or gunk that doesn't come off with a light wipe of a dry cloth. This stubborn residue could be anything from caked-on sweat to a spilled beverage that you didn't wipe away thoroughly (hey, it happens to the best of us). Fretboards are especially susceptible to human-produced gunk because your fingers and hands are in constant contact with them.

In these cases, use a very light coating of furniture polish (the aerosol kind) or a specially made liquid guitar polish, available at your local music store. Take care not to spray anything in an aerosol can directly onto the guitar itself. Instead, spray a little onto a non-abrasive cloth, let it soak in for a few seconds, and then wipe the affected area lightly. After applying the wet cloth, go over the area with a dry cloth to soak up any residual moisture.

If your strings get gummy or grungy, you can wipe them down with a cloth, but the best maintenance is preventative: Wipe them off just after you finish playing, before your bodily fluids have had a chance to do their corrosive, gunky damage.

Changing the Strings on Your Classical Guitar

Changing strings is one of those tasks that may sometimes seem like a hassle, but at least you can take comfort in knowing that everyone has to do it. And the good news is, nothing in the world compares to a new set of strings on your guitar. After you get them on and tuned up and you play that first arpeggio or melody, the new strings — and the new, improved tone they bring with them — make you realize it was well worth the effort.

Practically speaking, you change strings for one or more of the following three reasons:

- The old strings are so worn and corroded that they've lost their luster and tone.
- The strings have lost their flexibility and no longer play in tune.
- A string breaks and you have to replace it immediately.

Stringing a classical guitar isn't like stringing other types of guitars, because the bridge and headstock constructions are different from both steel-string acoustic and electric guitars. Unlike steel-string acoustics, classical guitars don't use bridge pins, so you have to tie the strings off at the bridge. And classical guitars use slotted headstocks, where the strings wrap around cylindrical rollers tucked between the slots, rather than posts coming upward from the solid headstocks that you find on both acoustic and electric guitars. In this appendix we show you how to attach your new strings to both ends of your classical guitar.

Before you set out to change your strings, have at least one set of new classical guitar strings ready. One new set means you can replace every single old string on the guitar with a new one. It's always best to replace all the strings at once, ensuring that every string is the same age. Having a second new set available is handy, too, in the event that you accidentally break a string while putting a new one on (it's rare, but it happens). If you break a new string, you can at least draw a spare from the additional new set. When you have either one or two sets of new strings, you're ready to change the old ones. Following is a three-step procedure for changing the strings on your classical guitar.

Step one: Remove the old string

Before you can put on a new string, you have to remove the old one. If the string is intact and tuned up, simply turn the tuning peg in the direction that loosens the string until the string is completely slack. That should free up the connections at the bridge and headstock enough that you can undo the ties and pull the string ends out of the holes. If you're replacing a broken string, just remove the parts that are still attached at the bridge and the roller. In either case, discard all remnants of the old string. (Note: Roommates and significant others are known to get very upset when you leave your old string bits lying around on the couch or carpet!)

A quicker way to remove the old string is to use wire cutters or snips to cut the string as close to the bridge or roller as possible. Then, with the tips of the cutters, pull the string remnants away and out of the holes. Cutting the string is faster than detuning and removing it with your bare fingers, but be sure you don't knick the surfaces of the guitar with the tips of your cutting tool. The disadvantage to cutting the string is that you no longer have the entire string length available, should you need the string as a spare. It's better to use a new string as a spare, but an old string is better than no string.

After the old strings are completely off the guitar and out of the way, you're ready to attach the new strings.

Step two: Tie off the string at the bridge

A classical guitar string has plain ends at either end (unlike acoustic and electric guitar strings, which have a ball at one end), so you can insert either end through the bridge. If, however, one end of the string looks different from the other, grasp the one that looks like the middle portion of the string, not the end that has the loosely coiled appearance. When you have the ends of the new string oriented, follow these steps:

1. **Be sure all traces of the old string are removed,** as we describe earlier in this chapter.

2. **Grasp one end of the new string and pass it through the bridge hole,** beginning at the side closest to the sound hole and coming out on the side that's away from the sound hole. Leave about an inch of string sticking out the back end of the bridge.

3. **Tie the string off by bringing the short end over the bridge and passing it under the long part of the string,** as shown in Figure A-1a. Then pass the short end under, over, and then under itself, on top of the bridge, as shown in Figure A-1b.

   Like tying a necktie, you may require a couple of tries to get the protruding part to be just the right length, where not too much excess is sticking out off the bridge. If you still have some excess that's a little too long (meaning it's touching the guitar top or looks funny sticking up in the air), you can always snip the end a bit. Just be careful not to ding the top with your cutting tool!

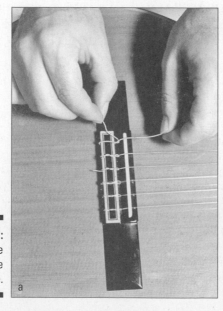

Figure A-1:
Tying off the string at the bridge.

a   b

4. **Pull on the long end of the string with one hand and adjust the knot with the other to remove the slack,** so that the knot lies flat against the top of the bridge.

Step three: Secure the string to the roller

After tying off one end of the string at the bridge, you can secure the string at the headstock. Classical guitars use rollers (as opposed to the posts on acoustic and electric guitars), which go horizontally (in the same direction as the nut and the frets) through slots in the headstock. Rollers provide the surface for the strings to wrap around. To attach the string to the roller inside the slotted headstock, follow these steps:

1. **Pass the string through the hole in the roller and bring the end of the string back over the top of the roller, or toward you.** Then pass the short end under the long end in front of the hole. Pull on the string end so that the long part of the string (the part attached to the bridge) sits in the U-shaped loop you just formed, as shown in Figure A-2a.

   Make your loop come from the outside (that is, approaching from the left on the three bass strings and from the right on the three treble strings).

2. **Pass the short end under and over itself,** creating two or three wraps. The wraps hold the loose end firmly against the roller (as shown in Figure A-2b), preventing the string end from slipping out of the hole.

3. **Wind the tuning peg so that the string wraps over the roller and on top of the loop you just formed,** forcing it down against the roller.

4. **Pull the string taut with one hand and turn the tuning peg with the other,** making sure to wrap the windings to the outside of the headstock, away from the guitar's center.

Repeat steps 1 through 4 for each string that needs replacing, noting the difference in direction between the bass and treble strings when forming the initial loop and when wrapping additional windings toward the outside of the headstock.

As you continue turning the tuning peg, the string becomes taut and slowly comes into tune. Be sure to continually check the pitch with your tuning device (electronic tuner, pitch pipe, keyboard, and so on); see Chapter 2 for instructions. Nylon strings (the kind used for classical guitars) require quite a bit of stretching until they hold their pitch, so after you get the string initially pulled up to pitch, grip it at various places along the fretboard and over the sound hole, pull on it with your fingers, and then tune up again. Repeat this process three or four times, or until the strings stop slipping out of tune after you pull on them with your fingers. Sometimes it takes a couple of days for the strings to stop slipping completely and to hold their tuning, even if you're careful to stretch them out.

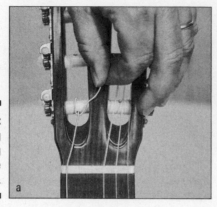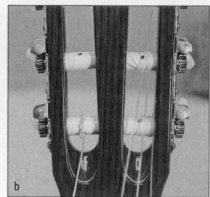

Figure A-2: Securing the string at the headstock.

a

b

Use your cutting tool to snip the string end after you're done putting on and tuning up all six strings, as the excess string may rattle during play. Besides, having loose string ends hanging out of the top of your guitar looks messy onstage!

Making Minor Repairs

Classical guitars are made mostly of wood, and any type of wood-based damage — including dents, cracks, scratches, gouges, deep stains, or joint separations — must be tended to by a qualified repair person. At the first sign of trouble, take your guitar in for evaluation, as often a crack on a guitar — just like a crack on a windshield — will spread over time, making the problem worse.

For the non-wood parts of your guitar, like the tuning machines, you can replace them yourself if they become damaged or worn — assuming you're handy with tools and have a clear idea of what to do. For example, a plastic tuning peg can break because of a fall or just because it wears out over time. You can order the replacement part and, with a couple of screwdrivers, perform the job yourself. You have to loosen the strings and remove the tuning machine assembly on the affected side of the headstock (by removing all the screws), but it's still a fairly easy repair to make. If you have any doubts about your competency, though, play it safe and take the guitar into the shop. Often, a repair person will advise you if this is a repair you can do yourself and give you some pointers in the process, saving you the labor fee.

If you hear something rattle inside your classical guitar, chances are it's a loose brace or some other wooden part that's become dislodged, meaning a glue joint has failed somewhere. Just as it is with your car, if you hear a rattle under the hood, take it into the shop!

Appendix B

How to Use the CD

This book comes with an audio CD so that you can hear how the exercises and pieces that appear in the text sound when played at a normal playing tempo. You can use the CD to give you an idea of how a piece sounds in its finished state, or you can play along with it to make sure you're playing the notes correctly and playing in tempo.

The CD contains over 140 recorded examples on 99 tracks. Every written music figure from Chapter 4 through Chapter 16 is performed on the CD. All you need to do to find which track a particular example falls on is to look at the black track box at the top of the figure.

 One fun way to use the CD is to flip through the book looking at just the written music while listening to the CD. That way, you can get an audio tour of the book without reading all that text! (Though to truly understand what you're listening to — and why — we're confident you'll read the text eventually.)

Relating the Text to the CD

Whenever you see written music in the book and you want to hear what it sounds like on the CD, refer to the box at the upper-right-hand corner of the figure. The box tells you the track number and, if present, the start time (in minutes and seconds) of the exercise within the track.

To select a given track, use the *track skip* control on your audio player (CD player, portable mp3 device, computer screen, and so on). If the exercise you want to listen to shares a track with other exercises, use the *cue/review* (also known as "fast forward/rewind") control to advance to the specific time within the track. For example, if the exercise you want to hear has a box that reads "Track 2, 0:32," it means the audio begins 32 seconds into Track 2. Use the track skip control to go to Track 2, then use the cue control to advance the counter to 32 seconds. We suggest that you stop a few seconds before the actual start time to give yourself a little time to get your hands into playing position before the audio starts.

Each exercise and piece on the CD is preceded by a *count-off,* which is the sound of a metronome clicking in rhythm before the music begins. The count-off provides the tempo (the speed at which the music is played), and, if you're playing along, allows you to enter exactly in time and simultaneously with the recorded guitar. The count-offs follow the time signature of the figure, so an exercise in 4/4 has a four-beat count-off, an exercise in 6/8 has six eighth notes in the count-off, and so on. If the piece begins with a pickup measure (an incomplete measure), the count-off equals the total number of beats in a normal measure minus the pickup figure. In other words, the count-off plays up to — but not including — the pickup notes.

As you read this book, keep in mind that the book and the CD are meant to act as a unit. Keep the CD with the book at all times, rather than letting the CD get mixed up with your regular CD collection. The clear plastic sleeve in the back of the book protects the CD from getting scratched or falling on the floor and rolling away. Returning the CD to its sleeve after every use will ensure that it's right there where you expect it to be the next time you pull out the book to practice some exercises or perform the full-length pieces.

When you listen to the CD, follow along with your eyes in the written music, even if your note-reading skills leave a little to be desired. Following along helps you memorize the piece a little faster, and you learn to read music a little better this way, whether you realize it or not. Reinforcing the reading part of music with the listening counterpart is a great way to get the most out of the text-and-CD combination.

Listening to the CD

The CD works just fine in any standard CD player — just put it into your home stereo system and refer to "Tracks on the CD," later in this appendix, for the track descriptions.

If you're using your computer to listen to the CD, insert the disc into your CD or DVD drive and use your media player (Windows Media Player, QuickTime Player, iTunes, and so on) to play the files. Any computer with a CD or DVD drive can play the CD's audio files. Following is a short list that tells you what you need in your computer to play the CD:

- ✔ A computer running Microsoft Windows, Mac OS, or Linux
- ✔ Software capable of playing WAV files or CD Audio (usually included with the computer)
- ✔ A CD-ROM drive (a DVD-ROM drive will also play a CD)
- ✔ A sound card for PCs (Mac OS computers have built-in sound support) or some way of plugging in headphones or speakers

Using the CD with Microsoft Windows

To listen to the CD on your Windows computer, follow these steps:

1. **Insert the CD into your computer's CD drive.** Your default media player automatically launches.

2. **Use the interface to navigate and play the tracks on the CD.**

If your media player doesn't appear after you insert the CD, follow these steps to access the CD:

1. **Click Start.**

2. **Choose a program from the Start Menu,** or click on All Programs to navigate to an audio player, such as Windows Media Player, iTunes, and so on. Then navigate to the CD drive.

Using the CD with Mac OS

To listen to the CD on your Macintosh computer, insert the CD into your computer's CD drive. iTunes automatically launches and displays the contents of the CD in the track window.

If iTunes doesn't launch after you insert the CD, follow these steps to access the CD:

1. **Go to the dock and click on the iTunes icon** (the two musical notes on top of a CD). You can also go to the top of the screen and click Go/Applications/iTunes.

2. **Select the CD title appearing under Devices.** You see the tracks displayed in the track window.

Tracks on the CD

Following is a list of the tracks on the CD, along with the figure numbers that they correspond to in the book. The first number of the figure indicates the chapter in which we explain how to play the example. Use this list to scan through the descriptions until you find the track you're interested in playing. In the book, the black boxes containing track numbers (and times, if present) that appear above the exercises help you find the exact location on the CD for the audio version.

Track	Figure Number	Description
1	4-3—4-10	Melody exercises
2	4-11—4-17	Melody exercises
3	4-18—4-23	Melody exercises
4		A Theme by Haydn
5		"Turkey in the Straw"
6		"Scarborough Fair"
7	5-1—5-5	Arpeggio exercises
8	5-6—5-10	Arpeggio exercises
9	5-11—5-14	Arpeggio exercises
10		"Walking Down and Up"
11		"Lowland Lullaby"
12		"Pinch Parade"
13		Prelude in D
14	6-2—6-6	Scales exercises
15	6-7—6-10	Scales exercises
16	6-11—6-14	Scales exercises
17		Scale Study in F
18		Scale Study in B Minor
19		Scale Study in G
20	7-1—7-5	Texture exercises
21		Minuet in G
22		Air in A Minor
23		"America (My Country 'Tis of Thee)"
24		Andante in G
25	8-3	Using the half barre in a simple progression
26	8-4	Using full and half barres in a simple progression
27		Minuet in B Minor
28		"Angels We Have Heard on High"
29	9-1	A variety of ascending slurs
30	9-2	A variety of descending slurs
31	9-3	Playing ascending and descending slurs in a scale
32	9-4	Playing ascending slurs in an arpeggiated figure
33	9-5	Playing descending slurs in an arpeggiated figure
34	9-6	Playing a trill
35	9-7	Playing trills in musical phrases
36		Passepied in A Minor
37		Ländler in C
38	10-2	Harmonics at the 5th, 7th, and 12th frets

Track	Figure Number	Description
39	10-3	"Taps" played in harmonics
40	10-5	"Londonderry Air" with vibrato
41	10-8	Changing tone by means of right-hand placement
42	10-9	Changing tone with pizzicato technique
43	10-10	Tremolo technique on a D minor chord
44	10-11	Tremolo exercise in D Minor
45		"In the Hall of the Mountain King"
46		Tremolo Study in A Minor
47	11-1	F major scale in 5th position
48	11-2	Sequence patterns for F major scale in 5th position
49	11-3	B♭ major scale in 5th position
50	11-4	D minor scale in 5th position
51	11-5	A major scale in 9th position
52	11-6	D major scale in 9th position
53	11-7	F♯ minor scale in 9th position
54	11-8	E major scale with one position shift
55	11-9	A♭ major scale with two position shifts
56	11-10	C♯ minor scale with one position shift
57	11-11	G♯ minor scale with two position shifts
58		"Silent Night"
59		"God Rest Ye Merry, Gentlemen"
60	12-1	Arpeggio exercise with melody in bass
61	12-2	Study in A Minor with melody in bass
62	12-3	Arpeggio exercise with melody in treble
63	12-4	Study in C with melody in treble
64	12-5	Arpeggio exercise with melody alternating between treble and bass
65	12-6	Waltz in E Minor with melody alternating between bass and treble
66		Ländler in D
67		"Romanza"
68		Andante in C
69	13-1	Counterpoint up the neck with barre chords
70	13-2	Prelude in D Minor
71	13-3	Melody and accompaniment up the neck with barres and slurs
72	13-4	Waltz in A Minor
73		Allemande in D Minor

(continued)

Track	Figure Number	Description
74		Study in F
75	14-1	Study in E Minor
76	14-2	"Adelita"
77	14-3	Maestoso in C
78	14-4	Study in E Minor
79		Study in B Minor
80		"Lagrima"
81		Andante in C
82		Study in A
83	15-1	"Greensleeves"
84	15-2	"Melancholy Galliard"
85	15-3	"Jesu, Joy of Man's Desiring"
86	15-4	"Hallelujah Chorus"
87		"The Three Ravens"
88		"Tarleton's Resurrection"
89		Bourrée in E Minor
90		"Joy to the World"
91	16-1	Aria from *Don Giovanni*
92	16-2	*Pathétique Sonata*
93	16-3	"Hungarian Dance No. 5"
94	16-4, 16-5	"The Little Shepherd," "The Girl with the Flaxen Hair"
95		Theme from *The Magic Flute*
96		"Für Elise"
97		"Lullaby"
98		"Clair de lune"
99		Tuning notes

Troubleshooting

If you have trouble with the CD, please call the Wiley Product Technical Support phone number: 800-762-2974. Outside the U.S., call 1-317-572-3994. You can also contact Wiley Product Technical Support at http://support.wiley.com/techsupport. Wiley Publishing provides technical support only for installation and other general quality control items.

Index

• M •

Wiley Publishing, Inc.
End-User License Agreement

READ THIS. You should carefully read these terms and conditions before opening the software packet(s) included with this book "Book". This is a license agreement "Agreement" between you and Wiley Publishing, Inc. "WPI". By opening the accompanying software packet(s), you acknowledge that you have read and accept the following terms and conditions. If you do not agree and do not want to be bound by such terms and conditions, promptly return the Book and the unopened software packet(s) to the place you obtained them for a full refund.

1. **License Grant.** WPI grants to you (either an individual or entity) a nonexclusive license to use one copy of the enclosed software program(s) (collectively, the "Software") solely for your own personal or business purposes on a single computer (whether a standard computer or a workstation component of a multi-user network). The Software is in use on a computer when it is loaded into temporary memory (RAM) or installed into permanent memory (hard disk, CD-ROM, or other storage device). WPI reserves all rights not expressly granted herein.

2. **Ownership.** WPI is the owner of all right, title, and interest, including copyright, in and to the compilation of the Software recorded on the physical packet included with this Book "Software Media". Copyright to the individual programs recorded on the Software Media is owned by the author or other authorized copyright owner of each program. Ownership of the Software and all proprietary rights relating thereto remain with WPI and its licensers.

3. **Restrictions on Use and Transfer.**

   (a) You may only (i) make one copy of the Software for backup or archival purposes, or (ii) transfer the Software to a single hard disk, provided that you keep the original for backup or archival purposes. You may not (i) rent or lease the Software, (ii) copy or reproduce the Software through a LAN or other network system or through any computer subscriber system or bulletin-board system, or (iii) modify, adapt, or create derivative works based on the Software.

   (b) You may not reverse engineer, decompile, or disassemble the Software. You may transfer the Software and user documentation on a permanent basis, provided that the transferee agrees to accept the terms and conditions of this Agreement and you retain no copies. If the Software is an update or has been updated, any transfer must include the most recent update and all prior versions.

4. **Restrictions on Use of Individual Programs.** You must follow the individual requirements and restrictions detailed for each individual program in the "About the CD" appendix of this Book or on the Software Media. These limitations are also contained in the individual license agreements recorded on the Software Media. These limitations may include a requirement that after using the program for a specified period of time, the user must pay a registration fee or discontinue use. By opening the Software packet(s), you agree to abide by the licenses and restrictions for these individual programs that are detailed in the "About the CD" appendix and/or on the Software Media. None of the material on this Software Media or listed in this Book may ever be redistributed, in original or modified form, for commercial purposes.

5. Limited Warranty.

(a) WPI warrants that the Software and Software Media are free from defects in materials and workmanship under normal use for a period of sixty (60) days from the date of purchase of this Book. If WPI receives notification within the warranty period of defects in materials or workmanship, WPI will replace the defective Software Media.

(b) WPI AND THE AUTHOR(S) OF THE BOOK DISCLAIM ALL OTHER WARRANTIES, EXPRESS OR IMPLIED, INCLUDING WITHOUT LIMITATION IMPLIED WARRANTIES OF MERCHANTABILITY AND FITNESS FOR A PARTICULAR PURPOSE, WITH RESPECT TO THE SOFTWARE, THE PROGRAMS, THE SOURCE CODE CONTAINED THEREIN, AND/OR THE TECHNIQUES DESCRIBED IN THIS BOOK. WPI DOES NOT WARRANT THAT THE FUNCTIONS CONTAINED IN THE SOFTWARE WILL MEET YOUR REQUIREMENTS OR THAT THE OPERATION OF THE SOFTWARE WILL BE ERROR FREE.

(c) This limited warranty gives you specific legal rights, and you may have other rights that vary from jurisdiction to jurisdiction.

6. Remedies.

(a) WPI's entire liability and your exclusive remedy for defects in materials and workmanship shall be limited to replacement of the Software Media, which may be returned to WPI with a copy of your receipt at the following address: Software Media Fulfillment Department, Attn.: *Classical Guitar For Dummies,* Wiley Publishing, Inc., 10475 Crosspoint Blvd., Indianapolis, IN 46256, or call 1-800-762-2974. Please allow four to six weeks for delivery. This Limited Warranty is void if failure of the Software Media has resulted from accident, abuse, or misapplication. Any replacement Software Media will be warranted for the remainder of the original warranty period or thirty (30) days, whichever is longer.

(b) In no event shall WPI or the author be liable for any damages whatsoever (including without limitation damages for loss of business profits, business interruption, loss of business information, or any other pecuniary loss) arising from the use of or inability to use the Book or the Software, even if WPI has been advised of the possibility of such damages.

(c) Because some jurisdictions do not allow the exclusion or limitation of liability for consequential or incidental damages, the above limitation or exclusion may not apply to you.

7. U.S. Government Restricted Rights.
Use, duplication, or disclosure of the Software for or on behalf of the United States of America, its agencies and/or instrumentalities "U.S. Government" is subject to restrictions as stated in paragraph (c)(1)(ii) of the Rights in Technical Data and Computer Software clause of DFARS 252.227-7013, or subparagraphs (c) (1) and (2) of the Commercial Computer Software - Restricted Rights clause at FAR 52.227-19, and in similar clauses in the NASA FAR supplement, as applicable.

8. General.
This Agreement constitutes the entire understanding of the parties and revokes and supersedes all prior agreements, oral or written, between them and may not be modified or amended except in a writing signed by both parties hereto that specifically refers to this Agreement. This Agreement shall take precedence over any other documents that may be in conflict herewith. If any one or more provisions contained in this Agreement are held by any court or tribunal to be invalid, illegal, or otherwise unenforceable, each and every other provision shall remain in full force and effect.

BUSINESS, CAREERS & PERSONAL FINANCE

Accounting For Dummies, 4th Edition*
978-0-470-24600-9

Bookkeeping Workbook For Dummies†
978-0-470-16983-4

Commodities For Dummies
978-0-470-04928-0

Doing Business in China For Dummies
978-0-470-04929-7

E-Mail Marketing For Dummies
978-0-470-19087-6

Job Interviews For Dummies, 3rd Edition*†
978-0-470-17748-8

Personal Finance Workbook For Dummies*†
978-0-470-09933-9

Real Estate License Exams For Dummies
978-0-7645-7623-2

Six Sigma For Dummies
978-0-7645-6798-8

Small Business Kit For Dummies, 2nd Edition*†
978-0-7645-5984-6

Telephone Sales For Dummies
978-0-470-16836-3

BUSINESS PRODUCTIVITY & MICROSOFT OFFICE

Access 2007 For Dummies
978-0-470-03649-5

Excel 2007 For Dummies
978-0-470-03737-9

Office 2007 For Dummies
978-0-470-00923-9

Outlook 2007 For Dummies
978-0-470-03830-7

PowerPoint 2007 For Dummies
978-0-470-04059-1

Project 2007 For Dummies
978-0-470-03651-8

QuickBooks 2008 For Dummies
978-0-470-18470-7

Quicken 2008 For Dummies
978-0-470-17473-9

Salesforce.com For Dummies, 2nd Edition
978-0-470-04893-1

Word 2007 For Dummies
978-0-470-03658-7

EDUCATION, HISTORY, REFERENCE & TEST PREPARATION

African American History For Dummies
978-0-7645-5469-8

Algebra For Dummies
978-0-7645-5325-7

Algebra Workbook For Dummies
978-0-7645-8467-1

Art History For Dummies
978-0-470-09910-0

ASVAB For Dummies, 2nd Edition
978-0-470-10671-6

British Military History For Dummies
978-0-470-03213-8

Calculus For Dummies
978-0-7645-2498-1

Canadian History For Dummies, 2nd Edition
978-0-470-83656-9

Geometry Workbook For Dummies
978-0-471-79940-5

The SAT I For Dummies, 6th Edition
978-0-7645-7193-0

Series 7 Exam For Dummies
978-0-470-09932-2

World History For Dummies
978-0-7645-5242-7

FOOD, GARDEN, HOBBIES & HOME

Bridge For Dummies, 2nd Edition
978-0-471-92426-5

Coin Collecting For Dummies, 2nd Edition
978-0-470-22275-1

Cooking Basics For Dummies, 3rd Edition
978-0-7645-7206-7

Drawing For Dummies
978-0-7645-5476-6

Etiquette For Dummies, 2nd Edition
978-0-470-10672-3

Gardening Basics For Dummies*†
978-0-470-03749-2

Knitting Patterns For Dummies
978-0-470-04556-5

Living Gluten-Free For Dummies†
978-0-471-77383-2

Painting Do-It-Yourself For Dummies
978-0-470-17533-0

HEALTH, SELF HELP, PARENTING & PETS

Anger Management For Dummies
978-0-470-03715-7

Anxiety & Depression Workbook For Dummies
978-0-7645-9793-0

Dieting For Dummies, 2nd Edition
978-0-7645-4149-0

Dog Training For Dummies, 2nd Edition
978-0-7645-8418-3

Horseback Riding For Dummies
978-0-470-09719-9

Infertility For Dummies†
978-0-470-11518-3

Meditation For Dummies with CD-ROM, 2nd Edition
978-0-471-77774-8

Post-Traumatic Stress Disorder For Dummies
978-0-470-04922-8

Puppies For Dummies, 2nd Edition
978-0-470-03717-1

Thyroid For Dummies, 2nd Edition†
978-0-471-78755-6

Type 1 Diabetes For Dummies*†
978-0-470-17811-9

INTERNET & DIGITAL MEDIA

AdWords For Dummies
978-0-470-15252-2

Blogging For Dummies, 2nd Edition
978-0-470-23017-6

**Digital Photography All-in-One
Desk Reference For Dummies, 3rd Edition**
978-0-470-03743-0

Digital Photography For Dummies, 5th Edition
978-0-7645-9802-9

**Digital SLR Cameras & Photography
For Dummies, 2nd Edition**
978-0-470-14927-0

**eBay Business All-in-One Desk Reference
For Dummies**
978-0-7645-8438-1

eBay For Dummies, 5th Edition*
978-0-470-04529-9

eBay Listings That Sell For Dummies
978-0-471-78912-3

Facebook For Dummies
978-0-470-26273-3

The Internet For Dummies, 11th Edition
978-0-470-12174-0

Investing Online For Dummies, 5th Edition
978-0-7645-8456-5

iPod & iTunes For Dummies, 5th Edition
978-0-470-17474-6

MySpace For Dummies
978-0-470-09529-4

Podcasting For Dummies
978-0-471-74898-4

**Search Engine Optimization
For Dummies, 2nd Edition**
978-0-471-97998-2

Second Life For Dummies
978-0-470-18025-9

**Starting an eBay Business For Dummies
3rd Edition†**
978-0-470-14924-9

GRAPHICS, DESIGN & WEB DEVELOPMENT

**Adobe Creative Suite 3 Design Premium
All-in-One Desk Reference For Dummies**
978-0-470-11724-8

**Adobe Web Suite CS3 All-in-One Desk
Reference For Dummies**
978-0-470-12099-6

AutoCAD 2008 For Dummies
978-0-470-11650-0

**Building a Web Site For Dummies,
3rd Edition**
978-0-470-14928-7

**Creating Web Pages All-in-One Desk
Reference For Dummies, 3rd Edition**
978-0-470-09629-1

**Creating Web Pages For Dummies,
8th Edition**
978-0-470-08030-6

Dreamweaver CS3 For Dummies
978-0-470-11490-2

Flash CS3 For Dummies
978-0-470-12100-9

Google SketchUp For Dummies
978-0-470-13744-4

InDesign CS3 For Dummies
978-0-470-11865-8

**Photoshop CS3 All-in-One
Desk Reference For Dummies**
978-0-470-11195-6

Photoshop CS3 For Dummies
978-0-470-11193-2

Photoshop Elements 5 For Dummies
978-0-470-09810-3

SolidWorks For Dummies
978-0-7645-9555-4

Visio 2007 For Dummies
978-0-470-08983-5

Web Design For Dummies, 2nd Editio
978-0-471-78117-2

Web Sites Do-It-Yourself For Dummie
978-0-470-16903-2

Web Stores Do-It-Yourself For Dummies
978-0-470-17443-2

LANGUAGES, RELIGION & SPIRITUALITY

Arabic For Dummies
978-0-471-77270-5

Chinese For Dummies, Audio Set
978-0-470-12766-7

French For Dummies
978-0-7645-5193-2

German For Dummies
978-0-7645-5195-6

Hebrew For Dummies
978-0-7645-5489-6

Ingles Para Dummies
978-0-7645-5427-8

Italian For Dummies, Audio Set
978-0-470-09586-7

Italian Verbs For Dummies
978-0-471-77389-4

Japanese For Dummies
978-0-7645-5429-2

Latin For Dummies
978-0-7645-5431-5

Portuguese For Dummies
978-0-471-78738-9

Russian For Dummies
978-0-471-78001-4

Spanish Phrases For Dummies
978-0-7645-7204-3

Spanish For Dummies
978-0-7645-5194-9

Spanish For Dummies, Audio Set
978-0-470-09585-0

The Bible For Dummies
978-0-7645-5296-0

Catholicism For Dummies
978-0-7645-5391-2

The Historical Jesus For Dummies
978-0-470-16785-4

Islam For Dummies
978-0-7645-5503-9

**Spirituality For Dummies,
2nd Edition**
978-0-470-19142-2

NETWORKING AND PROGRAMMING

ASP.NET 3.5 For Dummies
978-0-470-19592-5

C# 2008 For Dummies
978-0-470-19109-5

Hacking For Dummies, 2nd Edition
978-0-470-05235-8

Home Networking For Dummies, 4th Edition
978-0-470-11806-1

Java For Dummies, 4th Edition
978-0-470-08716-9

**Microsoft® SQL Server™ 2008 All-in-One
Desk Reference For Dummies**
978-0-470-17954-3

**Networking All-in-One Desk Reference
For Dummies, 2nd Edition**
978-0-7645-9939-2

**Networking For Dummies,
8th Edition**
978-0-470-05620-2

SharePoint 2007 For Dummies
978-0-470-09941-4

**Wireless Home Networking
For Dummies, 2nd Edition**
978-0-471-74940-0

OPERATING SYSTEMS & COMPUTER BASICS

Mac For Dummies, 5th Edition
78-0-7645-8458-9

Laptops For Dummies, 2nd Edition
78-0-470-05432-1

Linux For Dummies, 8th Edition
78-0-470-11649-4

MacBook For Dummies
78-0-470-04859-7

Mac OS X Leopard All-in-One
Desk Reference For Dummies
78-0-470-05434-5

Mac OS X Leopard For Dummies
978-0-470-05433-8

Macs For Dummies, 9th Edition
978-0-470-04849-8

PCs For Dummies, 11th Edition
978-0-470-13728-4

Windows® Home Server For Dummies
978-0-470-18592-6

Windows Server 2008 For Dummies
978-0-470-18043-3

Windows Vista All-in-One
Desk Reference For Dummies
978-0-471-74941-7

Windows Vista For Dummies
978-0-471-75421-3

Windows Vista Security For Dummies
978-0-470-11805-4

SPORTS, FITNESS & MUSIC

Coaching Hockey For Dummies
78-0-470-83685-9

Coaching Soccer For Dummies
78-0-471-77381-8

Fitness For Dummies, 3rd Edition
78-0-7645-7851-9

Football For Dummies, 3rd Edition
78-0-470-12536-6

GarageBand For Dummies
978-0-7645-7323-1

Golf For Dummies, 3rd Edition
978-0-471-76871-5

Guitar For Dummies, 2nd Edition
978-0-7645-9904-0

Home Recording For Musicians
For Dummies, 2nd Edition
978-0-7645-8884-6

iPod & iTunes For Dummies,
5th Edition
978-0-470-17474-6

Music Theory For Dummies
978-0-7645-7838-0

Stretching For Dummies
978-0-470-06741-3

Get smart @ dummies.com®

- Find a full list of Dummies titles
- Look into loads of FREE on-site articles
- Sign up for FREE eTips e-mailed to you weekly
- See what other products carry the Dummies name
- Shop directly from the Dummies bookstore
- Enter to win new prizes every month!

Separate Canadian edition also available
Separate U.K. edition also available